REVELATION

Preparing for and Uncovering Your Destiny

GERALD S. MELTON

ISBN 978-1-0980-3769-7 (paperback)
ISBN 978-1-0980-3770-3 (digital)

Christian Faith Publishing, Inc.
832 Park Avenue
Meadville, PA 16335
www.christianfaithpublishing.com

Printed in the United States of America

Contents

PREFACE

The book of Revelation is about the time when Jesus, worldwide, becomes known as the King of kings and Lord of lords. Up to the present time for many millions of persons, Satan has blinded them to this truth. Satan will lead a rebellion of deceived collaborators to fight the One True God. But as the last days' end, it will become more and more apparent that God's judgment will prevail over the forces of darkness. Jesus will lock Satan up in the abyss for a thousand years, humble or destroy nations, and judge the world. The futuristic literal time of the descriptions within the book of Revelation in chapters 4 to 20 will end the moral and spiritual conflict of the ages. And at the glorious appearing of Jesus Christ at the Second Advent will bring in a new order for humankind. This book is about the destinies and desolations of men on this planet.

As I write this book, there is a sorrow in my heart for the many peoples who have chosen one of Satan's lies to reverence in place of Bible truth. For all humankind are citizens of eternity; the only problem is that there are only two destinations which all men enter when their probationary period is over (this natural life on earth.) A soul either goes to heaven or hell. To simplify it, let me put it this way—those who accepted Jesus Christ as their Lord and Savior and followed him go to heaven (the place he is King over). And those who chose to reverence one of Satan's many lies and follow him will go where God has assigned him, the doom of punishment in hell. Tell me, where will you go when you enter your eternal state? Eternity is waiting the day to claim each one of us. We must be ready.

I've done my dividing of this book into three sections so that you can easily understand the things that are going on within the text.

Chapters 1 through 3 describe what was and the present realities.

Chapters 4 through 20 describe what takes place on planet earth within the context of heaven. I call these chapters heavenly assessment.

Chapters 21 through 22 describe the future age.

Let me give two scripture verses for us before we begin this remarkable book.

"So that ye come behind in no gift; waiting for the coming of our Lord Jesus Christ" (1 Corinthians 1:7, KJV).

"That the trial of your faith, being much more precious than of gold that perishes, though it be tried with fire, might be found unto praise and honor and glory at the appearing of Jesus Christ" (1 Peter 1:7, KJV).

To me, these two verses give us good advice for those who follow God now and those who come to faith after the snatching away. In the first verse, we consistently labor to win souls for God's glory until we are gone. Then we see that should we experience suffering for God's cause; we are to endure to the end for the sake of our faith. That includes those who come to follow Jesus after the catching away of the saints. We are always to be prepared to suffer for the testimony of Jesus Christ. We must keep a faithful testimony of our relationship with Jesus Christ. Let me warn you though, if you come to faith after all the Christians are gone, most likely you will end up dying for your loyalty. The Antichrist and false prophet will hunt down any known to be the followers of Jesus Christ.

We will be going over this book passage by passage. I feel that that is one of the best ways to break down the complexities in the book and make it practical. My teaching on Revelation is not technical. May God bless you as you study with me in the book of Revelation.

Sincerely,
Gerald Melton

DIVISION 1

The Past and Present Realities

CHAPTER 1

W̲e must discover this revelation of Jesus Christ for ourselves! Can we genuinely understand prophecy without studying the book of Revelation? This book will open you up to what prophecy is. It will prepare you for your future. I encourage you to let the book of Revelation reveal Jesus Christ in his glory and his plan for you.

As we look at Revelation 1:1–3, begin to envision what a revelation of Jesus Christ entails. So then, why should we study the book of Revelation? Let's examine this question now.

We should study the book of Revelation because this book reveals what must shortly come to pass.

"The Revelation of Jesus Christ, which God gave unto him, to show unto his servants' things which must shortly come to pass; and he sent and signified *it* by his angel unto his servant John" (Revelation 1:1, KJV).

God gave this revelation to Jesus Christ, then to his angel, and shown to the apostle John to show us (his servants) things which must shortly come to pass. It will happen! We are to live with an expectancy of the fulfillment of God's plans. Part of this plan includes the rapture and the coming lie of Satan (Antichrist), the tribulation, and the final judgment, etc.

The revelation of Jesus Christ is a mystery from God, opening the divine events to the reader, which brings in the close of the Church age, the end of man's reign apart from God, sins influence, Satan's rampage, and all attacks on Israel end. A readiness and a sense of immanency concerning the coming of Jesus Christ should motivate us to stay prepared. Since these things must shortly come to pass, Jesus said that this time would trap the whole world.

Jesus told us to pray that we are counted worthy to escape all that is coming upon the earth and standing before the Son of man.

We see events unfold today at an accelerated rate, which points to the soon return of Christ. We see catastrophes, tsunamis, hurricanes, tornadoes, earthquakes, famines, hunger, pestilences, diseases, economic woes, the rise of revived Rome, Israel as a nation, anti-Semitism, the atomic bomb, world cults and religions, the rise of communist Russia and China, etc.

Let's quicken our hearts by zealously repenting. If anything is wrong, let's get it right and turn to God through faith in Jesus Christ. If you turn to Jesus as you read this book, God will help you get prepared for the catching up of the saints.

We should study the book of Revelation because we are co-witnesses of the revelation of Jesus Christ.

"Who bare record of the word of God, and of the testimony of Jesus Christ, and of all things that he saw" (Revelation 1:2, KJV).

We, like the apostle John, bear witness that Jesus Christ is the Word of God. We share in and take the gospel to the world. This gospel consists of all Jesus said and did and who he is. The Holy Ghost overshadowed the Virgin Mary, and she conceived and bore the Son of God. The Son of God was from eternity and came into time, lived a sinless life, died in our place, and arose from the dead, ascended into heaven, and defeated Satan by his sacrificial offering of himself on the cross. Satan had nothing against Christ at his death because he was sinless. Satan's sentence remains to be carried out at the time of the Second Coming; eventually, he will end up in the lake of fire. We together bear witness of these things with the old faithful apostle John.

We also testify to and bear record (witness to) of the fact that Jesus is God's chosen Messiah; therefore, he is Savior, Lord, and the soon coming King. We are those who testify of Jesus Christ. He is good news to man. Whoever repents to God and comes to him through the Lord Jesus Christ shall be saved.

We testify to what we have seen, heard, and know about Jesus. We boldly take our stand for Christ because we are followers of Jesus. We are not ashamed of him even if we suffer from this testimony.

Jesus said that if we deny him before our neighbors, that he would deny us before his heavenly Father in heaven. We must never cower away before adversity.

We must build up our firm footing and be bold over our testimony of Jesus Christ. When we share our experience in Christ, we will have good and bad responses and both positive and negative results.

We should study the book of Revelation because we are blessed if we examine what the book of Revelation contains.

"Blessed *is* he that reads, and they that hear the words of this prophecy, and keep those things which are written therein: for the time *is* at hand" (Revelation 1:3, KJV).

Reading and studying Revelation will open us to the awareness of God's triumphant coming program for the world and planet earth. Understanding this program will help us see the winning side more clearly so that we can prepare our lives by living with eternally minded priorities and keeping in mind that the time is at hand.

So you are truly blessed if you read this book. Your motivation will help you take proper measures for your security. Let's pay attention to the things written within this book. The study of prophecy should be practical, as well as technically accurate, so that we can adjust our lives in a manner consistent with the program of God.

God wants us to know that the consummation of the present order and world system is ending so that all should prepare themselves. We must think about the ramifications that such a turn in conditions will have on humanity so that we make ready for our eternity.

Let's consider ourselves blessed as we see in the events in life that genuinely the time is at hand; the Second Coming of Christ is casting its shadow upon humankind. As we study this book, we will know the attitudes and responses to take. We will also know how to help others as they seemingly are overwhelmed by the changes coming.

Let's try to set time aside at regular intervals so we can get an understanding of the book. We may have to read the book several times. That is a great way to get the things God wants us to know so we can always stay ready for all and anything we may face that has to do with faith.

Therefore, let us study for ourselves about the revelation of Jesus Christ as contained in the book of Revelation, and then we will see through doors that will give us insight into our life.

We need to get into the book of Revelation so that we realize that it is God's message from above. If we read this book, then we will be stirred to change. Revelation provokes correction and repentance. This book can be practical in the influence it has on our turning to God.

We see in Revelation 1:4–6 that revelation is a message from above. Why do we recognize that this message is from above? Let's look at that now.

Revelation addresses all of us in the church.

"John to the seven churches which are in Asia: Grace *be* unto you, and peace, from him which is, and which was, and which is to come; and from the seven Spirits which are before his throne" (Revelation 1:4, KJV).

In the first part of the verse, the apostle John wrote to seven specific churches. Since seven is the number of perfection, the full scope addresses all Churches over the whole church age. The author of the book is John, who wrote what was told, given, and shown to him. Even though John wrote to the Churches in Asia Minor, the book goes out to all churches. These churches, in chapters 1 to 3 of Revelation, had issues that relate to all churches from then to now. It applies to all churches and individuals. Since the scriptures by the Holy Ghost tell everyone who has an ear to hear, then that means all of us are to understand. So we better tune in and listen. We better pay great heed to this book, so we are prepared for all that is coming. Our preparedness will allow us to make adapting adjustments.

This message comes from Almighty God.

> John to the seven churches which are in Asia:
> Grace *be* unto you, and peace, from him which is,
> and which was, and which is to come; and from

the seven Spirits which are before his throne; And from Jesus Christ, *who is* the faithful witness, *and* the first begotten of the dead, and the prince of the kings of the earth. Unto him, that loved us, and washed us from our sins in his own blood. (Revelation 1:4–5, KJV)

These verses express the trinity. The scripture says grace unto you. Part of this grace is God giving us the book of Revelation, which communicates to us that he is in control. We are to be at peace, knowing we are in his grace. The verses express the Father, who is, was, and is to come. The seven spirits is a title denoting the perfection of the Holy Spirit. And of course, the message is from Jesus Christ. The purpose_is to let us know that God sent his Word to prepare us for things to come.

Revelation can be a useful and informative book to help us get our life right with God and to take our stand for Jesus Christ. Chapters 1–3 give practical advice to the churches to get right with God. As we study the book of Revelation, let's look for how the book brings corrective action to our walk with God and our stand for Jesus. Let's apply those things to ourselves, and we will be an overcomer.

This message expresses Jesus's works and high position.

"And from Jesus Christ, *who is* the faithful witness, *and* the first begotten of the dead, and the prince of the kings of the earth. Unto him that loved us, and washed us from our sins in his own blood" (Revelation 1:5, KJV).

This verse tells us that Jesus is that faithful witness upon whom we can depend on our salvation and expresses his work. He is the first begotten from the dead (he who died for our sins and rose from the dead) and is the Prince of the kings of the earth. Psalms 2:7–9 expresses that the Son will rule the world with an iron scepter. He came at his First Advent in love and compassion for humankind. But at his Second Advent, he will return in judgment as a conquering King to destroy those who refuse to repent and believe. As the King of kings and Lord of lords, our Prince Jesus has preeminence over the world and will judge the nations at his coming. It is Jesus who loves us in this verse, this loving and suffering Jesus will come as judge and pour out God's wrath.

This book expresses the fulfillment of all prophecy, which is accomplished in Jesus Christ. The doctrine of the Second Coming of Jesus Christ reveals the terrible times up ahead, especially for those who shunned the good news. Once again, if we need repentance in some area, then do it today. Let's call on God to forgive us and save us and change us for our preservation and God's glory.

This message expresses God's empowerment for the believer.

"And hath made us kings and priests unto God and his Father; to him *be* glory and dominion forever and ever. Amen" (Revelation 1:6, KJV).

This verse states our position and empowers us for that work. We will be a kingdom of priests unto God. We will serve him forever. As kings and priests, we will rule with Christ to intercede to God on people's behalf and to talk to people on God's behalf. We will exalt and uphold his dominion and glory.

God empowers us to do this work even as we face the changing future. The book of Revelation expresses that Jesus is coming quickly! We then must align our lives up with the Word of God and do his bidding. Put the Word into motion in your life. Get into the study and apply it to your life. The leading of the Holy Spirit conforms us to God's way and the message prepares us for Christ's coming.

Upon realizing that Revelation is a message from above, we need to treat our study in the book as a message from God. It's God's Word about our future and for our practical application today. This book invokes change in us and helps us adjust and causes us to prepare ourselves for Christ's coming.

Jesus is coming again, so that means we need to get ready and stay ready.

Will you be ready for Christ's coming? Are you unsure about this? Are you unprepared for his coming? Do you know if you're saved and prepared to meet him? John the Apostle lays out visions of what will happen to make us ready.

In Revelation 1:7–8, the Bible declares that Jesus shall soon come. But how will the Second Coming be perceived? Let's look at some ways that the Second Coming of Jesus Christ will be regarded.

The Bible declares that Jesus Christ's Second Coming will be in glory.

"Behold, he cometh with clouds; and every eye shall see him, and they *also* which pierced him: and all kindred of the earth shall wail because of him. Even so, Amen" (Revelation 1:7, KJV).

The first part of this verse refers to the glory of Christ's majesty surrounded by clouds, saints, and angels. Jesus, with a word from his mouth, will judge the wicked. The word *behold* means to observe or take note or prepare. Jesus is coming in a splendor that all nationalities of people will see.

Since at Jesus's Second Coming, he will set up his millennial kingdom, judge nations, and put an end to wickedness. We need to live in a state of readiness to meet him on good terms of peace. These clouds that surround the Lord Jesus represent divine activity as in Daniel 7:13. Vigilance should characterize our sense of preparedness. As we get vigilant, we will prepare ourselves in any manner that God's Word and Spirit tell us.

The Bible declares that all people shall see Jesus Christ at his coming.

Nobody will be in the dark over this Second Coming of Jesus because it is the day of the Lord, a dreadful day. The Bible says here that every eye will see him. Everybody on the earth will behold him. The revealing of Jesus will significantly change everyone's lives and eternity.

If people have been fighting with God, then they will be consigned to hell. They who reject Jesus Christ will find themselves rejected. So when Jesus comes back, all people will see him. We should desire to be a saint who is on his side. And if you will be on his side, then you must personally receive him as your Lord and Savior.

The Bible declares that Jesus Christ's enemies shall wail because of him.

In the previous verse, the very end part, the people wail because they made themselves Jesus Christ's enemy. Now it is their doomsday. When it speaks of all kindreds, it is referring to all who have rejected the good news. There will be a vexation of the soul with a fear of their end fate.

Since these persons have rejected the good news of Jesus Christ, they are gripped with great fear as they await their end. Jesus declared in a parable that when the king comes back that he will have those killed who didn't want the king to be ruler over them. It's our privilege and responsibility to submit to Christ's lordship today. Let's use our will to do God's bidding now!

The Bible declares that Jesus Christ is God and is in sovereign control.

"I am Alpha and Omega, the beginning and the ending, saith the Lord, which is, and which was, and which is to come, the Almighty" (Revelation 1:8, KJV).

In this verse, Jesus declares his authority and approval over the message in this revelation given to John, stating his Second Coming. As Jesus proclaimed to John, he is the beginning and end. The deity of Jesus means that before all things were, he was and always will be God (God the Son). He is in control and guiding all events to their completion.

This fact of Jesus Christ's complete authority is why we have been given the book of Revelation ahead of time, so we could be prepared to meet him on good terms. Trust in God and don't let your heart be troubled. Stay in good standing with God through faith in Jesus Christ, for your redemption draws near. Focus on your confidence and walk with God. If you are up to speed on exercising your fellowship with Jesus, you'll be good to go. So realize that Jesus Christ is soon coming, and we need to take steps to prepare. Examine your life today to be sure all is well between you and God.

We need to acquire a vision of the triumphant Jesus Christ to endure in the last days.

Is a vision (or its enlargement) of Jesus Christ necessary? We cannot experience salvation without a knowledge of the work of Christ on the cross. We cannot prepare without insight or understanding of Jesus's teachings. Likewise, for full preparation, we need a view of the triumphant Jesus Christ.

In Revelation 1:9–11, we see we need a vision of the revealed Jesus Christ. So let's look at some reasons why we need a view of the glory of (as the book of Revelation speaks of him) Jesus Christ.

We must get a vision of the revealed Jesus Christ because of the suffering that belongs to the believers in Jesus Christ or followers of Jesus Christ.

"I John, who also am your brother, and companion in tribulation, and in the kingdom and patience of Jesus Christ, was in the isle that is called Patmos, for the word of God, and for the testimony of Jesus Christ" (Revelation 1:9, KJV).

The early church was undergoing some severe persecution! Jesus Christ came to John with the revelation of himself concerning the coming day of the Lord so that the church would not faint and retract from their faith in him. Revelation is about Jesus Christ coming back as King of kings and Lord of lords. John calls himself our brother in tribulation. If we are in Christ (born again), we are a brother or sister in the family of God. We are called to suffer and carry our cross with Jesus knowing he is coming one day to set up his throne. At that time, we will rule with Jesus. The Bible says John received this revelation while exiled for the Word of God and the testimony of Jesus Christ. We must not be afraid to speak the Word of God and share our testimony of Jesus Christ. We live in a society where our expression about Jesus and the Bible is contended against and frowned upon, but let's not fail our Savior who gave all to save us.

The vision that revelation gives us of our soon revealed and triumphant Jesus Christ will carry us through our trials in life. When people see competitions, they align themselves with the winning team. We have been told in advance of the triumph of Jesus so we would not get discouraged and quit. Now we can align ourselves with God's will for us in Jesus Christ. We must take steps to grow in the knowledge of Jesus Christ by reading the Bible and the book of Revelation as a good start toward a vision of our triumphant Lord. With this kind of understanding of the truth, we will endure and bear fruit season by season.

It is necessary we get a vision of the revealed Jesus Christ, also for a sense of reverent fear for the greatness of our God.

"I was in the Spirit on the Lord's day, and heard behind me a great voice, as of a trumpet" (Revelation 1:10, KJV).

Here is the recording of the initial encounter of the apostle John with Jesus, which Revelation speaks. From this verse, we get a vision of the greatness of our God, whose voice is like a trumpet. He truly is a God to be feared, followed, and obeyed. It is this Jesus we are waiting to come. John was in the Spirit when the vision came to him. How exactly this took place, I don't know? Either the Lord lifted him to the third heaven or God gave him the revelation within himself. Again, I don't know. The Lord's Day probably has the meaning of the day of the Lord rather than the Sabbath because the whole revelation in the book is about preparation for this day and what happens when it comes. John heard a mighty and great voice! It was the mighty Jesus Christ in his glory!

We need to acquire this vision of Jesus so we can give due reverence and worship to our awesome God. We know Jesus as the savior, but Revelation portrays Jesus as the soon coming triumphant Lord God of the universe! Jesus's greatness means we need to live out our lives in a way we give full honor and loyalty to him. By taking steps to do so, we will prepare our hearts for the day we see the King!

It is also necessary to get a vision of the revealed Jesus Christ for knowledge of the critical message of our God.

"Saying, I am Alpha and Omega, the first and the last: and, What thou sees, write in a book, and send *it* unto the seven churches which are in Asia; unto Ephesus, and unto Smyrna, and unto Pergamos, and unto Thyatira, and unto Sardis, and unto Philadelphia, and unto Laodicea" (Revelation 1:11, KJV).

Jesus Christ had a message for these seven churches that encompasses all churches and individual believers in all generations. This message was addressed to believers to reveal who Jesus is, warns them to keep their faith alive and to know what would transpire throughout the Church age, especially the time of its end. Jesus declared he is the Alpha and Omega. Jesus was the beginning, and he is the end. Jesus being so is a declaration of godhood. Jesus is God the Son. He tells John to write what he sees to the churches of Asia. What Jesus is saying to the churches is significantly important because it prepares us to keep our lamp's burning and retain our place in God's kingdom. It also makes us ready to meet our Lord and Savior when he returns unannounced!

Jesus is giving us instructions for the needed preparation to make in being ready to see him face-to-face! The world will be unprepared because of their unbelief. We are believers who are the just who live by faith. We have God's warning and apply it to our lives to prepare us. If you believe, you will get ready by doing what God's Word says. Read through the letters of the churches and see how they apply to you, then do it. Getting prepared is listening to what the Spirit says to the churches.

So let us acquire our vision of the revealed Jesus Christ by continuing to study the book of Revelation, and then we can know for ourselves God's plan and program for the future.

We find that no man (in the flesh) can stand before the Son of God's mighty countenance.

Does Jesus have an equal evil counterpart? No, Satan was created and had no godly attributes. Neither do the nations compare to Jesus Christ. We live in a world where lies flourish, and people assume the characteristics of God unto themselves.

In Revelation 1:12–16, we see that human beings are to heed the warning that no enemy can, nor will stand up to the brilliant countenance of Jesus Christ. Let's examine some reasons why Jesus Christ's enemies will not stand up against him.

The enemies of God cannot stand because Jesus Christ holds the church in his hand.

"And I turned to see the voice that spoke with me. And being turned, I saw seven golden candlesticks" (Revelation 1:12, KJV).

The gates of hell have not prevailed against the church for two thousand years because Jesus Christ is the builder and sustainer of the church. He is keeping her. I realize that as John turned to see the voice speaking to him, if our lives are to reflect Jesus Christ in these last days, we must be converted to Jesus and listen to him. The seven golden candlesticks represent the church and her light.

Revelation reveals the coming time when Jesus Christ is show-ing through judgments and his Second Coming that no unbeliever will stand up to him. Psalms 2:7–9 bears this out. Just by asking shall the Father give to Jesus Christ the nations, and he shall dash them to pieces. It behooves us all to align ourselves with Jesus Christ's cause. If we get on Jesus's side today, we may suffer a little in this present age but gain Jesus's approval for eternity.

The enemies of God cannot stand because Jesus Christ is the High Priest of his church.

"And in the midst of the seven candlesticks *one* like unto the Son of man, clothed with a garment down to the foot, and girt about the paps with a golden girdle" (Revelation 1:13, KJV).

The enemies of God have not only tried to destroy the church from the outside, but from within, they have attempted to corrupt the church. Thanks be to God that Jesus Christ has cleansed the church and brought her to usefulness. Jesus is the Son of man or God's appointed Messiah and God-man, the Savior. He wears a gar-ment down to his feet which speaks of his priestly office on behalf of his people. Because of Jesus's sacrifice, he has cleansed the church at his first advent.

Jesus is continually cleansing those who repent and believe upon him. The High Priest woes us to repent and accept God's planned sacrifice for our sins. There does not have to be another way; in fact, there is no other way! Jesus intercedes for those who come to him by faith. Jesus Christ is still and always will be our High Priest who intercedes for us on our behalf unto the Father. We will ever recall his atoning sacrifice on our behalf.

The enemies of God cannot stand because Jesus Christ's bril-liance is a reminder of the defeat of all God's enemies.

"His head and *his* hairs *were* white like wool, as white as snow; and his eyes *were* as a flame of fire; And his feet like unto fine brass, as if they burned in a furnace; and his voice as the sound of many waters" (Revelation 1:14–15, KJV).

Again, we read in Psalms 2 the rebellion of the nations against God's Christ. We also see in that Psalm how there will be at a certain point in time when the Father's anointed will crush God's enemies.

The book of Revelation opens our conscience to the awareness of these things. It is a book that reveals Christ's coming conquest! The verse speaks of Christ's white hair, referring to his deity, holiness, and majesty. No adversary can stand up against his brilliance which means a supernaturally strong countenance. Jesus has eyes as flames of fire! We must repent because we cannot hide our sin from God's eyes; neither can the world. Do you expect anything less than such magnificence from God?

You can repent. The world won't repent; therefore, it won't endure. The Bible declares Jesus to be the stone of stumbling; thus, whoever refuses to believe stumbles and gets crushed, so don't ignore to place your faith in him. If you keep putting off turning to Jesus, your time is running out. Run to Jesus, confess your sins, and believe upon him and live.

The enemies of God cannot stand because Jesus Christ makes us know that it is he who will rule for a thousand years (crushing the nations and ruling them with a rod of iron).

"And he had in his right hand seven stars: and out of his mouth went a sharp two-edged sword: and his countenance *was* as the sun shineth in his strength" (Revelation 1:16, KJV).

It is this Jesus speaking to John, letting the churches know that it is he who has been appointed the coming king who will reign over the earth for a thousand years. He will judge the nations and rule from Jerusalem. He holds the seven stars. Jesus holds the leaders of the churches in his hands, and our security rests in the condition that we remain in him. He can keep us if we continue to believe. The verse speaks about the two-edged sword and his excellent countenance, which refers to the sword of Jesus and his brilliance that will judge the nations instantly upon his coming.

Revelation reveals the Second Advent of Jesus Christ in brilliance, power, and great glory. Jesus will return with his hosts of angels and saints. The rapture is when Christ takes up his church before the wrath of God falls upon and ensnares the whole earth. The hope of the evacuation is our incentive for victorious living in these last days of the church age. Knowing that Jesus Christ is going to triumph, we have the power to live.

So let's not align ourselves with the cultural unbelief of the day by refusing to submit to Jesus Christ's lordship. Let's turn to him now and live, and then we will escape the snare that will trap an unbelieving world.

We need to get a grasp on the book of Revelation.

Can you get a grasp on the book of Revelation? If you're willing, attentive, and put in the time, then you can get a grip on this book. Revelation is for whoever has a mind or ear where they hear what the Spirit says to the churches (or an intention to read).

In Revelation 1:17–20, we see that we can comprehend Jesus's explanation of things to be revealed. Let's look at some aspects of Jesus's statement concerning things to be announced.

We examine first the things that have been seen.

"And when I saw him, I fell at his feet as dead. And he laid his right hand upon me, saying unto me, Fear not; I am the first and the last: I *am* he that lives, and was dead; and, behold, I am alive forevermore, Amen; and have the keys of hell and of death. Write the things which thou hast seen, and the things which are, and the things which shall be hereafter" (Revelation 1:17–19, KJV).

The things that John had seen were the truth and revelation of the person of Jesus Christ, which he imparted to John concerning himself. The things that John saw was Christ himself in high power and who is the one revealing the whole of the Revelation that's in this book. Jesus is he who lived, died, and rose again, ascended into heaven, and now as our great God lives to make intercession for us. One day, he will come back as King of kings and Lord of lords.

John saw the glorified Christ, who would impart the revelation of the future. Jesus had first to reveal his glory to John, so John would be able to communicate the announcement. If we are going to comprehend what will come, we must understand Jesus Christ's glory. The revelation will show us how all events relate to Christ.

Next, we examine secondly the things which are. In my first division of the book, I include both the things that have been seen and the things that are.

"Write the things which thou hast seen, and the things which are, and the things which shall be hereafter; the mystery of the seven stars which thou sawest in my right hand, and the seven golden candlesticks. The seven stars are the angels of the seven churches: and the seven candlesticks which thou sawest are the seven churches" (Revelation 1:19–20, KJV).

John received a word for the seven churches, which includes all the churches in the church age. The word to the seven churches remains that which is until the church age ends. The mystery consists of Jesus's word to warn and prepare church leaders and members to take heed so they can overcome through the help of their great God, Savior, and coming King.

The instructions to the churches are for the Christians of all ages so we can prepare ourselves for the coming future days leading up to the church's departure. The key is to stay awake so we can come to a place where we are ready to meet Jesus at any time. Making ourselves available includes repenting, obeying, and rekindling our passion for Jesus Christ. It's our job and duty and task to read the letters to the churches and apply them to our lives. As we listen and respond, we will be prepared for the evaluation Jesus will give over our lives.

Finally, we examine the things which shall be. Included in this part are the two divisions of the way I outlined this book for simplified reading, heavenly assessment (chapters 4–20) and the future age (chapters 21–22).

Looking at verses 19–20, we see that as John got a vision of the overcoming Christ, we learn that it is this One, who overcame at his first advent, to save people from sin, who will be dealing with the nations during the period following the tribulation. Jesus judges the nations in preparation for the millennial kingdom, where he rules for one thousand years. John tells us he fell as dead when he saw Jesus. If Jesus came now in his glory, it would be the end of all of us. No man can see God in the flesh and live; God must have placed his hand on John to preserve him. The reason there will be a seven-year period of testing on earth is to allow humankind to discover what they want when they choose Satan as their leader. No, God does not desire the death of the wicked, but they prefer that over life in Jesus Christ.

Satan will take his devotees to their end along with him, and the world won't be able to point the finger and say God's ways are ridiculous. We need to seriously consider it has always been God's good will for men by preserving them. Let's continue to study the book of revelation to become aware of the upcoming drama and why we want to escape the wrath to come! Let this enforce faith in Jesus and a personal relationship with him. The preciousness of the soul is incredible, and our work for Jesus is urgent.

So let's become awakened and vigilant over biblical truth so that we study to be fully prepared and ready to meet Jesus Christ.

CHAPTER 2

We, as we read the book, realize we need to stir up our love for Jesus Christ.

Has your love grown cold toward Jesus? Do you go through the motions when it comes to spiritual disciplines and churchgoing? Is your passion alive or waning? Jesus warns that those whose love grows cold will lose out.

We see in Revelation 2:1–7, that it is essential we heed the warning to return to our first love.

We read that the all-knowing coming King addresses us.

"Unto the angel of the church of Ephesus write; These things saith he that holdeth the seven stars in his right hand, who walketh in the midst of the seven golden candlesticks" (Revelation 2:1, KJV).

It is this one which the book of Revelation describes. Jesus will come from heaven upon an unprepared world. Jesus is what this book is all about, and it is addressing the churches of all generations and times. Jesus holds the seven stars, which means he has appointed Christian leaders and lifts them or puts them down. He walks among us and observes all things that go on.

Jesus wrote these letters with the intent of addressing us personally. We then should get our act together and be ready to meet him. Jesus spoke in parables about the time when the master returns home to his house. Will we, his servants, have lived accountable? Let us each examine our lives thoroughly to be prepared to meet Jesus upon his return.

We need to know that God notices our good qualities.

"I know thy works, and thy labor, and thy patience, and how thou canst not bear them which are evil: and thou hast tried them which say they are apostles, and are not, and hast found them liars: And hast borne, and hast patience, and for my name's sake hast labored, and hast not fainted" (Revelation 2:2–3, KJV).

Jesus truly notices those who are busy doing his work and laboring for his cause. Our actions and labor for God are that which we appointed to do. These Christians were not only working, but they tested the spirits. They wouldn't let heretics lead them astray. We would do well to watch that also. For Jesus's name's sake, they just kept going for him.

These are great qualities, and Jesus was pleased with those qualities, but as the Christians went on, this began to die out because their love and passion for Jesus Christ grew cold and died out. When that happened, I assume that their works became a tradition of going through the motions. If we lose our passion for a vibrant walk with God, then our practices for God fades into oblivion.

We are admonished to return to our undiluted passion for Jesus Christ.

"Nevertheless, I have *somewhat* against thee, because thou hast left thy first love" (Revelation 2:4, KJV).

Jesus rebukes them here by warning that their love, not their works, for God, Jesus Christ, and their fellow Christians has grown cold, and the flame went out. This lack of passion for Jesus brought criticism against them. Have you ever seen someone do something without desire for it? Jesus told them that they left their love for him. Obedience is better than sacrifice; we are to live the law of Christ, which is Christ's passion, toward one another. How can we have that passion if our relationship with God has grown cold?

Let's stir up the flame and passion for Christ and his cause again. Having motivation may mean that we retain our position in Jesus. Let's begin to meet God in prayer, turn up our passion for spiritual things, get excited over the Word of God, and tell people the good news again. Let's take steps, and our love will burn again.

We need to take the steps necessary for repentance.

"Remember therefore from whence thou art fallen, and repent, and do the first works; or else I will come unto thee quickly, and will remove thy candlestick out of his place, except thou repent" (Revelation 2:5, KJV).

God is calling for immediate and drastic repentance, or people will lose out. Jesus tells the church to remember! Do you remember the joy of your salvation and the deep love for Jesus as your Lord that you once had? Jesus tells us to go back to that love for him. We are urged to repent. To go back to what you had and did and do those things again. Respond again to the relationship you have with God. If we don't, we stand the chance of having our candlestick removed. That means we must engage in our walk with God because if we go through the motions and don't know him, then he can remove the flame of his love within us. We could lose out forever.

Our initiative remains necessary for our preservation. Do we know God? Have we had a real born-again experience with God? Are we still walking with God? Again, don't assume others are in need, and you got it all together. You make sure of your calling first! Look at your own life and make the changes. Examine your love (is it real and producing)? Give your love expression to the Lord Jesus Christ, our Savior.

We need to take care not to be carnally minded.

"But this thou hast, that thou hatest the deeds of the Nicolaitans, which I also hate" (Revelation 2:6, KJV).

Jesus also agrees that the church should continue to hate the deeds of the carnal Nicolaitans. These were possibly a Gnostic sect with immoral practices or a group of leaders who put superiority of clergy over laity. Either way, such behaviors are works of the flesh.

Because Jesus declared that he hates such practices, we must avoid taking advantage of our fellow Christians. We need to learn the secret of putting to death the flesh nature and stir up the love for the Spirit of God in us.

We need to be overcomers.

"He that hath an ear, let him hear what the Spirit saith unto the churches; to him that overcomes will I give to eat of the tree of life, which is in the midst of the paradise of God" (Revelation 2:7, KJV).

If we have a mind, we are to put effort into hearing and comprehending what God is saying to the church. We can be overcomers if we take heed to Jesus's words. If we walk with Jesus and obey him, we may freely eat of the tree of life. It is rational that we have ears and can hear, so we should comprehend what Jesus is saying to us and apply it to our lives. If we overcome by keeping a good testimony through walking with God and obeying him, God will give of the tree of life.

Don't we want to partake of heaven's best? We must pass the test to be loyal to Jesus. That is the whole purpose of our life in the flesh. The earthly probationary period is a stage for eternity, where our destination is and our status there. Live this life well for the next phase of your existence. No matter what we believe, upon our decease, we go on to exist forever in eternity. But I say again, whatever you made your master on earth is what you follow to your eternal home. Ultimately, it's either Satan's lies and whoever follows him goes to hell. That is his consigned place for eternity. Or you follow Jesus Christ, who is the King of heaven, and you go there forever. Heaven is going to be wherever Jesus is, ultimately on the new earth. So you make your decision. By the time we die, we have already made it. If we neglect and put off making the decision, that is our decision. Do you see why you must overcome according to who you choose to follow? Continue in the faith then and be diligent in service and vigilant over Christ's cause so you will be the kind of overcomer of whom Jesus speaks.

So we must do all in our power to return to our pure and passionate love for Jesus Christ. A vigilant love is a response that the Spirit is looking for when the scriptures say, "Let him hear what the Spirit says to the churches."

We need to prepare for Satan's strategies.

Are you prepared for Satan's encroachments? Have you learned to stand and fight off his attacks? Could you learn more about how to keep the victory? Jesus expresses that our faith will indeed experience testing. The question is, "Are you ready for an attack from Satan?"

We see in Revelation 2:8–11 that we can prepare for the coming persecutions from Satan that will engulf the whole world because of Satan's collaborators. Yes, this is about a church that has already gone through the fire; we can learn valuable lessons from them for the future fight. How can we prepare? Let's look at four ways we can make ready for this coming persecution that the book of Revelation warns.

We can listen to the words of the Spirit of Christ to his church.

"And unto the angel of the church in Smyrna write; these things saith the first and the last, which was dead, and is alive" (Revelation 2:8, KJV).

It's ironic, but this church is still alive and vibrant today. Christians in this city still suffer for their faith; their voice roars that they are a Christian. If the spirit of this church can endure for two millennia of trials, it is a testimony that we also, by Christ's help, can make it to the end and overcome. Jesus addressed them, and the letter comes down to us today for our benefit.

Jesus addresses this church, and the church throughout the dispensation of grace to hear and overcome. If we look at Revelation 12:11, we will find that the overcomer did so by Jesus's shed blood, the word of their testimony, and choosing the cross over worldly security. Only the assurance of Holy Scripture will prepare us for what is quickly approaching. We must secure our position by hearing the Bible's testimony.

We can continue in fidelity to the Christian faith throughout our trials.

"I know thy works, and tribulation, and poverty, [but thou art rich] and *I know* the blasphemy of them which say they are Jews, and are not, but *are* the synagogue of Satan" (Revelation 2:9, KJV).

Jesus saw the condition that would occur upon these Christians for their faith. He told them that he took note of the synagogue of Satan, those opposing Christ, his message, and his people. Jesus said to them that they were rich. If we stay faithful to Jesus throughout our trials and life, then we will be made rich spiritually and in all ways. These Christians faced those of Satan's synagogue, those who pretended to be of God but fought him. These opposers of God vehemently attacked and vexed God's people and collaborated with Satan.

If we stay true to Jesus Christ, we will run into contentious collaborators of Satan. We must remain faithful to Jesus Christ. Just as God has his church doing his business, so Satan has a network of those who do his bidding as well. So let's beware. We must not let trials, enemies, ill-intentioned friends, pressures of life, or anything else steal our crown and cause us to quit and forfeit our prize. Let's always be determined to serve Jesus Christ in all situations.

We can keep our eyes on the crown of life given to those who endure Satan's encroachments.

"Fear none of those things which thou shalt suffer: behold, the devil shall cast *some* of you into prison, that ye may be tried; and ye shall have tribulation ten days: be thou faithful unto death, and I will give thee a crown of life" (Revelation 2:10, KJV).

We are to behold or take careful consideration of what is coming upon the church. It is the trying of our faith to test the quality of it. We must predetermine to be wholly committed and faithful to the end if we would have Jesus's approval. Jesus tells his church to fear not. Jesus suffered and overcame, so we need this same mindset. Jesus indicated that the devil would persecute members of the Smyrna church. Satan's collaborators will work overtime to put people through all manner of tests. We must be, like Jesus told Smyrna, be faithful even if we die. Have fidelity to Jesus by keeping your eye on the crown of life.

The crown of life is the eternal life we have in Jesus through the born-again experience, but this life is also waiting for us in heaven to enjoy. It is for the overcomers. What is an overcomer? It is each believer who knows Jesus and walks in the faith. It includes adhering to the truth of the deity of Jesus Christ and continuing to take our stand for him. We must remain in the life of Christ during our earthly journey if we lay hold of the awaiting things of life in heaven.

We can overcome in Jesus Christ so that we won't face the second death.

"He that hath an ear, let him hear what the Spirit saith unto the churches; He that overcomes shall not be hurt of the second death" (Revelation 2:11, KJV).

If we listen to God and stay true to Jesus and keep the apostolic Christian faith, we don't have to worry about the second death, eternal damnation, and separation from God. So if we have an ear, we should engage our mind to the will of God as described in scripture. The Spirit's voice is expressing all Jesus said and did and who he is, but especially the warnings Jesus made to the churches. To overcome means, we hear and keep Christ's words.

We must own our faith when under pressure of contention to win the victory. We must continue in our faith to prevent someone from stealing our crown. Faithful unto death means both until we die and fidelity to the faith even in persecution, suffering, and death. Take ownership of your faith in Jesus Christ. Let the scripture guide and grow it and help you bear the marks of the consequences of it. Your crown will cost you marks. Remember, we live by our faith.

Therefore, be fully prepared to face off with the enemy's strategy by determining to be true to Jesus Christ, and as you press on in faithfulness to Jesus, you'll obtain the crown of life.

We can be faithful witnesses.

Faithful Antipas gave his life as a testimony for Jesus Christ. Can we uphold an honest confession in honor of those who shed their blood for Jesus Christ? Our Christian heritage came at a high cost through blood, trials, and persecutions. Let's be faithful to Jesus Christ. We can live a life that cooperates with their testimony and sacrifice.

In Revelation 2:12–17, we see that we, as part of the church, can follow the example of the faithful. Let's see how we can follow the legacy of the faithful in Jesus Christ.

The faithful followers of Jesus walk in fear of the Lord.

"And to the angel of the church in Pergamos write; these things saith he which hath the sharp sword with two edges" (Revelation 2:12, KJV).

Jesus appeared to John as one with a double-edged sword. He ultimately decides the fate of the faithful, sincere, and unfaithful. We are to walk in fear of him, seeking to do those things he approves. The verse tells us Jesus speaks, "These things saith he." God is giving us an appraisal so that we will get our lives in line with his will. Now

31

the verse tells us that Jesus has a sword. Jesus's Word is no ordinary sword, for whatever Jesus speaks is done. His tongue is that sword. We will go on in God's plan as Jesus commands.

You might be thinking, "Who wants to serve such a fearful and mighty God like him?" But serving God is why I am writing this book. For sure, Jesus will conquer sin, evil, the wicked nations, and Satan. Ultimately, everyone chooses either to follow Jesus or some other things (one of Satan's lies). It's our choice. But if you want Jesus to continue to read this book because the book of Revelation gives the disciple of Jesus great hope and leverage to weather the storm. If we are unfaithful, then our light will be removed. Stay in the light of the Word of God. The Word will either judge us or preserve us depending upon our response to it in the days of grace. Our attitude toward God's Word is of paramount importance to being in his will. There is a call to reverence the Word by hearing, responding, repenting, and believing.

The faithful continue to stand and face satanic opposition.

"I know thy works, and where thou dwellest, *even* where Satan's seat *is*: and thou holdest fast my name, and hast not denied my faith, even in those days wherein Antipas *was* my faithful martyr, who was slain among you, where Satan dwelleth" (Revelation 2:13, KJV).

We must live a life that reflects the testimony of those who shed their blood for Christ's cause and our Christian heritage. When Jesus tells us that he knows our work, he is saying that he sees everything about us. Jesus was pleased that this church held fast his name. Even among Satan's influence, they held fast. We do not deny Christ's name even under dire situations. Antipas was a martyr of that time. Our testimony in life should complement the heritage of the cross because our salvation came by blood.

Those who died stood up to Satan. We must keep our testimony in Word and conduct and not deny Christ. We need to proclaim salvation through Jesus Christ and his shed blood at the cross. God gives the overcomer a promise that they will eat of Christ's hidden manna for eternity. If Satan rises, then engage and attack using your sword and armor by resisting Satan, he will either flee or attempt to inflict pain on you—you will have won a victory.

The faithful will always conduct themselves godly.

"But I have a few things against thee, because thou hast there them that hold the doctrine of Balaam, who taught Balac to cast a stumbling block before the children of Israel, to eat things sacrificed unto idols, and to commit fornication. So hast thou also them that hold the doctrine of the Nicolaitans, which thing I hate" (Revelation 2:14–15, KJV).

We do not cause others to stumble, let us not engage in practices that are heathenistic or break God's commands. All of a sudden, Jesus comes and tells this Church that he has some things against them. We will do well to examine our lives to make sure it matches God's Word. My friends, the Word of God, is not outdated! It is the most up to date, and precious book humanity has. If our lives don't match the Bible, change that. We have got to watch out for stumbling blocks. We don't use our spiritual gifts to cause others to fall. Concerning the Nicolaitans, we reject immoral and unbiblical practices.

Anything contrary to Christlikeness, we discard. Jesus left us an example that we could always please the Father. With the indwelling Holy Spirit, we can still do those things that God wants. I'm not saying we are sinless or won't mess up from time to time, nor am I making excuses, but the church has let down her standard very low. Discern the good from the bad by knowing and practicing the good, not by becoming familiar with bad and developing immunity. That is unbiblical—stay clear of evil. Evil is, in my opinion, a state of ungodliness (wanting to live without God). We need to separate ourselves from that which corrupts. We are to be separated from the acts of sin, not brushing up and developing immunity—that is not a biblical view.

The faithful remove all forms of wickedness out of their lives.

"Repent; or else I will come unto thee quickly and will fight against them with the sword of my mouth" (Revelation 2:16, KJV).

We are to get zealous and repent, believe and turn to God through Jesus Christ. Those who knew and departed from the truth, who won't heed the warnings, will be judged and take part in the wrath that will trap the entire world. We are to repent, that is what this book is about, and if men don't repent, then Jesus will fight against them. Let's recognize our wrongs. Be honest with yourself and God. Systematically hand it over to God. Jesus will turn unrepentant over to God's wrath.

Many preachers have said that judgment starts in the house of the Lord. Notice in Revelation that Jesus first addressed the church, and then the book goes on to discuss and judge the world. We ought to be open to God's criticism of our behavior by receiving his word and making the corrections, following the Holy Spirit's leading.

If we know of anything in our life, then let the Holy Spirit point it out and repent and correct it. Rededicate your life to Jesus Christ. That's what this book addresses.

The loyal followers of Jesus win victories all the time.

"He that hath an ear, let him hear what the Spirit saith unto the churches; to him that overcomes will I give to eat of the hidden manna, and will give him a white stone, and in the stone a new name written, which no man knows saving he that receives *it*" (Revelation 2:17, KJV).

To him, who continually wins victories and proves his faith is real, Christ will give the eternal food and a personal reminder of heaven's backing. We need to hear what the Spirit is saying to us because we cannot overcome unless the Spirit operates through us. Will we eat of the hidden manna? If we overcome, we will eat for eternity and being sustained on the person and words of Jesus Christ. Each who overcomes will be given a stone from Jesus with a personal message just for them.

It is because the faithful allow the Spirit to work through them all the time that they obtain many victories under their belt. Romans 12:2 speaks of proving what the goodwill of God is. Dependency is how we live our faith out. God gives us many creative ways to express and live out our faith. Let's stay open to opportunities and cooperate.

So if we live a life that corresponds to those who were faithful before us, we will obtain Jesus's approval by expressing all he did for us in our life.

We must pass the test of the heart (that test, in my opinion, is that our belief is demonstrated by what we did in and with this life).

Did you know that life is a trust? On accountability day, our honesty and works and compassion will come under examination. Yes, our actions and experience and what we did with it will be considered and critiqued by Jesus Christ.

If we examine Revelation 2:18–23, we should realize that Jesus will consider our life as demonstrated by what we did with it. So let's look at some ways we can prepare for this examination.

We cannot escape Jesus Christ's oversight.

"And unto the angel of the church in Thyatira write; These things saith the Son of God, who hath his eyes like unto a flame of fire, and his feet *are* like fine brass" (Revelation 2:18, KJV).

This description expresses one who watches all our actions and will judge accordingly in righteousness. Jesus is the one we are to fear and stay in a relationship. The verse tells us, thus saith the Son of God. Jesus has a word to give everybody. Each person will give an account of themselves to him.

Jesus will determine our citizenship status based on how we lived for him here. If we abused or neglected our trust, then Jesus will recompense accordingly. Jesus is all-seeing and all-knowing; this is a call to repent and reform to get it right with God. What are we making happen for the cause of Christ? Employ your potential for Jesus Christ's approval.

The Lord commends any progress we have.

"I know thy works, and charity, and service, and faith, and thy patience, and thy works; and the last *to be* more than the first" (Revelation 2:19, KJV).

The Lord complimented the Thyatira church for some great qualities, works, charity, service, and faith. The Thyatira church was vibrant. God takes into account our service. Jesus told this church that he knew their actions. We will all get our life examined by Jesus. These Christians were on fire.

The Lord commends our efforts, so we continue to grow this way. So let's take inventory of our gifts and blessings and turn them over to God's use. The Lord is not a tyrant. He commends, as well as rebukes, his people so they will get their lives right. The Lord is doing what is just in this.

Teaming up with bad influences brings us into contention with God.

"Notwithstanding I have a few things against thee, because thou sufferest that woman Jezebel, which calleth herself a prophetess, to teach and to seduce my servants to commit fornication and to eat things sacrificed unto idols" (Revelation 2:20, KJV).

The Lord despises people who call themselves by his name and join themselves to his Church and then dare to corrupt his people and pervert his word in any way.

Jesus tells this church that he has a few things against them. If we want to make it to heaven with our light burning, then we need to take heed and repent. Jesus was not happy that this lady was seducing his servants. We are not to do anything to cause any of God's people to fall.

It makes God angry enough to remove our light when we corrupt our brothers and sisters in Christ. Our light should shine in the darkness, not putting out the fire in others. We need to watch and observe who is around us. If people are immoral and break God's commands, we should not hang with them.

Let's consider how God judges unrepentant sin.

"And I gave her space to repent of her fornication, and she repented not. Behold, I will cast her into a bed, and them that commit adultery with her into great tribulation, except they repent of their deeds" (Revelation 2:21–22, KJV).

This woman would not repent of her Jezebel ways and found God's judgment. God is not going to tolerate hypocrites in his church. We must repent and get our hearts right. Jesus said that he gave space for her to repent. How long do we need before we change? A judgment day is coming. Jesus said he would cast her into a bed, perhaps of tribulation or troubles.

Jesus can remove light just as readily as putting fire in us. Do not be one whose light turns into darkness. Let's turn to Jesus so we can be forgiven and live. Then we will do those things that please God's heart.

We need to guard where our heart's dwell.

"And I will kill her children with death; and all the churches shall know that I am he who searches the reins and hearts: and I will give unto every one of you according to your works" (Revelation 2:23, KJV).

We must set our hearts upon the doing of God's will and then guard the godly deposit God placed in us through others. God searches the hearts. God will draw out what motivated our hearts and the counsels that were within us.

Let's allow this to cause us to elevate ourselves to godly principles so we may have things that last into eternity. Second Corinthians 5:10 describes how we will receive according to all we have done while in our earthly period of testing. We need to make sure our sights are set high enough to acquire Jesus Christ's compliment, or we are wasting time.

Let's realize that what we do in our earthly period of testing matters to God and our future destiny. We still may reform if we will listen and repent by letting God work through us. Let's give full diligence to the Word of God and its application.

We can be overcomers.

Does it matter if we are an overcomer? It matters if you want to keep the victory or stay consecrated. Likewise, overcoming is a prerequisite to our reward.

In Revelation 2:24–29, we see that as we overcome, we receive rewards. You might be asking, "What rewards will we gain if we exercise victory in Christ?" Let's look at some prizes. This passage points out as we overcome in Christ Jesus.

There is the reward of eased burdens (rest).

"But unto you I say, and unto the rest in Thyatira, as many as have not this doctrine, and which have not known the depths of Satan, as they speak; I will put upon you none other burden" (Revelation 2:24, KJV).

To have the reward of "no other burden," we must avoid the teachings of the depths of Satan, such things as immorality, satanic snares, false teachings, etc. Those who avoid and do not know evil doctrine by escaping and staying innocent of it avoid becoming corrupt by it.

Jesus's words embark a vigilant stand on our part for our soul. It is a battle for our soul. Do not accept the depths of Satan, whatever they are. Satan has many religious systems also. Stay clear of it. Do not have such doctrines and evil teachings. By overcoming, we will experience Jesus Christ's help through the Holy Spirit. No other burden is God's help for us who overcome the error.

There is the reward of strength to stand fast.

"But that which ye have *already* hold fast till I come" (Revelation 2:25, KJV).

Jesus says if we continue in him, diligently holding fast, he will give us a spirit of vigilance to hold our place in Christ. Jesus can keep what we have committed to him. On accountability day when we give account, the Holy Spirit will be with us because we were vigilant here with our stewardship unto God.

Let's ask God for a spirit of patient endurance to obtain victory. Gentle patience and faithfulness will give us the edge. Applying ourselves to continue in Jesus Christ will allow us to gain strength to stand fast. Jesus is waiting to show himself strong on our behalf for exercising our faith in him.

There is the reward of the empowerment of authority.

"And he that overcomes, and keeps my works unto the end, to him will I give power over the nations" (Revelation 2:26, KJV).

Because we did the works of Jesus, he will provide us with the rod of authority to rule with him over the nations. But the condition is that we overcome through him. We listen and obey what Christ says to the churches. When we do that all our lives, Jesus will give us power over the nations. We will share in Christ's authority if we are faithful.

Sharing in Jesus's authority is a way of rewarding those loyal to his cause. Having power over the nations is to be in a position of authority and dominion. We should then have the incentive to press on for Jesus Christ. Let's exercise our gifts for Jesus now. We will rule with him in his kingdom.

There is a reward for the position of authority.

"And he shall rule them with a rod of iron; as the vessels of a potter shall they be broken to shivers: even as I received of my Father. And I will give him the morning star" (Revelation 2:27–28, KJV).

Jesus says because we overcome, we will be in his rulership judging and ruling nations with a rod of iron or authority, having positions of power. In dealing with vessels like a potter, we shall be instrumental in governing what goes on in the nations. It is appointed for the faithful to become heirs with Christ. Are we able to see why we should be committed? If we are reliable, we will receive a reward.

There is the reward of an open ear to the Spirit of Christ.

"He that hath an ear, let him hear what the Spirit saith unto the churches" (Revelation 2:29, KJV).

If we are willing, the Spirit will open our ear to his instructions for his church. We can tune into his voice. If we have an ear, we can comprehend and do the will of God.

The Spirit is waiting to help us overcome. Will we let him? Let's apply ourselves to study these letters to hear the Spirit talking to us. Let's put in the effort to open our ears to biblical truth and the signs of the times. This will prepare us for God's work and will.

So work for those rewards by staying true to Jesus Christ. God's prizes will be an enduring crown on accountability day.

CHAPTER 3

We need to turn our slack into watchfulness.

Can a lax attitude over spiritual things hurt us? Slackness could mean the difference between a flickering light and a bright and vibrant light. Slackness could cause us to walk out of fellowship with God. Jesus sounds the alarm to get slack out now in our walk with God and begin walking in the light!

In Revelation 3:1–6, we notice that it is essential for our preparedness to turn our slack into watchfulness. I'm going to define slack as slow to respond. I'll identify watchfulness as a tenacious observance. Why is it necessary to transition from slackness to vigilance? Let's look at some reasons that help us transition from slackness to diligence.

We need God's help to come to life if we are dead.

"And unto the angel of the church in Sardis write; These things saith he that hath the seven Spirits of God, and the seven stars; I know thy works, that thou hast a name that thou livest, and art dead" (Revelation 3:1, KJV).

Jesus can impart life from the Spirit to stir up the flame so that we won't be in a state of slackness. We, along with God's help, need to watch. It is he who hath the seven Spirits of God that can impart his life to you. For this Church, Jesus pronounced them dead. That is fearful if we are slack, then we must have an awakening.

As we do this drift from God independently, we fall from our high position; therefore, it will be necessary that we obtain God's favor for our restoration. This slack is drifting from God's expectations for us. Let's turn back to the urgency of the response to Jesus.

We should become a watcher over what God has given us.

"Be watchful, and strengthen the things which remain, that are ready to die: for I have not found thy works perfect before God" (Revelation 3:2, KJV).

Jesus rebukes this slackness or spiritual sluggishness. Such sloth is a nonworking attitude. Jesus commands this church to strengthen what remains. Jesus commands this church to be watchful! We must be watchers over those things imparted by God. We must reinforce what is acceptable to God. Exercise it or use it, stabilizes the gifts God gave us.

We need to do the exact opposite of slack! We should get the fire burning for God now! Military people undergo training to prepare for war. We need to initiate into the program of exercising ourselves unto godliness to be ready for Christ's visitation. Readiness requires our attention, decision, and action, then we will stir up ourselves to God's activities with our determined response.

We must return to the gospel truth and continue in it.

"Remember therefore how thou hast received and heard, and hold fast, and repent. If therefore thou shall not watch, I will come on thee as a thief, and thou shall not know what hour I will come upon thee" (Revelation 3:3, KJV).

Jesus warns us to remember how we heard the good news and responded as he addresses this church. We should return to the truth and walk with God. He tells them to remember how they received and heard the good news. Let us recall our fervency when we initially received the truth. We desperately need to stir up the flame within us and return to the plow again.

We are to become a watcher. We are to vigilantly hold and practice the truth of the Word of God. Let's continue in this way. Jesus let us know that those who hold to his truth will know his doctrine, and the truth will set them free. Again, let's return to the reading and studying of scripture and prayer.

We are to keep our garments and walk in victory.

"Thou hast a few names even in Sardis which have not defiled their garments, and they shall walk with me in white: for they are worthy" (Revelation 3:4, KJV).

We must keep sound theological teaching and continue laboring for Jesus. We need to overcome through his Spirit if we are those who walk with the Lord in white clothing. There were a few names in Sardis that did not soil their soul with the world. We must be vigilant if we want to be counted with the faithful ones. These have not defiled their garments. They kept their labors untainted for the Lord Jesus.

Jesus calls us to awake and make sure our light is burning. Jesus said to walk in the light why we have the light, let's return to the fire today. We can choose to avoid spiritual deadness like the general populous. They are dead because they reject Jesus Christ. Through Jesus, we are counted worthy.

We must remain in Christ and assure that our name remains in God's book.

"He that overcomes, the same shall be clothed in white raiment; and I will not blot out his name out of the book of life, but I will confess his name before my Father, and before his angels" (Revelation 3:5, KJV).

We overcome by continuing to abide in Jesus Christ. Then our name will remain in God's book of life. Jesus talked about the one who overcomes. We stay true to and abide in faith in Jesus Christ. If we remain faithful to Jesus, then he will not blot out our name because we continue in the faith, and we are registered citizens of heaven.

So we must stay true to the doctrine of Christ. In John 15, Jesus tells us that we should remain in him and let him stay our source; this is our responsibility. We need to ask for the Holy Spirit's help to assist us to always continue in the Lord Jesus Christ. He is our source of fellowship in Christ.

We must continue in the Spirit's leading.

"He that hath an ear, let him hear what the Spirit saith unto the churches" (Revelation 3:6, KJV).

It is the leading and power of the Holy Spirit who will prepare us to be ready for Christ's appearing. The scriptures tell us to hear! We need to get into the presence of God and allow him to make us.

Only by the Holy Spirit's help will our preparation be acceptable. One of the things the Holy Spirit does is to conform us into Christ's image. Let's be open to God's leading and follow the unction of the Holy Spirit to prepare us, and we will become alive again.

So as we turn our slack into watchfulness, we receive the help of the Holy Spirit, and our light will continue to burn brightly.

We need to stay connected to Jesus Christ.

Does fidelity matter to God? Will God accept half-hazard loyalty? Is your intentional devotion acceptable to him? Jesus places a high price on our commitment to him.

In Revelation 3:7–13, we see Jesus Christ is setting an open door of opportunity for those who demonstrate fidelity to God. What blessings will Jesus give to those who are faithful to him? Let's examine the benefits Jesus gives to the faithful.

Ultimately, we see that it is Jesus Christ who determines who will abide in the eternal heaven.

"And to the angel of the church in Philadelphia write; These things saith he that is holy, he that is true, he that hath the key of David, he that openeth, and no man shutteth; and shutteth, and no man openeth" (Revelation 3:7, KJV).

Jesus is the only way anyone can get in and be a citizen of heaven. Jesus is the door of entry and the way that keeps souls out. It is he who is the Holy One who says this. Because Jesus is the Son of God, he has full rights to determine who goes to heaven and who won't. As it speaks of the key of David, it could be referring to the eternal throne of David. God told King David that he would have an heir sit forever on his throne.

Psalms chapter 2 describes God giving the throne to his Son. We are to kiss the Son's feet why there is peace with him. Those who repent and trust in Jesus for their salvation have entry into the eternal heaven. John 3:16 expresses the necessity of placing our trust in Jesus for our salvation and eternal hope. It is time to get our hearts right with God. We need to settle the sinful account by believing in the merits of Jesus Christ's work to redeem us.

Jesus Christ has opened a door of opportunity for his followers who stay faithful to him.

"I know thy works: behold, I have set before thee an open door, and no man can shut it: for thou hast a little strength, and hast kept my word, and hast not denied my name" (Revelation 3:8, KJV).

Jesus is giving his church time to fulfill his work while he waits in heaven. We have an open door also of the opportunity to work for Jesus. By being faithful, we are given more significant opportunities to co-labor with Christ in his work. We must go through this open door by responding to Jesus Christ's letter to the churches. If we are faithful, then more excellent opportunities will be given to us to serve Jesus. This church has little strength and keeps Jesus's Word. These are people who stay true to Jesus Christ and faith.

Jesus is keeping this door open for this church so that the faithful can excel in opportunity for him. The open door is called occupying for God. We stay in service and are busy fulfilling Jesus Christ's will while we await him to come back. Let us continue to be faithful so that doors of opportunity will open so that we may seize them. Doing this will enhance our stewardship and glorify God.

Jesus Christ will humble our enemies, who ridicule us for our loyalty to him.

"Behold, I will make them of the synagogue of Satan, which say they are Jews, and are not, but do lie; behold, I will make them to come and worship before thy feet, and to know that I have loved thee" (Revelation 3:9, KJV).

It is those who keep Jesus's commandments and do the will of the Father who is ridiculed by the world. God will cause those who mock us to bow before us and honor our God. God will make these mockers to worship God before us. They will see that God has loved us.

It is time God sets all records straight. God has never abandoned those who are loyal to him. Therefore, let's continue to be operating with an authentic, heartfelt fidelity to Jesus Christ. If we do this, we won't shrink but shine when we give account to Jesus.

Jesus Christ will keep us from the hour of temptation that will overtake the whole world because we continue to abide in him.

"Because thou hast kept the word of my patience, I also will keep thee from the hour of temptation, which shall come upon the entire world, to try them that dwell upon the earth" (Revelation 3:10, KJV).

This word *from* is (Ek) in the Greek and means to come out. Check out the Greek Strong's #1537. EK says Jesus will remove us out of the snare about to engulf the whole world. Jesus is speaking to those who keep his word. If we follow the work and doctrine Jesus did and taught, we can expect God's protection. Jesus said he would save us. Jesus will secure our souls. I believe this refers to the catching away of the saints in 1 Thessalonians 4:13–18.

Because we have clung to him, he will put divine guidance on us. God looks for those he can show himself big on their behalf. Let's stay joined to Jesus by living out our faith all our life. Then we will be delivered from the trial that's coming upon the whole world.

Jesus Christ warns us to keep our salvation in him by allowing nothing or nobody to take it away.

"Behold, I come quickly: hold that fast which thou hast, that no man takes thy crown" (Revelation 3:11, KJV).

We must not abandon our confidence in Jesus Christ but hold fast to the salvation and good news he gave us so that we will pass our earthly sojourn and receive the eternal home as part of our salvation. We must not allow any people or persons to snatch away the knowledge of the truth so that we can hold our confidence in Jesus Christ.

We need to make sure we are growing in the knowledge of the truth. Paul tells his mentees to guard that good deposit within them. Let's see to it that the truth abides within and continue to live within us. Do not put out the fire or light Jesus gave you.

Jesus Christ will establish us in his eternal plans if we will hear the voice of the Spirit and overcome.

"Him that overcomes will I make a pillar in the temple of my God, and he shall go no more out: and I will write upon him the name of my God, and the name of the city of my God, *which is* new Jerusalem, which cometh down out of heaven from my God: and *I will write upon him* my new name. He that hath an ear let him hear what the Spirit saith unto the churches" (Revelation 3:12–13, KJV).

Jesus gives precious promises to the overcomer (winner in the contest of life by exercising faith in Jesus Christ), a pillar in his house and citizenship in his city. We will go no more out; we will have an eternal home of our own in his city. Therefore, hear what God is saying through the Spirit! If we want these things, we must open our hearts to God and stay true to him or cling to him.

The Spirit empowers us to overcome. We do this by the Spirit's power. Let's stay close to God, and he will fulfill his will in our life.

So let's stay faithful to God, and we can partake of Jesus's open door.

Spiritual wretchedness is dangerous to our place in Jesus Christ and heaven.

How do we gauge our spiritual condition? Can we be compared to a tree that is fruitless or dry and barren? Do the things of Christ bore us? We must deal with spiritual wretchedness, or our light will go out.

We see in Revelation 3:14–22 that we are able with Jesus Christ's help to correct our spiritual wretchedness. Do we need to ask ourselves what we can do to fix our condition? Today, let's examine the things Jesus pointed out, which we can do to alter our wretchedness condition.

We need to let Jesus be the real source of retrospection.

"And unto the angel of the church of the Laodiceans write; These things saith the Amen, the faithful and true witness, the beginning of the creation of God" (Revelation 3:14, KJV).

Since Jesus made creation, he has preeminence; therefore, he is our source for guidance. Jesus addressed this vibrant church called Laodicean. We will find that this church was the furthest from Christlikeness and earned the most forceful criticism. Many writers tell us that this church characterizes the last days' church since it is the very last church mentioned. Jesus would not have rebuked this church so sharply if he did not have the hope of redemption in mind should some repent and turn back to him. As we examine this church, let's examine ourselves considering the Word of God to see if our lives aligned with the nature, character, and Word of God.

It is needful for us to judge whether we are in Jesus or not, so we won't be classified as lukewarm. Lukewarm or tipped is a deplorable state in the spiritual setting. A significant problem with lukewarmness is its unfitness for usefulness. If we are inactive in faith and useless in exercising our gifts for God's cause, we will be in trouble, and we need to judge ourselves to make sure we are in the faith.

Let us reform or we may lose out with God.

"I know thy works, that thou art neither cold nor hot: I would thou wert cold or hot. So then because thou art lukewarm, and neither cold nor hot, I will spew thee out of my mouth" (Revelation 3:15–16, KJV).

If we refuse to examine our Christianity and spiritual life and we remain deplorable (useless), Jesus will release us. Indeed, we are saved by faith by God's grace; this I wholeheartedly believe, but what we have is stern rebuke by Jesus to change our hearts. Let's examine the situation. Was our salvation a real heart-changing experience in Jesus or are we just Christians in name only? Let me tell you Jesus knows the difference. Jesus knows our works, so we ought not to pretend that we are the real deal when Jesus knows we are neither cold nor hot. Many Christians could care less about making any impact whatsoever. But if that's our attitude, then we lose out because we are to be in busy service while we wait for Christ to return.

Jesus didn't save us to be a lame duck in his kingdom; we are all called to bear fruit that lasts. Many CEOs lose their jobs because they won't reform. We are the CEO of our walk with God. Let it be real and fruitful. Only you can make yourself draw nearer to God. The Bible tells us to exercise godliness and stir our gift up. Doing this will cause us to bear fruit.

We need to acknowledge our condition.

"Because thou sayest, I am rich, and increased with goods, and have need of nothing; and knows not that thou art wretched, and miserable, and poor, and blind, and naked" (Revelation 3:17, KJV).

We got to get honest with ourselves and our condition if we will get out of our complacency. We do not think well to assume that just because we have all we need physically, spiritually, and all other things that we do not need God. That is a deadly and false sense of security. It is tragic when religion and individuals assume the work without God. Trying to work and walk the walk apart from God will never work. This church thought it needed nothing. Many of us remain complacent in yesterday's blessings. We become wretched without God and slaves to our complacency.

We mislead ourselves into thinking that if everything is comfortable, then everything must be all right. We are comfortably wrong. We must break this condition or habit. Jesus tells this church that it is deplorable, blind, naked, and wretched. Let's identify our complacency so we can correct ourselves, and then God won't judge us for not correcting ourselves.

We need to turn to Jesus Christ for our healing.

"I counsel thee to buy of me gold tried in the fire, that thou mayest be rich; and white raiment, that thou mayest be clothed, and *that* the shame of thy nakedness does not appear; and anoint thine eyes with eye salve, that thou mayest see" (Revelation 3:18, KJV).

Jesus urges us to get a heart checkup and turn to him for everything we need for healing in our soul. Jesus is counseling us or confronting us to be made well through him. We must turn to him for the true riches, attire, and sight.

Only through faith in Jesus Christ will we possess our soul. It must be an active faith. Jesus told the religious leaders that they needed to believe in him for salvation, and that those who do God's will are God's children. We need to be busy carrying out the will and commands of God (seeking and obeying his Word). Our responsibility is to love God and others.

We must become zealous over Christ's work.

"As many as I love, I rebuke and chasten: be zealous therefore, and repent. Behold, I stand at the door and knock: if any man hears my voice and opens the door, I will come into him and will sup with him, and he with me" (Revelation 3:19–20, KJV).

Only an interactive relationship is the source of life fellowship with Jesus Christ. From this relationship, we are motivated to do what we can for the cause of Jesus and the gospel. Jesus commands us to be zealous. If we stay complacent, then we lose our fellowship. Ironically, Jesus is outside this church asking to come it. The Church belongs to Jesus, and she put him out! If we keep growing in our fellowship with Jesus, we will bear precious fruit. The key is to do as Mary did and sit at Jesus's feet. Jesus told Martha that she was worried about many things, but what Mary did would not be taken from her. If we draw close to God, then he will draw close to us.

Our zeal cannot come from self-generated influence, but it is from above or from Jesus Christ. When we sit at Jesus's feet, then we get a Christ-centered relational power. Our fellowship with Jesus will move us to love one another. Will we get excited over the things of God? Let's ask God for a fresh excitement over our relationship with him and doing his will. We must stir ourselves to activity.

Let us obey and overcome.

"To him that overcomes will I grant to sit with me in my throne, even as I also overcame, and am set down with my Father in his throne. He that hath an ear, let him hear what the Spirit saith unto the churches" (Revelation 3:21–22, KJV).

Jesus calls us to hear, obey, and put into motion the things which bring spiritual breakthrough and victory. We must walk in the presence of God for the divine favor for our behavior. Jesus told this Church that if they would overcome, they must be determined to continue in Christ's victory. He promised that those who overcome would be granted a reward for obedience, a high place of authority ruling with Christ. Jesus urges us again to hear if we have an ear. To understand is saying that we should listen and obey the Spirit. We need to understand and repent so Jesus can come and heal us.

When we listen and obey, God will cooperate with us to bring our breakthrough and victory into our life. Deuteronomy stresses faith and obedience, so if we break through our complacency, we will need confidence and willingness. So let's listen to what the Spirit says to the churches, then we will put ourselves into a position of victory.

So let's start now to correct our lukewarm, loathsome condition by calling on Jesus to help us and stir up our passion for him and become useful to his cause. We can be an overcomer who put on Jesus Christ and entered eternity victoriously.

DIVISION 2

Heavenly Assessment

CHAPTER 4

Heaven disclosed.
Have you ever had a secret revealed to you? Maybe someone told of a plan unfolding that involved you? Perhaps someone gave you a lead in which brought you to a good thing? John expresses to us that God has a will for our eternal state. God's eternal will for us unfolds in the book of Revelation and culminates on the renovated earth. The sequences of events must happen in this book if God's people reach their destination. These events also include the full measure of martyrs that must come in according to God's decree.

In Revelation 4:1–4, we can get an understanding of how heaven will be made known to the people of God. How will God's people view the eternal realm? Let's look at some aspects in which God's people will see heaven's view.

There will be a call-up.

"After this I looked, and, behold, a door *was* opened in heaven: and the first voice which I heard *was* as it were of a trumpet talking with me; which said, come up hither, and I will shew thee things which must be hereafter" (Revelation 4:1, KJV).

Many people believe that this is the verse that describes the calling up of God's glorious Church to himself. After this verse, the Church isn't addressed on the earth again, except probably as a participator in heaven in various places (we will look at that as it comes up). This verse shows us a time heaven will open, and the Church will be translated out of the earth. The door in heaven reminds me of 1 Corinthians 15:52–53 and 1 Thessalonians 4:16–17, where the catching up to heaven occurs. Jesus Christ will call his Church home.

when we are raptured

The first voice that spoke to John now tells him (a representation of the church), "Come up hither!" Come out of your earthly existence into your eternal realm within the heavens. First John 3:1–3 reminds us that when this rapture occurs, we will see Jesus in his glorified state, and we will be like him. We will be in our eternal, sinless state.

This call that John received should stir our responsibility and readiness for our call home. When at that time, we will be full-fledged participators of the domain of the heavens. We will worship God. The Bible asks us what manner of men we should be? Indeed, we should be a Church waiting with anticipation for Jesus Christ's coming. We should certainly be paying close attention to how we walk with our God. What can we do then to stay prepared? First, let's make sure we are in Jesus and continue to be in him. We know for sure that he has saved us, and now we abide with him daily. We need to make sure we are practicing a walk with him. The second thing we need to make sure is that we are laboring for Jesus. Let's be busy fulfilling the purpose God has given us.

There will be a beholding of God's glory.

"And immediately I was in the spirit: and, behold, a throne was set in heaven, and *one* sat on the throne. And he that sat was to look upon like a jasper and a sardine stone: and *there was* a rainbow round about the throne, in sight like unto an emerald" (Revelation 4:2–3, KJV).

These verses state the royalty, majesty, and nobility of our God. We will behold him. He is pure and holy and takes great pains to sustain his creation. Not as though it is hard for him, but he does all that is right, just, good, and wise so that we can come into his presence to worship. The calling home is the time we obtain our resurrected spiritual bodies. John was caught up and was in the Spirit. He saw a throne. The only one who will ever sit upon the throne of heaven is God. I believe that the rainbow around God's throne reflects his great care toward humankind, like the rainbow in the sky, reminding him never to bring a worldwide flood again.

All who believe (those who hear and respond to God's call to trust in the Son) will see God and be one of the privileged who worship God forever. We don't have to wait to get into God's presence.

Psalm

Jesus said whoever is thirsty should come to him and drink. We can worship and adore God now. Let us practice and perfect our praise now. The best preparation for our praise and adoration is to enter his presence in prayer and praise continually. If we are prepared to be with him, then we must spend time with him now.

There will be a heavenly counsel.

"And round about the throne *were* four and twenty seats: and upon the seats I saw four and twenty elders sitting, clothed in white raiment; and they had on their head's crowns of gold" (Revelation 4:4, KJV).

Here God has set up divine representatives (priests) who are all nobility and who represent the church of the redeemed of all ages. They will be partners in God's heavenly counsel for his redeemed. They will have high authority, power, and influence. This counsel sits around the throne. These twenty-four elders will always abide in the presence of God. They will have seats in the presence of God, denoting dominion over divisions of the redeemed. Their white raiment and crowns of gold mean they are from those redeemed by God and are God's counselors of God for his people. That opinion is just my speculative observation.

These will be in God's heavenly counsel to carry out God's will. We recall boardroom settings where counsels have objectives drawn up and carry them out. Such will be the case and with authority. Our best preparation for a good account is to live by the authoritative rule—the Holy Bible. The Word alone will procure God's favor then.

So as we contemplate how God will disclose (open) heaven to his redeemed, determine to live pleasing to him by abiding in his will.

We should do all things in adoration to God.

In your occupation, do you do all in the worship of your God? Do you joyfully carry out your work in praise to God? Do you thank God for giving you work to do? In heaven, all things are carried out or done in adoration to God.

We see in Revelation 4:5–11 that it is necessary to know that the occupants of heaven do all of heaven's business out of worship unto God. Why is it essential to know that heaven's occupation is to do all of heaven's business out of communion with God? Let's look at this now.

Heaven's occupants do all of heaven's business out of worship unto God because the glory of God fills all of heaven.

"And out of the throne proceeded lightnings and thundering's and voices: and *there were* seven lamps of fire burning before the throne, which are the seven Spirits of God" (Revelation 4:5, KJV).

This verse stresses that all the activity and life elements of heaven proceed out of God unto his creation. The sevenfold manifestation of God's Spirit keeps all the holy activity going and is God's manifestation of himself to each of his creatures. They gladly give worship and praise to God. The verse tells us that these various things proceed out of the throne. This says that all of heaven is a God-centered place of worship and activity. A great theocracy. The seven lamps that were burning and the seven Spirits of God express the movement of God throughout all his creation by sustaining and activating it for his purposes by his Holy Spirit.

Heaven is glorious because we will be suited to know, worship, and enjoy the Lord God in the fullest. We will intimately participate in his presence. Paul said here we know in part, but there we will know in full. Having spiritual understanding like the angels should be a source of joy and excitement for us. As we entertain this excitement, it should direct our life to live intimately with God now. Intimacy will be the difference of a life lived in fellowship with God or out of the divine favor.

Heaven's occupants do all of heaven's business out of worship unto God because out of God's throne proceeds the sea of living water.

> And before the throne *there was* a sea of glass
> like unto crystal: and in the midst of the throne,
> and round about the throne, *were* four beasts full
> of eyes before and behind. And the first beast
> *was* like a lion, and the second beast like a calf,
> and the third beast had a face as a man, and the
> fourth beast *was* like a flying eagle. And the four

beasts had each of them six wings about *him*; and *they were* full of eyes within: and they rest not day and night, saying, Holy, holy, holy, Lord God Almighty, which was, and is, and is to come. (Revelation 4:6–8, KJV)

This living water is symbolic of God's sustaining providence and his purity because of the water proceeding from the throne. From the throne proceeds this sea of glass, declaring the holiness and life that comes from God and sustains us all. The four beasts are guardians of the throne. If you know about famous people, they need guards to protect them from intrusions or excited people. It this case coming to close to God could bring death and separation from God. Why dare come close to the Creator who is like total fire or a blazing inferno?

It will be and is our pleasure to thank and praise God for his life-giving and -sustaining providence. God sustains us by his providence. It is God's foresight and preparation in the care of his creation. Let us acknowledge our being comes from God and is sustained by him. Having the knowledge that God is our life should be incorporated into our worship of God.

Heaven's occupants do all of heaven's business out of worship unto God because total reverence is due to our Holy God.

"And the four beasts had each of them six wings about *him*; and *they were* full of eyes within: and they rest not day and night, saying, Holy, holy, holy, Lord God Almighty, which was, and is, and is to come. And when those beasts give glory and honor and thanks to him that sat on the throne, who lives for ever and ever" (Revelation 4:8–9, KJV).

The seen in Heaven is each person and every creature will join in on their appointed time to bring and exercise their worship to God. That will be the natural state. We will acknowledge God and his attributes. We will see clearly! We will join in the shouting "Holy, holy, holy." We will recognize the eternality of God.

We will be ecstatic over our praise for him. One reason will be evident in the truth that he created and sustains all things. We will be elated over our appreciation for him. Why don't we get out of our comfort zone and praise him now! Get in the habit of worshipping God now.

Heaven's occupants do all of heaven's business out of worship unto God because worshipping God is why he made us.

"The four and twenty elders fall down before him that sat on the throne, and worship him that lives for ever and ever, and cast their crowns before the throne, saying, Thou art worthy, O Lord, to receive glory and honor and power: for thou hast created all things, and for thy pleasure, they are and were created" (Revelation 4:10–11, KJV).

These twenty-four elders represent us as the Church of all ages. All of us will be casting our crowns before God and joyfully worshipping him. Like the twenty-four elders, we shall give our worship to our God and Savior. We will shout thou are worthy, O God. We do this because God is the Creator.

Not only will we be carrying out our positions of responsibilities, but we will do so in total allegiance and worship of God. We can't fathom this kind of devotion to God in a whole community setting on earth.

But that is how it will be in heaven. The Church or gathering of saints is the only thing that resembles this. Let us practice the assembling of ourselves to worship God. Worship is right now one of our foretaste of heaven's realities.

Let us learn then to do all we do out of worship to God, and we will be acting as citizens of heaven.

CHAPTER 5

Is He Worthy?

God is going to solve the unsolvable mystery.
Have you ever experienced an unsolvable problem? Was there a math problem you couldn't figure out? Did you ever have a relationship problem that continually irked you? There are insolvable mysteries that only Jesus Christ can solve.

In Revelation 5:1–5, we can contemplate why Jesus Christ is the only one who can read from God's book and make known God's unsolvable mysteries about earth's future. We are going to look at why Jesus Christ is the only one able to disclose God's unsolvable mystery about the earth's future. Essentially, Jesus Christ is the only one able to reveal God's unsolvable mystery relating to the future of the planet because he alone is found worthy. Let's examine why this is so.

We will see that within heaven is a book of wrath and mystery over the future of planet earth.

"And I saw in the right hand of him that sat on the throne a book written within and on the backside, sealed with seven seals" (Revelation 5:1, KJV).

Here God has a book that contains the mysteries of the revelation of the future and events that close the age and discloses the future direction of earth and its people. This book tells what will happen to the world as we know it. It covers such things as what will transpire concerning the gentile rulership of the world and God's purpose for Israel. It mentions God sitting on his throne holding this book, and God the Father will only give it to that worthy candidate who can unlock its secrets. It's a book of mysteries and judgment.

God has disclosed in a sealed book what will happen to our world and the future of humanity. God is known as our Sovereign Lord, who creates and judges. It makes sense for him to make known his judgments and counsel to heaven's viewers. That's why I labeled chapters 4–20 the heavenly analysis. Humanity's only hope comes from the One who overcame it! My friend there is only one who was never tainted by Satan, and that is the one who defeated him, the Lord Jesus Christ. All other people are not good enough to open this book. May I be bold enough to say that not even God's great angels are good enough to open this book? Somehow Satan's taint will be wiped out of heaven's cosmos also. I want to stress that we will want to be on the winning side. As I read Revelation, I notice that Satan puts forth his deceptive valiant effort to cloak all the things going on until he outright builds an army to fight God. Ultimately, he ends in a thousand-year cell until the last rebellion and from there cast into the lake of fire. The problem is that people cannot see the whole scheme of things since they live as common men and not illuminated by God's Word. They go with the flow until consumed by the deception.

We see, also, that it takes a certain one to open the book; that person has to be worthy.

"And I saw a strong angel proclaiming with a loud voice, who is worthy to open the book, and to lose the seals thereof?" (Revelation 5:2 (KJV).

Again, we see the scene in heaven for a search that gets underway! In this search, heaven looks for the presence of a worthy victor! One sinless who overcame Satan and his corruption. No one steps forward because there is none good enough, except Jesus Christ. Jesus steps forward to open the book. Who is worthy? In a sense, all of heaven and earth became stained with Satan's filth. But, thank God, the second Adam overcame and cleansed the places that where Satan's lies spread. It is this Jesus Christ who is worthy to disclose the contents of this book.

The Father will only hand the book to one worthy of reading it because only one worthy can pronounce judgment and future events—one without sin. Being in Jesus Christ, we see and know that it is he who cleanses us and makes us worthy of heaven.

Let us contemplate that no one in heaven or the earth is found able or worthy to open the book.

"And no man in heaven, nor in earth, neither under the earth, was able to open the book, neither to look thereon. And I wept much, because no man was found worthy to open and to read the book, neither to look thereon" (Revelation 5:3–4 (KJV).

Because no one was worthy goes to show how deep Satan's influence became. Satan usurped all at one time or another by his sinful power, and thus, no one was found worthy. No one was able to open the book. Only by the triumph of Jesus Christ was the future possible. Satan would have prevented it, but Jesus overcame and inherited creation.

Therefore, judgment on Satan and the world is fitting to make way for God's coming kingdom on earth and his future eternal plans for creation. Jesus regained and restored what Satan took away from men and the angels. Let us thank Jesus Christ for restoring us to God's plan for us, in us, etc. Give great thanks for God's salvation.

Let's look again at how Jesus Christ alone is found worthy to open the book.

"And one of the elders saith unto me, Weep not: behold, the Lion of the tribe of Juda, the Root of David, hath prevailed to open the book, and to lose the seven seals thereof" (Revelation 5:5, KJV).

Here Jesus triumphantly steps up to open God's book of future revelation so that God's will may go forward. My friend, if this doesn't happen, then kiss our godly inheritance in Jesus goodbye. But the lion of the tribe of Judah, Jesus, is pictured as the sovereign king who has crushed his enemies after a great struggle. Jesus has prevailed by way of the cross. Jesus has defeated Satan through the shedding of his righteous blood and made many righteous by faith in him.

The victory came at a high cost to the Son of God. He took on Gospel a body and suffered for men, died, and rose again. Men, being finite and sinful, could not reverse the fall. Men did not know how to get to heaven, they were already tainted with sin, their walk with God became corrupted, death had the prospect of a fiery grave for them,

Adam &
Eve

and no hope of a resurrection. Do you see the plight of men without Jesus Christ? The big clincher is that there is no ascension for men to go to God without Christ because upon the battles of life, they are left defeated and hopeless. Only through Jesus Christ is there hope of God calling them to himself in the future. Jesus redeemed a great host out of the clutches of Satan's lies. We are known as the Church, meaning a called-out assembly of redeemed ones. Jesus is, therefore, our key to prophecy who unlocks the future for us. Let us examine all that he speaks to us concerning the future and how to prepare our lives for his coming.

So for us to have revelation over future events, let us go to the scripture for its disclosure of our triumphant Lord. Scripture is that which points to Jesus Christ.

Understand what the redeemed look like in heaven.

What is the difference in the eternal state of the believer and the unbeliever? The nonbeliever suffers eternal punishment and separation from God. The believer is in the joys of heaven, worshipping their Creator. Let us grasp, then the truth that repentance and faith in Jesus Christ are necessary.

In Revelation 5:6–10, we see that we can comprehend the redeemed worshipping in heaven. Let's look at how the Bible pictures the redeemed worshipping Jesus in heaven.

The marks of Jesus Christ's work at Calvary is visible in heaven.

"And I beheld, and, lo, in the midst of the throne and of the four beasts, and in the midst of the elders, stood a Lamb as it had been slain, having seven horns and seven eyes, which are the seven Spirits of God sent forth into all the earth" (Revelation 5:6, KJV).

Jesus Christ emerges as the redeemer triumphant, being God the Son and having the fullness of the Holy Spirit. Jesus is worthy. He is that Lamb who had died on the cross. We will recognize him as the redeemer who purchased our salvation and procured our right to be in heaven. He has seven horns. He has exercised total victory over evil, Satan, and sin; hence, he is worthy to take the scroll. The seven Spirits of God indicate the fullness of Spirit.

In heaven, we will be present because of Jesus Christ redeeming work at Calvary. There has not been a presence in heaven, testifying of the great grace of God in such a magnitude. We will always be the reminder in heaven of God's great redemption and love. We should realize our vision of Calvary is an enduring vision. Thus, Christ is always our redeemer and Savior.

Jesus Christ is worthy to open God's scroll.

"And he came and took the book out of the right hand of him that sat upon the throne" (Revelation 5:7, KJV).

Jesus is worthy alone who can open the scroll. Jesus had to be blameless if he would be an administrator of the manuscript of wrath that God pours upon the world. Jesus took the book. This as the triumphant one and who has the full right to rule the earth Hebrews 1:2. Jesus took the scroll; Jesus being God the Son was the only one qualified to take it.

Jesus's superiority shows us that our redemption is fully secured, and that those who have rejected salvation through Jesus Christ must suffer God's wrath. The present work of the Holy Spirit is a work of comfort to the believer but a warning of judgment to the unbeliever. This points to the coming day of the beginning of wrath poured upon a Christ-rejecting world. It behooves the unbeliever to pour out his condemnation and sin unto God and settle the sin account.

All of heaven worships Jesus Christ.

"And when he had taken the book, the four beasts and four *and* twenty elders fell down before the Lamb, having every one of them harps, and golden vials full of odors, which are the prayers of saints" (Revelation 5:8, KJV).

This small vision shows that all of creation, and all the redeemed partake together in the worship of Jesus Christ, proving, once again, of Jesus deity. Only God is worthy of worship. I believe that the four beasts are representative of all creation in my opinion, while the twenty-four elders represent the redeemed of all ages. And all these fell before the lamb to give worship to him. They carried with them golden veils full of the prayers of the saints. The elders assist in the administering of the prayers of the saints. They are priests unto God.

The redeemed and creation joins in the greatness of God's good-will for men. Romans 8:19 speaks of all the nature awaiting the completion of the salvation of believers. Though this is judgment time for the inhabitants of the earth, the created order, along with all the redeemed, will join in worship over God's great benevolence in his redeeming love for man. We, as believers, will be worshipping God.

The redeemed will also be partaking in the worship of Jesus Christ.

"And they sung a new song, saying, thou art worthy to take the book, and to open the seals thereof: for thou were slain, and hast redeemed us to God by thy blood out of every kindred, and tongue, and people, and nation; And hast made us unto our God kings and priests: and we shall reign on the earth" (Revelation 5:9–10, KJV).

Here, we, as the redeemed in heaven, partake in the adoration and worship of Jesus Christ with a new song. New because heaven never had songs of redemption before the resurrection took place. God made the redeemed kings and priests unto him. We, at that time, are given positions of responsibilities. The redeemed will rule with Jesus Christ on the earth; we will be given authority in his future kingdom.

We won't want to miss the opportunity always to thank our God. His death for our life will resonate in our praise for all eternity. Let us make up our mind to fully follow Jesus Christ because once the Church is gone, all the earth will experience the wrath of God for rejecting Jesus Christ's work of salvation on their behalf.

So we must decide now to be one of the redeemed who worships God in heaven, and then we will be participators with all the redeemed and all creation in offering our uninterrupted services to our Creator.

The worship of God goes on forever.

Will you make worshipping God a part of your walk with him? Try to set a time to worship God every day. Bowing your knee and subordinating all things to do so? Worship is the greatest joy heavenly beings exercise in eternity.

In Revelation 5:11–14, we see how worship in heaven goes on forever. What is religion about in heaven? Let's examine this now.

Innumerable hosts worship God forever.

"And I beheld, and I heard the voice of many angels' round about the throne and the beasts and the elders: and the number of them was ten thousand times ten thousand, and thousand sands" (Revelation 5:11, KJV).

In eternity, our primary goal is to worship our Creator! Legions will come in their order to pay homage to the great God and Creator of heaven and earth. There will be there the voice of many angels. They also worship God in unison. The beasts and elders also are there, representing all creation worshipping God. There will be an innumerable company, the hosts of heaven.

The Lord is worthy who has endowed us with the joys of heaven. Daniel 7:10 expresses the innumerable company again before God. It is expedient to anticipate and be ready for our calling home. When we wait for this day watchfully, we show our applause to the worshipped God.

The Lamb of God is the object of worship.

"Saying with a loud voice, Worthy is the Lamb that was slain to receive power, and riches, and wisdom, and strength, and honor, and glory, and blessing" (Revelation 5:12, KJV).

Because of Jesus Christ's offering of himself to redeem men, all of heaven joins in worshiping the Lamb. He is the object of our worship. We will forever adore and attribute all glory to him. Jesus has all the power in the universe, and through his riches, he enriches heaven. He directs all affairs by his wisdom, and he has the strength to accomplish anything. We, as heavenly citizens, will ascribe to Jesus honor, glory, and blessings because he has saved us fully.

He is the agent of God in creation and salvation, fully worthy of all the things that are ascribed to him. Psalms chapter 2 describes how God the Father gives all things unto his Son upon his asking. Is Jesus the center of attention in your life? Does your schedule revolve around him? If not, reprioritize your goals to make Jesus first.

Homage will go to God for all he has done.

"And every creature which is in heaven, and on the earth, and under the earth, and such as are in the sea, and all that are in them, heard I saying Blessing, and honor, and glory, and power, *be* unto him that sits upon the throne, and unto the Lamb forever and ever" (Revelation 5:13, KJV).

All of heaven joins in on the heavenly worship of God; for all have experienced his love and goodness, so he is worshipped as their God. Each creature has representation there. This celebration and worship are unto to God and his Son, Jesus Christ.

Since Jesus Christ justly sustains all things by his power, he is worthy of our worship. Will you, even now, contemplate God's goodness to you? Let us now practice humbling ourselves and ascribing true worth to our God. As we exercise our adoration and praise to God, we will get accustomed to doing it.

All will give worship to our God.

"And the four beasts said, Amen. And the four *and* twenty elders fell down and worshipped him that lives for ever and ever" (Revelation 5:14, KJV).

These twenty-four elders represent man. The beasts represent the creation. All approve of the adoration of God by the whole host of heaven. These persons worshipped God also and gave their loving devotion to him and joined in the consent to God. Such will be the hearts we will have in heaven.

They are the heavenly representatives, so all heaven follows them to worship God. Will we fall prostrate unto God? Could we not find time to bow to our God? Let's break our pride and bend our knee.

This type of worship will go on in heaven forever! So let's allow the worship of God to be part of our life priorities, and then we will put God first in your business.

CHAPTER 6

(handwritten margin note: one of the four living creatures said, "Come.")

L ooking at the Antichrist's reign.

How will Satan's Antichrist come to power? Will he come on a peace platform? Will he deceive the world? We need to get a grasp on how this wicked ruler comes to be.

In Revelation 6:1–2, we come to understand how the opposer (Satan's Antichrist) of Jesus Christ will come. What do we know about the Antichrist? Let us examine some things concerning this Antichrist.

We must not get this opposer confused with Jesus Christ.

(handwritten margin note: Check Bible)

"And I saw when the Lamb opened one of the seals, and I heard, as it were the noise of thunder, one of the four beasts saying, Come and see" (Revelation 6:1, KJV).

This coming conqueror could not be Jesus Christ since Jesus is the one opening the seven seals. It is a futuristic time, occurring after the "Come up hither" of the church in chapter 4. The lamb opened the seal. The lamb is the real conqueror as we have already seen. He is the only one found worthy to open the scroll, giving him the title deed to the earth. As the beasts tell John to come and see, he will observe what will take place in the future and not the past. We are still awaiting these things to happen. We may see signs of them already, but the scenario is yet to happen.

As we see the future unfold before us, it is an expression to us of the providence and sovereignty of Jesus Christ. All the things that are appointed to happen will happen according to his oversight. For the believers to inherit their future blessings, these judgments must happen. God is just in his decisions. Please, remember that Jesus is the victor in heaven and not a satanic-appointed leader. Do not get upset or overcome by the circumstances of life, continue to exercise faith in Jesus Christ, then you'll be all right. The believer can expect protection from wrath.

This opposer overcomes without fighting.

"And I saw, and behold a white horse: and he that sat on him had a bow, and a crown was given unto him: and he went forth conquering, and to conquer" (Revelation 6:2, KJV).

Here is the introduction of Satan's Antichrist (meaning instead of or against or both), who comes riding on the scene. With the help of Satan's agents, he is part of the last world government system. He comes to power without fighting. He comes with a bow but no arrows which signify a bloodless acquiring of dominion. He comes to power without war, or he comes in peace-ably. Deceptively

Because he comes in on a peace platform, although it is outright war later, he deceives the people. I believe that position and power are given to him. Beware, God never sanctioned world peace through a human-made world government. Instead order won't come until Jesus Christ's Second Advent. When the entire world is crying peace and then comes sudden destruction.

This opposer establishes a one-world order.

The verse tells us a crown was given to him. There is a coming day this world leader sets up or takes the throne of the world government. He is picked by Satan and the world to rule the world lawlessly. Then soon, all hell breaks loose.

This world government begins peaceably but then engulfs the world with war. First Thessalonians 5:3 tells us that war will come like a woman with a child. Do not, if you're here, participate in his mark for food program because it's a program of death eternally. Rather starve and die and gain heaven.

This opposer has acquired the power to conquer.

The verse tells us he goes forth conquering and to conquer. Soon after the false sense of peace ends, all hell breaks loose, and the true nature and color of this madman come out. He has the color of blood and comes to conquer all lands. His rule engulfs the whole world with his agenda. Anyone who opposes him, he attacks and kills. Evil is his true nature, and he demands worship by the world. He is Satan's lie, who demands worship, and those who oppose will die. If you find yourself in the tribulation, die instead of worshipping him, or you'll suffer eternal judgment. Do not consent to Satan's plans to dominate, or you'll perish eternally. *yes please*

This opposer is Satan's lie (the Antichrist and false hope for the world). He comes to deceive and destroy the world; therefore, do not give your allegiance to him.

Chaos on the horizon.

Would you prepare if you knew chaos was coming? Perhaps you would set your spiritual affairs in order? Or maybe you would amend your relationships. There is coming such a time of war and chaos that it will engulf the whole world.

In Revelation 6:3–4, we see that a time of war and chaos is coming to planet earth. What time of war is this that is coming to the planet? Let us examine this time of war and chaos that is coming.

The opening of the second seal begins this time of war and chaos.

"And when he had opened the second seal, I heard the second beast say, Come and see" (Revelation 6:3, KJV).

John is summoned to observe another catastrophe upon the earth that comes with the opening of the second seal. The opening of this seal begins a time of chaos and war unlike any other time in the earth's history. All peace will be removed from humanity. As Jesus opens the second seal, we see that this is God's doing. So whether followers at that time suffer or not, we are to know God is allowing this to transpire. Praise the Lord! As John is summoned to observe, it is a time of persecution and bloodshed upon the believers. Know ahead of time that God does allow this to elevate his people. Be prepared for suffering if you miss the rapture. *please receive*

God is doing this (allowing it) because he is closing this age and showing he is sovereign, and that apart from him, men will be in complete chaos and war. At this, time is war and confusion, and peace will not return until Jesus's Second Coming. Regardless of our take on end-times, concerning how we believe, let's live in a way we are not surprised but ready to give our lives for the Lord Jesus Christ.

Oh yes

We cannot be sure what we will experience before the catching up occurs.

The red horse signifies bloodshed and persecution. *war*

"And there went out another red horse: and *power* was given to him that sat thereon to take peace from the earth, and that they should kill one another: and there was given unto him a great sword" (Revelation 6:4, KJV).

This horse is a specific force of evil that moves upon the earth, which takes away all peace and brings chaos and war and persecution to the saints. We have been given this warning to solidify our faith so that we are not caught off guard and turn away from God. The horse follows the demonic dictator. This judgment from God is for a world that has rejected the good news, therefore, tenaciously hold to Christ.

It comes because the world chose this over peace with God through Jesus Christ. Let God be true and every man a liar. A world that rejects Jesus Christ will stumble to its demise on the stumbling stone. The ironic thing is that the world refuses to repent, but many do. We, therefore, must be ready to bring in the crop. It is harvest time, and we must be busy during this harvest.

Man's security of peace is gone.

In the same verse, we see that this time creates a vacuum where no peace remains. It will be insane, and people will tear one another up. Have we ever seen an environment with no order? That is a foretaste of this time. This rider on the red horse takes peace away; he will touch all the earth. He will remove peace wherever it is; no matter where you live, there will be no peace.

Security is removed also because men refuse to repent and come to the prince of peace. The nation that forgets its God becomes a living hell. In truth, all countries during this time have rejected Jesus. We, in our relative time of peace, can choose to trust in the prince of peace, Jesus Christ! Will you give him your life today?

The people of the earth fight each other.

It is the people who kill each other and those who follow God. There is complete negation for the value of life. No value for life is the dominant power of wickedness that moves through the heart of the world or this season. The inhabitants of earth kill each other. The people get insane and do the killing. There was also given to the rider a great sword. Could that be nuclear bombs? Everywhere in the world, there will be bloodshed.

Millions will become victims of their countrymen. Jesus said this day would be like the day before the flood. How was that day? The world will be filled with violence. Be prepared by knowing God and knowing your Bible. We have not arrived at heaven yet, so be always ready.

So know that a very particular time of chaos and war is coming that will engulf the whole earth. Knowing ahead of time will help you prepare by being right with God through Jesus Christ. *3rd*

There is coming a physical and spiritual famine. *Horse*

What would you do if you were in a famine? Are you prepared to live physically in such a state? Can you go forward spiritually in your walk in such a state? Revelation says there is coming such a time upon the earth. *Thank You, Jesus, that I won't*

In Revelation 6:5–6, we learn that a time is coming when fam- *be* ine is going to break out upon the earth. What does this passage say *on* about the coming time of worldwide famine that is going to break *earth* out upon the earth? Let's look at this passage to see what it says about *because I* this. *received*

We need to observe what God is saying and prepare! *you*

"And when he had opened the third seal, I heard the third beast *into* say, Come and see. And I beheld, and lo a black horse; and he that *my* sat on him had a pair of balances in his hand" (Revelation 6:5, KJV). *life*

The famine will be a worldwide end-time judgment which will cover the whole land. It will cover all the earth. People who believed that through hard work and self-reliance can produce the dream of wealth will soon experience great grievous disappointment. Only in God will there be provision. John heard a voice that came from heaven. I want you to know that this whole famine is from God. John was told to come and see this. John saw the hunger and how it comes to earth. It engulfs the land and tries all men that are upon the earth.

If you are living in such days, do not take offense at God and his judgments, instead worship him through it. The goal is to exercise abundant grace spiritually. Let's set our two houses in order, the physical home and all its elements and the spiritual house. We better lay aside the resources to sustain us. Let's practice our growth pattern now and be ready to share our abundance with others. If we have our house in order, then we will be set to be a house of survival for ourselves and others.

Hard times are going to occur in all the earth.

This black horse goes forth to the earth as a sign of the great woe, distress, famine, and scarcity, which will fall upon it. This black horse symbolizes suffering and hunger. Heaven calls for a pair of balances to measure the foodstuff of the earth.

There will be no place to hide, and it will be worldwide. There will be few controlling what's available, and they will be powerful and wealthy. Distress such as anxiety, difficult circumstances, and suffering will be many people's lot. Let us waste no time with our preparations over our home and spiritual house and affairs. If we find that we are well-fed spiritually, then we will have the life needed to encourage the many hopeless people.

The decree of famine comes from heaven.

"And I heard a voice in the midst of the four beasts say, a measure of wheat for a penny, and three measures of barley for a penny; and *see* thou hurt not the oil and the wine" (Revelation 6:6, KJV).

Why do I bring this to your attention again? It is because this comes on a gospel-rejecting world. If we are going to be ready, then we must be prepared spiritually by walking in Jesus Christ. John hears a voice of one of the beasts which signify God's righteousness over all his creation to bless or to judge.

As these judgments unfold, all heaven praises God and backs them. Heaven awaits God's fulfillment of his plans for the earth. These plans come through punishment. So are we pressing into the kingdom of God? Let's practice that which allows us to produce for Christ's cause so that we won't have a spiritual famine.

A day's wage will only purchase a meal.

The money will be worthless, and the ability to acquire food and things will be slim. People will put in a whole day of work to eat a meal and stay alive. They will be forced to put in camps possibly; this will be drudgery. It speaks of a measure of wheat, meaning that your whole day at work will be worth a loaf of bread. Three measures of barley are a little better wage but less quality food.

The famine will end the dream of working hard to make something of yourself. I do not call it the American dream, though others do. I believe the American dream of our forefathers was to have religious freedom and live it out for God without government interference. Since the deceived people withhold their best from God (by rejecting him and his ways), God will do so to them. Prepare your pantry for a period of scarcity of six months or more if you are able, food and the good news equal response to Jesus by others.

The famine will be the spiritual characteristic, as well as the physical.

In the last part of verse 6, we can deduce that the oil (word of God) and the wine (the presence of the Holy Spirit) will be in short supply. You can be sure Satan will make every attempt to stop the influence of the Word of God. It will be Satan's seven-year period to destroy his enemies as well. The oil and wine are spiritual characteristics that produce grace in those who believe in God. Most people will not hear or allow the Holy Spirit to move them; many will though.

Instead of turning to the Word of God, people will sneer at God and blame their woes on him. Revelation emphatically says most people will not repent. Let's prepare our Bible and store up spiritual resources, so we have life to impart to our neighbors.

So know and be prepared for the coming time of worldwide famine; if you miss the rapture, then you need to be ready to bring people to Jesus Christ. I do believe the Church is not appointed for wrath, so we receive the call up before the very end seven-year wrath deluge 1 Thessalonians 5:9 and 1 Thessalonians 4:13–18.

agree

We need to know that there will be death befalling many on earth.

Do you believe that massive amounts of lives will die in a short period? I believe it, although I don't know any technical aspects of it. We must be ready to meet the Lord. What about the tsunami in Southwest Asia claiming over 150,000 souls? The 9/11 claims three thousand plus souls in a matter of hours. On and on, I could go. Such catastrophe is chump change in comparison to what will occur on earth. Although these were real and wrested our hearts, what's coming will baffle understanding.

In Revelation 6:7–8, we see that there is coming a time when death is going to take one-fourth of the earth's population. How is it possible for death to claim so many people? Let's look at that today.

We see that the heavenly council approves this judgment.

"And when he had opened the fourth seal, I heard the voice of the fourth beast say, Come and see" Revelation 6:7, KJV).

Massive dying is going on before all the heavenly council. This beast and the other beasts and twenty-four elders, as well as the host of heaven, all consent to God carrying out his judgments. Jesus opens this seal that brings the decision. It is the fourth seal now, Jesus unsealing the scroll of wrath and the title deed to the earth. As he does this, the judgments are automatically happening. Jesus Christ is worthy and holds the scroll and title deed to the earth. This title deed brings in the millennial kingdom on earth through judgment.

Because this will be the heavenly timetable, and because the measure of the world's sin is filled up by rejecting God's goodness, all of chapter 5 expresses the heavenly harmony over this. Do not be a scorner. Repent and believe the good news today. Today is our chance to settle the sin account with God through faith in Jesus Christ and his work at Calvary. We have little time left to be prepared to meet Jesus, for he is coming soon.

As we read the book of Revelation, we realize death, and hell are going to claim a whole lot of people.

"And I looked and behold a pale horse: and his name that sat on him was Death, and Hell followed with him. And power was given unto them over the fourth part of the earth, to kill with sword, and with hunger, and with death, and with the beasts of the earth" (Revelation 6:8, KJV).

This rider goes out with the power to take life from the earth. This rider is death who will take one-fourth of the earth's population, and hell will swallow up the souls of those who refuse to believe. This pale horse is the color of death; it is an angel of death. It says that hell followed him. Hell waits and enlarges itself to swallow its victims.

Remember, God allows this, so those who die in this time who trust in God are covered by Calvary's love also. Think in terms of tribulation (great afflictions, trials, and distress) of the like that earth has never seen. Prepare now because when this starts, if someone rejects the good news, they probably will miss the rapture because it makes accepting Jesus harder, not easier. One thing after another will happen (the likes that are unfixable). People won't have time to get right.

One-fourth of the earth's population will die.

In the same verse, we see that this judgment alone destroys one-fourth of the population on planet earth. Everyone in the world will feel the effects of this in a personal way. Power was given to death and hell to claim all these lives. So many dies because this is the great test that was to come upon the earth, to test all who live on the planet, and to purge it of all that offends and bring in the kingdom.

Why would God do this? Why instead won't people repent? The hardness of people's hearts is not acceptable, to be saved, they must humble themselves before God. Let God be true and every man a liar. Do not die spiritually, either in peace or under judgment and tribulation. Do not die lost. Respond today to the good news.

Death will wield his powerful instruments of killing.

In some way after all, judgment comes to pass; every person will be affected some way. If you refuse to believe, you won't make it. There will be innumerable ways that the death angel will apply his instruments of war and weapons to kill. The sword could be instruments of war and arms and any natural cause, etc. Hunger waves will sweep the world. The consequences of misfortune will bring death. The beasts of the earth will once again multiply and take the lives of countless numbers of people, perhaps through diseases of the animals as well.

The examples above are my illustration of many instruments that death will be using. Think of the numerous ways people die and multiply that in a short space of time, one-fourth will decrease.

People assume that they can fix the crises and go on. That won't be so in the tribulation. One trial after another will come in a way that decimates lives. Repentance is the only option because the end of the age is ending. Therefore, repentance is the only solution God accepts for man's preservation.

So escape the trap of thinking all things will continue like they are according to the good old days because bad days are coming, and many people will die. Turn to Jesus Christ and live.

What Is the Cry of the Martyrs?

Do martyr's cry after their death? Able's righteous blood cried out to God. Martyr's in heaven call before God's altar in heaven. The call of the martyrs is for God's justice to prevail on earth.

In Revelation 6:9–11, we see that we should know what the heavenly cry of the martyrs is. What is the roar of the martyrs in heaven? Let's examine that in this passage.

There is a special place in heaven just for martyrs.

"And when he had opened the fifth seal, I saw under the altar the souls of them that were slain for the word of God, and for the testimony which they held" (Revelation 6:9, KJV).

These souls experienced death, not because they spoke an excellent presentation, but because they held the truth as Christ has given it. They also lived the truth out in such a way that God's enemies rose and slew them. There is a big difference between a professor and a committed Christian. The professor has no truth to back his testimony, but the faithful Christian has Christ's Spirit within. Here the martyrs are under the altar. This place under the altar is where the prayers of the saints come up to God. It's as if these martyrs were living sacrifices poured out to God. These martyrs lived out the Word of God.

The sacrifice God requires is one in which a person has been transformed and by Christ's Spirit testifies by both Word and lifestyle about who Jesus Christ is. Millions end up martyred because of the truth about who Christ is and what he has done. These martyrs are all represented by John's vision of the fifth seal. The verse says they are there because of the testimony of Jesus Christ that they bore witness too. The meaning of these martyrs is that justice will eventually and truly be meaded out upon the earth. So such martyrdom will never occur again. The only way that can happen is at Christ's Second Coming. I am not encouraging martyrdom for us, but we should be faithful even unto death for the truth that is in Christ Jesus. It is of the Christian faith to partake of Christ's sufferings.

The martyrs are crying for God's justice and God's kingdom on earth. *from Heaven*

"And they cried with a loud voice, saying, how long, O Lord, holy and true, dost thou not judge and avenge our blood on them that dwell on the earth?" (Revelation 6:10, KJV). *martyrs*

We are commanded to pray for God's kingdom to come. Will these martyrs do this always because martyrdom will not cease until Jesus Christ's government is on earth and wicked men are totally out of power? When will this happen? The overthrowing of the wicked happens at Christ's Second Coming, so they are told to wait a little longer. They ask God how long it will be before his justice reigns on earth. When will you avenge our blood, they ask? It's not for personal vengeance but a reordering or remaking of the world order. Their blood cries that man must change.

They cry this so God will hasten the coming of his order and kingdom on earth. God's plan is in motion, and very soon, end-time events will unfold. We have a justice system; one function of this system is to enforce the law so that a bad thing won't happen again. We cannot stop martyrdom until evil's purpose is complete, and it cannot rise again. Jesus will come and take vengeance on this world because of those who rejected the gospel and fought God and killed his people. If we have not believed the good news, we lose out.

Martyrs are clothed and held in waiting for the fulfillment of God's plan on earth. *in heaven where*

"And white robes were given unto every one of them, and it was said unto them that they should rest yet for a little season, until their fellow servants also and their brethren, that should be killed as they *were*, should be fulfilled Revelation 6:11, KJV). *Trib? martyrs*

+ righteousness

White robes signify victory, protection, and rest, which they are in now. But retribution won't be carried out until all the other forthcoming martyrs are killed in like fashion. They then all will witness God's judgment upon gospel-rejecting people. They are commanded to rest for a season. Just wait a little longer because justice is coming. They must wait until their fellow servants become martyred for the faith. Wait for those. There will be more deaths for the gospel, so let us, along with them, hold our peace and persevere in the faith.

These martyrs are invaluable reminders to God of his eternal plan for the redeemed humankind and the planet earth. The martyrs will hasten God's plan forward. The hastening of God's plan is so because they remind God what the real solution is—the end-time plan of God to establish his kingdom. Let us pray for God's kingdom to come and be always ready to die for the faith. We have them as a cloud of witnesses to the courage of our walk.

So realize the heavenly cry of the martyrs in heaven is for the fulfillment of God's righteousness and kingdom on earth when evil will rule no more.

There is coming the day of the Lord when all will see Jesus Christ.

Are we able to know what the day of Christ's revealing will be like at his Second Advent? Who will be on earth when this day comes? What kind of indications or signs will spell out this day? The Bible calls the Second Advent of Jesus Christ a day of wrath that will consume the whole earth.

In Revelation 6:12–17, we see that the Bible declares what it will be like when the great day of God's wrath comes. Just what will take place when the great day of God's wrath comes? Let's see what will take place when the great day of God's wrath comes.

There will be mighty signs in the heavens.

"And I beheld when he had opened the sixth seal, and, lo, there was a great earthquake; and the sun became black as sackcloth of hair, and the moon became as blood; And the stars of heaven fell unto the earth, even as a fig tree casts her untimely figs when she is shaken of a mighty wind" (Revelation 6:12–13, KJV).

earthquake ushers...

REVELATION

A catastrophic sign occurs, which engulfs the whole earth, causing a great earthquake. This earthquake affects all peoples of the earth. At this time, the sun becomes black, the moon becomes bloody, and meteors fall to the ground. These seal judgments are the indication to all inhabitants of the planet that the day of the Lord's judgment has come. The sun becoming black means the end of the present order has arrived. Then the moon won't give her light. Just a fearful expectation of God's wrath comes upon people.

Jesus Christ's first coming presence moved the heavens; there was a star in the sky. In this case, since he comes in his Second Advent in judgment, the heavens are becoming a sign of terror. Matthew 24:29 describes this as the time immediately after those days. It is in the days of the tribulation and the days of great turmoil that engulfs the whole world where the unrepentant are deceived into joining forces with Antichrist.

raptured typo

At this point, the Church will have been ruptured out of the way of God's wrath. But these earthlings present during this whole course of seven years of tribulation refuse to repent. The time for repenting and turning to Jesus Christ is today. Don't put it off for a later time. If, you do get saved in the tribulation, you may have to die for your testimony.

The natural shape of the earth will change.

"And the heaven departed as a scroll when it is rolled together; and every mountain and island were moved out of their places" (Revelation 6:14, KJV).

The cataclysmic catastrophe that happens causes such strain upon earth that its mountains and islands and land features are altered. No doubt, countless people will die by this alone. Every mountain and island moved out of their place. However, when God's presence is manifested, it causes immense changes upon earth.

The change in landscape occurs because it is the great day of God's wrath; it encompasses the seven years of tribulation and literal day of Advent and millennial reign. Who can bear God's presence, especially his enemies within his wrath? How many have heard similar messages and mocked his soon return? They did that because they made the world their home. Turn from the world and make God your all and all.

Every living person will hide from the presence of God.

"And the kings of the earth, and the great men, and the rich men, and the chief captains, and the mighty men, and every bondman, and every free man, hid themselves in the dens and in the rocks of the mountains" (Revelation 6:15, KJV).

The great day of Jesus Christ's revealing will be absolute destruction to those who refused to believe and repent. Since they chose to rebel by teaming up with Antichrist and rejecting the good news, they lose out. Such honoraries as kings, great men, chief captains, and mighty men will be the people who have no strength to help or secure favor with the Lord Jesus Christ. Every slave and freeman upon the earth will be gathered up for either damnation or God's good purposes.

All people will hide because of pure sheer fear and dread of God's coming. This coming will be a terror that we cannot comprehend, utter confusion. It says they hid in dens and the rocks of the mountains. We see in this that God's sovereignty will sum up the age and fulfill his program now and in the future. Let us then align ourselves with his will.

Each unsaved person will plead for death to take them from the coming presence of God.

"And said to the mountains and rocks, fall on us, and hide us from the face of him that sits on the throne, and from the wrath of the Lamb: For the great day of his wrath is come; and who shall be able to stand?" (Revelation 6:16–17, KJV).

The Lamb of God will come in glory, who gave his life a ransom for many, who will destroy all dissenters. The people who have rejected the good news by refusing Jesus Christ and his offer of forgiveness through the cross will cry for the rocks to fall on them. All will attempt suicide rather than face the coming Lord. These souls will be utterly terrified because they have trampled the Son of man underfoot, so now they will be judged by him.

Can you imagine the terror and utter chaos in their hearts as God's wrath consumes them? Probably all they can think about in such terror is get me away. There have been armies that Israel has fought in which God caused their destruction through great states of confusion-this will be the case. Those who miss the rapture find themselves entangled in the strong delusion. Don't put off your salvation any longer.

The day of God's wrath and revealing will overthrow all remaining dissenters; if you have been rejecting Jesus Christ, I urge you to make your peace with God through him.

CHAPTER 7

Whose seal will be on your head?

When God's wrath comes, who will stand? Unrepentant and unbelieving sinners won't make it. Those who obtain the mark of the beast won't survive. But God sends his angels to seal those who belong to him, so they are protected from the divine wrath.

We see in Revelation 7:1–3 that God will seal his tribulation servants from divine wrath. Let look at why God seals his servants from the divine wrath.

God will seal his servants because divine wrath will befall earth during the tribulation time.

"And after these things I saw four angels standing on the four corners of the earth, holding the four winds of the earth, that the wind should not blow on the earth, nor on the sea, nor on any tree" (Revelation 7:1, KJV).

Here angels are dispensed to bring cataclysmic destruction upon the earth. This message is a response to chapter 6:17, "Who shall be able to stand?" Many will die because repeatedly they have rejected God's offer of pardon through faith in the Lord Jesus Christ. The angels that stand at the corners of the earth have been dispensed to bring great devastation. They are holding back the judgment until God's servants become sealed in verse 3.

It seems that humanity is at a state where they both identify with God and live for him, or they break all ties with God and proclaim their independents from him. I asked a man several years ago if he believed in God to start a conversation with him and introduce Jesus to him. He stopped me and said that he believed in himself, and that he would take care of himself, not God. Such answers go to show the permeation of Satan's false teachings into society. Because of the lies of Satan, which his sympathizers indoctrinate through TV and various other methods, there is a nationwide rebellion and revolt against Jehovah God. Again, let me state why this divine wrath comes. It comes because the people of the world refuse to turn to God. God will judge them as he sums up the age.

God will seal his servants because those who would not turn to God will die.

"And I saw another angel ascending from the east, having the seal of the living God: and he cried with a loud voice to the four angels, to whom it was given to hurt the earth and the sea" (Revelation 7:2, KJV).

Let us look a little further at this judgment that will befall those who reject Jesus Christ's gospel and revolt against God. Here is an angel with the seal of God, who will place that protection upon the servants of Jehovah. The worldly unbelieving people are sealed by Satan's mark of the beast already. The mark will designate them as God's enemy. The seal of the living God saves God's own from the darkness of Antichrist's fate. While Antichrist is blaspheming God and destroying his people, the judgment of God falls on his kingdom, and Antichrist's kingdom turns into darkness.

Because the seven years will sum up the end of the age and Jesus ushers in the kingdom of heaven, only those saved (sealed) will escape the death and wrath of God and enter the kingdom. Two types of angels go forth, angels to seal and preserve God's servants and angels who kill God's enemies. Jesus says in the gospel of Mark to repent and believe the good news for the kingdom of heaven is at hand. Repentance and faith in Jesus Christ are the only means of becoming sealed and saved and the entrance into the kingdom.

God will seal his servants because the followers of Jesus need protection from this judgment, which will befall the earth.

"Saying, hurt not the earth, neither the sea, nor the trees, till we have sealed the servants of our God in their foreheads" (Revelation 7:3, KJV).

There is going to come great wind, cyclones, and storms which shall cover all the earth and do complete devastation along with other judgments which bring an end to sins purpose and the continuation of rebellion against God. These coming judgments are from the rock (Christ), who crushes human rulership that is apart from God. The angels were told not to hurt the earth. This judgment will be held back long enough until God's servants get sealed. Thus, we see in the end that it is wiser to serve God even in death on earth so that we inherit eternal life.

These judgments are not going to allow any unbeliever or dissenter from God to partake of his good future if they have determined the rejection of his salvation and lordship over their lives. Are you a servant of God's? Because the drama of the ages is unfolding, and your choices are determining which side you're on. If you've spurned God, you're on the wrong side.

So understand why God seals his servants. He has not appointed them to divine wrath, but those who reject the gospel of Jesus Christ will perish.

God will have a witness.

Will God have witnesses to testify of himself during the tribulation period? God has always had a witness. At those times, many believed and repented, also many hardened their hearts. So know God too will have a witness during the tribulation period.

We see in Revelation 7:4–8 that God will have a witness to himself during the Tribulation period. Who will be God's witness during the tribulation period? Let us examine who will be God's witness during the tribulation time.

God will raise Jewish witnesses.

"And I heard the number of them which were sealed: *and there were* sealed a hundred *and* forty *and* four thousand of all the tribes of the children of Israel" (Revelation 7:4, KJV).

God rises Jewish witnesses that proselytize much of the world during this time, signifying Israel's true calling to convert the world to God. That was also why the Church came to be; 144,000 Jews set apart to witness for Jesus Christ. These Jewish saints get sealed. There is a special seal put upon them to protect them from the judgments of God.

Since this period, God is singling out Israel; the Jewish people should become God's witness to the world. After chapter 4:1, when God calls the Church home, Israel again is fulfilling what God calls her to be his witnesses to the world. God will have a witness to himself among men. Will you be his witness while you travel on your journey here? Don't miss your opportunity to share the truth about Jesus. *yes*

Judah will take the lead.

"Of the tribe of Judah *was* sealed twelve thousand. Of the tribe of Reuben *were* sealed twelve thousand. Of the tribe of Gad *were* sealed twelve thousand" (Revelation 7:5, KJV).

Judah again takes the lead in this witnessing for God. But notice that probably all the Jewish tribes are represented. We also ought to prepare ourselves for God's work so we can witness more effectively. God will use us according to how we have prepared. Judah takes the lead in witnessing. All the Jewish people are represented in verses 4–8. I don't know if that means no Danites are present; possibly they are intermingled in the other tribes.

There must be a strong leadership charge by the jadeites—to encourage the other tribes in such a hostile world. Taking the initiative and command of the witness campaign is a huge undertaking. Will you mobilize to witness to your neighbors at home, work, etc.? You can make a difference.

Levi's tribe has a place.

"Of the tribe of Simeon *was* sealed twelve thousand. Of the tribe of Levi *were* sealed twelve thousand. Of the tribe of Issachar *were* sealed twelve thousand" (Revelation 7:7, KJV).

Each tribe is taking their place as witnesses, probably dispersing to the four corners of the earth to witness to all regions, which will result in a great many coming into the faith. Millions will get saved on account of these Jewish witnesses. Levi is no longer the one held within the temple. Now they are a part of God's evangelizing plan to reach the entire world.— *yes*

We are each called to reach our place of occupation. The first place we must reach is our dominion in the entire world. Make a goal to tell a person a day, try. You will then so a seed into others' lives.

Ephraim has a place.

"Of the tribe of Zabulon *was* sealed twelve thousand. Of the tribe of Joseph *was* sealed twelve thousand. Of the tribe of Benjamin *was* sealed twelve thousand" (Revelation 7:8, KJV).

So we see not one tribe is lost here; they fervently share the good news with the world. Ephraim, who was lost since Assyria, is present as Joseph. Ephraim is the meaning because Manasseh, his brother, was mentioned in verse 6. So no longer are there any lost tribes. No matter what your sin is turn back to Jesus through repentance and faith. God is faithful to forgive you.

Why should you fail to have a place in God's plan? You should seek God's will out and do that. Again, we are looking forward to the rapture. We don't look for what takes place in the tribulation period. Settle your sin account with Jesus Christ.

So know God will have a witness to himself during the tribulation period. Let's allow this to stir us up to witness for God in our sphere of influence.

We shall worship God.

What will heaven's citizens be doing? We know there will be positions and authority given. We also know there will be a reunion and fellowship with God. But in heaven, the number one activity is worship centered on God.

Looking at Revelation 7:9–12, we can know how heaven's citizens will celebrate God's salvation. Let's look at how heaven's citizens celebrate God's salvation.

Heaven's citizens will rejoice in the presence of God.

"After this I beheld, and, lo, a great multitude, which no man could number, of all nations, and kindred's, and people, and tongues, stood before the throne, and before the Lamb, clothed with white robes, and palms in their hands" (Revelation 7:9, KJV).

Here is a countless multitude of all ages and races that come in adoration of God and his salvation. They get to appear before God in worship. All of the earth's redeemed being a great multitude of all

cludes all intelligent beings in heaven. God created us to worship and glorify God.

Heaven's citizens will express God's greatness and glory exuberantly.

"Saying, amen: Blessing, and glory, and wisdom, and thanksgiving, and honor, and power, and might, *be* unto our God forever and ever. Amen" (Revelation 7:12, KJV).

The focus goes from celebration of our salvation to the sincere worship of our God. We will all adore God in unity. As the angels say what they say, the focus over all the gifts which God employed to redeem us is to completely give thanks and credit to God as Redeemer, Savior, Creator, Lord, and the Author of our faith. Forever we will glorify God.

Since God exercised all these things in redeeming us and they have their existence in God, we give God adoration and thanks. Be quick to glorify God because all our pleasant things and our life come from him. We will no longer credit ourselves.

So let us participate with heaven in all-out worship of God. We should know that this is the thing we were created for and will do forever in heaven, along with all God's bidding.

We need to know what the destiny of the tribulation saints is.

What happens to tribulation saints who stand for Jesus? Do they miss God's good plan for them? Will they be received into heaven's victory for them? John tells us that they will not lose God's goodwill for them.

In Revelation 7:13–17, we see that it is essentially the right thing for the tribulation saints to stand for Jesus Christ. Why should these tribulation saints take their stand for Jesus Christ? Let's see why this is.

There appears a new group in the heaven's stage.

"And one of the elders answered, saying unto me, what are these which are arrayed in white robes? And whence came they?" (Revelation 7:13, KJV).

Because these believers are a new group (the angel asks what these are), we assume it is those who stood for Christ in the great tribulation. I believe these came out of both the great tribulation and the long Christian history of affliction that the saints had to endure being martyred by Satan's collaborators.

So along with John and the martyred saints of the whole Church age, there comes a host of martyred saints out of the great tribulation. They come in after the rapture because that's when they believed. But realize the cost of salvation in the tribulation is martyrdom. The question is then, what does God give to the tribulation martyrs for their testimony of Jesus Christ by which they suffer? When they die for Jesus, he gives them a glorious eternity.

These are the ones who came to faith after the rapture of the Church.

"And I said unto him, Sir, thou knowest. And he said to me, these are they which came out of great tribulation, and have washed their robes, and made them white in the blood of the Lamb" (Revelation 7:14, KJV).

So John was unsure of this addition to the saints of all the ages. He said you tell me who they are. Thus, the angel said that it is earth's last harvest of the age of grace. These are those who, in the tribulation, place their faith in Jesus and his shed blood on their behalf. These martyrs settled their sin account with God through Christ's shed blood before they died. They either were martyred or killed in the great tribulation.

This group who joins the heavenly hosts of saints of past generations is latecomers but who do place their faith in Jesus Christ. It is better to be late than never. Please consider receiving Jesus Christ as your Savior and Lord and boldly stand for him.

These tribulation saints receive positions of service.

"Therefore are they before the throne of God, and serve him day and night in his temple: and he that sits on the throne shall dwell among them" (Revelation 7:15, KJV).

For all these saints in heaven, they will serve the Lord in a state of no lack. They will have honorable positions. Serving God is why he called and made us. The verse tells us that they are before the throne serving God day and night. Can you imagine the joy of being in God's presence all the time serving him? That would be pure joy.

Because service is a part of God's plan for a meaningful existence, such a plan will be part of our eternal happiness. In eternity,
we won't be happy unless we are serving God. Our stand for Christ
now will equate to an exact position then.

These tribulation saints shall suffer no lack ever again.

"They shall hunger no more, neither thirst anymore; neither
shall the sun light on them, nor any heat. For the Lamb which is
amid the throne shall feed them, and shall lead them unto living
fountains of waters: and God shall wipe away all tears from their
eyes" (Revelation 7:16–17, KJV).

Never again shall these believers experience hardships. The good
shepherd will lead them. God will feed, water them, guide them, and
remove all tears. For these, the tribulations of the earthly existence
are over. The Lamb of God shall feed them. Because of their choice
for Jesus Christ, Jesus will shepherd them and care for them.

Because they stood for Jesus Christ here on earth, in Heaven,
Jesus stands for them. Whoever is ashamed of Jesus while living out
their lives here, Jesus will be ashamed of them there. Because of our
position of faith, we will experience such joys. We must not recant
our faith in Jesus Christ.

We must understand then that it is essentially the right thing
for all believers to stand for Jesus Christ. And when we hold to
our position of faith in Jesus Christ, heaven prepares our welcome.
Tribulation saints take your stand.

CHAPTER 8

Prayer has a part to play in end-time events.

Do our prayers matter to God? Does God listen when we pray? What kind of priority does God give to our prayers? Let's see how prayer affects the great tribulation.

In Revelation 8:1–5, we see that it is necessary to know how the prayers of the saints affect the coming judgment. Let's look at how prayer affects the coming judgment.

Prayers are offered in heaven's most quiet time.

"And when he had opened the seventh seal, there was silence in heaven about the space of half an hour" (Revelation 8:1, KJV).

The opening of the seventh seal leaves heaven in silence and expectation of the great wrath of God prepared to be poured upon the earth. There was silence in heaven. This silence is not prayerlessness but space to receive prayer as prioritized above heaven's activities. For half an hour, prayer is offered in this quiet time and is necessary for the hope of God's saints to remind God of their concerns in him. So the need to judge the world's wickedness has come before God.

Only through judgment will the kingdom be established. Daniel 2:34–35, 44–45 reminds us that heaven's kingdom will crush the kingdom and world powers of this rebellious earth. It is expedient for us to pray over the circumstances of our lives because we see that in God's priority system, the prayers of the saints take priority over conditions.

Prayer will be offered in heaven's preparation for judgment.

"And I saw the seven angels which stood before God; and to them were given seven trumpets" (Revelation 8:2, KJV).

These trumpets were war-calling instruments. Heaven receives their call to battle! This war called proceeded the angel who would offer up the prayers of the saints in the next verse to show that they had a part in the orders that influence the direction the war will go. These seven angels must be high-authoritative servants of God because they are given the seven trumpets to sound. These trumpets prepare and summons heaven's weapons of wrath.

This wrath is that which will occur upon all unbelievers and those opposed to God on earth. None of this takes place until the prayers are offered up to God in the next verse. These prayers inspire the wrath. We must always remember that when we treat others kindly, we are doing it as unto Christ. So let's love others because Christ first loved us. The world has forgotten that the Father hears the prayers of his people and knows how to respond.

Prayer is precious to God.

"And another angel came and stood at the altar, having a golden censer; and there was given unto him much incense, that he should offer *it* with the prayers of all saints upon the golden altar which was before the throne" (Revelation 8:3, KJV).

Here is an angel designated as a servant to offer up the prayers of the saints. The association of the prayers with the golden altar indicates the value of the prayers of the saints to God. Heaven silently waits and listens as the prayers of God's saints go up to him. No trumpet is allowed to blow until God receives the prayers. The golden altar represents the work Christ did on our behalf and our prayers going up from there.

The ascending prayers are from the saints of all ages as all heaven awaits God to judge the earth so they can take their places in the new kingdom. All heaven is silent as these prayers ascend to God. So let's not listen to Satan's intimidation, which attempts to dissuade us from praying. Our prayers are important to God, and Satan knows this.

Prayer influences God's decisions.

"And the smoke of the incense, *which came* with the prayers of the saints, ascended before God out of the angel's hand" (Revelation 8:4, KJV).

These prayers will be influential factors of heaven's response to judging the earth. God will consider all things. The verse talks about the smoke of the incense, which came with the prayers. This tells us that God will consider each prayer ever prayed. As the prayer and incense ascend to God, he considers all of them. Now what an awesome God we serve!

This participation of prayer between the citizens of heaven and God is the far-reaching influence that sets in motion God's plans. Did you ever pray and see circumstances change? It will bring change to the earth. Pray big prayers and develop your vision through excellent communication with God.

Prayer initiates the judgments to come.

"And the angel took the censer, and filled it with fire of the altar, and cast *it* into the earth: and there were voices, and thundering's, and lightnings, and an earthquake" (Revelation 8:5, KJV).

All of a sudden, after the offering of the prayers of the saints, great sounds are again heard in heaven. This time is a summons to war and judgment upon planet earth. As the angel caste the censer to the surface, there is a purging of evil through wrath. Great confusion upon earth comes on people because the trumpets have begun.

Those who do evil and those who promote it and live it must enter judgment. No unbeliever and unconverted will make it into the millennium. If God dealt with all the Hebrews twenty years and older in the desert wanderings, he would also deal with unbelieving objectors. In this way, God's kingdom will come in by way of judgment.

There is coming a day that saints will pray the curses of God down on the unbelieving unrepentant sinners. God will do it so that he can bring in his kingdom.

Divine wrath begins.

How does God's wrath begin? It hits humankind when he is most vulnerable before God. It takes away man's sense of security of existence. What I am talking about is God's judgment begins with a blow to the ecosystem.

Revelation 8:6–7 warns us and the whole world to take warning of how God's divine wrath begins with devastation to all vegetation. Let's examine how God's wrath devastates the earth's vegetation.

Let us note that this wrath originates from heaven, which means that man cannot fix it.

"And the seven angels which had the seven trumpets prepared themselves to sound" (Revelation 8:6, KJV).

These trumpets, which start in Revelation 8:6, go to Revelation 16. Four of the trumpets deal with judgments on man physically, and the other three deal with spiritual judgments. As we see in this wrath, men made the earth their home. They think they do not need God or his kingdom. God, therefore, shows man that he owns the land and can do with it as he pleases. God turns man's oasis into hell on earth. Seven angels prepare to sound. This divine wrath from heaven will devastate the land. But we know how man is, in his stupidity, always assumes that he can fix things and go on with life. There will be no repairing the earth when God judges it. The armies of heaven aim their attack on earth when God tells them to blow the trumpets; great devastations come upon all the earth, home of humankind.

A lot of people say I choose some other god than Jehovah because he kills people. But I tell you he has reached out in love (the cross of Jesus Christ), yet it is the cross rejecters who have sinned and offended God and won't repent and turn to God through Jesus. God tells us to come and reason together. God wants to reconcile us back to him, but it is not possible if people won't lay aside their offenses toward God. The application is for today; people are offended in the lordship of God because he demands they live as unto him. They find fault because they are unwilling to make God Lord of their lives. So they will perish instead of repent and receive God's forgiveness.

Man's home becomes a towering inferno.

"The first angel sounded, and there followed hail and fire mingled with blood, and they were cast upon the earth: and the third part of trees was burnt up, and all green grass was burnt up" (Revelation 8:7, KJV).

Suddenly in a soon future time, the wrath of God is uniquely poured upon this earth. The earth's trees, grass, and vegetation are

God must deal with people who won't repent in order to bring His Kingdom to a new earth (heaven) = no sin + to reward

burned up. This is the condition which becomes the state of man's home, this earth, a planet in crises. Such a situation will put man's life is on the line. Man's existence hangs in the balance, hail and firefall. I don't have any clue whether this is nuclear war or devastation by meteors. This book is a practical study, not technical. But what I see in this verse is that God plunges the earth into the ecosystem crises. Why? Because man thought that he could manage the earth's affairs without God's help. *I believe that God gives everyone a choice*

Believer

God is going to show man that apart from God, man's existence becomes a living hell. Remember, these are judgments that the saints have implored God to pour upon a God-rejecting world. God is not at fault. These people won't repent, and they are hindering the fulfill-ment of God's future for the earth. They still want to run the planet without God.

? really ??? check

Green vegetation becomes a scarce commodity.

The very essence of what sets earth apart within the solar system is its bioecology or the ability to produce vegetation life. One-third of this disappears, meaning many animals and people will die. For our bodies to live, we depend on the vegetation of the earth. The vegetation becomes burnt up, so how will man's fix-it ability do then? Man will still not repent. Just like in the day of Pharaoh, people harden their hearts. This trumpet judgment affects one-third of all vegetation life-forms on planet earth. This plague from heaven is fire and hail which rains upon the land for a time.

Man needs to realize God is the source of our life. He made us and gave us the breath of life and sustains us through the ecosystem that is now present on earth. This ecosystem will enter into crises, and God will show that man will still not repent. So, therefore, God will have to go on with further judgments. Let us consider then why we persevere in our faith. It is to reject the Antichrist. He is Satan's lie, which blinds men to their need for God and his Son.

So foreknowledge is a forewarning. Let us seek God in our time of grace and blessing so we can avoid God's wrath by genuinely knowing Jesus Christ, God's Son. *Yes*

Man's existence becomes further threatened.

God is just, loving, merciful

Could judgments threaten man's existence further? Will judgments continue to threaten humanity as they reject God? Will, their rejection of the gospel, put their life into a crisis? All the decisions of God are upon an unrepentant world.

In Revelation 8:8–9, we observe how the second trumpet brings devastation to the waters. What destruction comes to the waters upon the second trumpet judgment? Let's look at that.

The Lord sends a large mountain into the sea.

"And the second angel sounded, and as it were a great mountain burning with fire was cast into the sea: and the third part of the sea became blood" (Revelation 8:8, KJV).

So we see God's judgment on the ecosystem continues. He is proving to those professors of evolution that the world didn't just evolve. God preciously governs life by his hand, and if he removes his grace, then our life will become extinct. These first four trumpets prove that God's hand is the guardian of man's life on earth. And though humankind sees all these devastations, he does not repent. The lie has so firmly entrenched his heart. When the second angel sounds, this lets us know that these judgments are from divine intervention upon the wickedness of men. God's wrath eventually brings the end to humankind's rule without God. God sends what is or is like a big mountain burning into the sea. Here is some massive object, possibly a comet, and it was burning and entered the earth's atmosphere and crashed into the sea.

We hear of men planning to intercept comets to deter them from impacting the earth. But when God sends a comet or mountain or object burning as judgment, know that it will change the planet. Remember the flood? Let me tell you God won't miss. Things won't be business as usual in the great tribulation. Not one person will be unaffected. The Bible says, "In the beginning, God..." Our responsibility is to believe and be reconciled to him. We must reject those teachings which illuminate or explain God away. So we don't get caught in the undertow of an unbelieving world that is sinking.

One-third of all, the sea becomes corrupt.

Can you imagine such devastation? The sea is big, but it becomes polluted. This plague is like the plague of blood in the Egyptian

waters. The master of education and religion thought they had it all figured out, but God was not in their routine. The verse tells us one-third become blood. A world without God in the tribulation, who put God out of their lives, this is the world in which God must show that their world will fall apart without him.

This world does attempt to move forward without God. Humankind is lost at this time as to what to do, and repentance is the last thing they want to do. As humanity's world comes crashing down within their sense of frustration and resentment, their sin accelerates more wrath. Let's break out of our cycle of unbelief by acknowledging God. Get acquainted with God because our future's foundation relies on a relationship with him.

One-third of all life in the sea dies.

"And the third part of the creatures which were in the sea, and had life, died; and the third part of the ships were destroyed" (Revelation 8:9, KJV).

Ironically, men are telling us that we need to establish space colonies. But God is not going to allow our sin to spread into outer space. Instead of humanity advancing into outer space, humankind regresses to a crisis of life on earth. All these judgments are about this crisis. The wrath of God causes the thread of life to be severely cut.

The verse tells us one-third of the sea becomes corrupted. This plague in the seas is a global scale unparalleled. Each phase of commerce of life, as usual, comes crashing down. There is no let's-fix-it-and-go-on. It means to repent and turn to God or lose your soul. Hell will swallow the victims.

One-third of all ships in the sea become destroyed.

Men's business and food supply are severed. This stopping of cargo is another crisis. It is one that is unfixable. This crisis isn't like the Alaskan oil spill or Gulf of Mexico spill or Persian Gulf oil dump. God corrupts one-third of the whole seas. Many ships become destroyed. This disaster will prove more loss of life yet. People going on with business as usual, who made no place for God, now will find a fiery end.

All those in this period entered it because they made no time or place for God in their lives. They purposely put God out of their life.

They don't want God; this is utterly foolish. This fragile ecosystem will enter into its max test. In today's world, it may seem as if these judgments are a fairy tale. But these judgments are coming, so I plead with you to not let daily life be business as usual. Make a place for God in your life today.

So this second trumpet judgment brings devastation to the seas of the earth, which threatens man's existence further. It is time for us to make a place for God in our lives. *3rd trumpet*

The drinking water becomes polluted.

What would happen if the drinking water on earth was polluted? How would this affect humanity? What devastation would this impose on men? There is coming a time when one-third of all the drinking water on earth becomes corrupted.

Revelation 8:10–11 tells us to take care to understand how the water supply becomes polluted. How will the earth's supply of water become corrupted? Today let's examine what happens to earth's water supplies. *3rd*

Divine judgment comes upon man's vital necessity (water).

"And the third angel sounded, and there fell a great star from heaven, burning as it were a lamp, and it fell upon the third part of the rivers, and upon the fountains of waters" (Revelation 8:10, KJV).

Now judgment hits land, and humankind's drinking water is affected. Water is a crucial component of life. As men die because the waters become undrinkable, we would assume man would realize that he needs God and would pray for God's intervention. But Satan's lie is at work, stirring up rebellion against God. The angel that sounded again indicates that this also is of divine origin, prepared for this moment by God. Now a star pollutes the earth's water supplies.

God is tightening the noose around the neck, showing man that he is going to lose his self-governing rights over the earth. The millennial reign of Jesus Christ brings the end to humanity's self-governing qualities. Jesus Christ will rule. Man, instead of turning to God, follows the Antichrist into great rebellion and tries to fight God. As if they think they can stop God's future program, they become defeated.

Most sources of freshwater supplies become polluted.

Can you imagine that there would be no safe water to drink or buy? Without taking the mark of the beast in a future message, men cannot buy earth's goods. Men die out quickly. This mark for food program again cannot fix men's loss. Men are forced to either call on God in repentance and need or curse him and die; men choose the latter.

One-third of the earth's drinking water becomes destroyed. As this star hits the fountains of waters, it corrupts the drinking water in the cisterns and underground springs its lousy news. I said that these devastating judgments would affect all people. Nobody is exempt no matter where they live. God must deal with all unbelieving people for the coming kingdom to begin in an entirely righteous state. God will deal with all the people. God will deal with all people by bringing them to a stand of either faith or rebellion. Which stand will you make? It is not our earth but Gods. Let's make our appeal for clemency today by repenting toward God and exercising faith in Jesus Christ.

One-third of all water supplies turn bitter.

"And the name of the star is called Wormwood: and the third part of the waters became wormwood; and many men died of the waters, because they were made bitter" (Revelation 8:11, KJV).

This verse implies great death upon earth. Remember, most people are pawns on the board and get destroyed. It doesn't mean they are guiltless or don't have to be responsible and turn to God. God allows this upon them to perhaps pursued some of them to repent. This star called wormwood becomes so named after it corrupts the waters. One-third of all earth's waters become undrinkable.

Life quickly comes to an end for many people. Perhaps God will give them a deathbed salvation if they are willing. But Antichrist's arrogance permeates their hearts. Can you imagine the panic upon the people with no water? Have you made your peace with God by settling your sin account? Please don't put it off any longer. God is waiting to take you into his family.

An innumerable host of men perish because they cannot drink the water.

This verse says to us that the waters were poisonous, and if people drink it, they will die. Millions died because of the waters. The waters were made bitter or poisoned because of the star. Men cannot save themselves. Many entered eternity and died lost. Because of the constant rejection of truth, men perish. Jesus said if you hold to his doctrine, you shall know the truth, and the truth will set you free. Are you turning to Bible truth? If not, you'll enter into this sinking ship of unbelief.

So understand that earth's water supplies will become poisoned, and that it will mean death to many. Let's prepare to meet our Maker. Let's prepare our hearts today by personally receiving Jesus Christ as our Lord and Savior.

There are dark days on earth.

What will happen if the earth turns dark? How will people live in a realm of darkness? Will they recognize it as God's wrath leading them to repent? The Bible warns of coming dark days and how the earth's inhabitants won't repent.

In Revelation 8:12–13, we see that the world takes heed because of the dark days that will cover the land. What will happen to the earth that causes days to become dark? Let's look at this right now.

One-third of the light of the sun, moon, and the stars is cut off.

"And the fourth angel sounded, and the third part of the sun was smitten, and the third part of the moon, and the third part of the stars; so as the third part of them was darkened, and the day shone not for a third part of it, and the night likewise" (Revelation 8:12, KJV).

These judgments are answers to the prayers of the saints, which bring in God's justice so his good plan can move forward. Here is another blow to the ecosystem-less light means less can grow to feed the people. It does not state how long this darkness lasts. This darkening is not just a shorter span of the light, but at night, darkness grows more significant as the heavenly bodies give off one-third less light. Gross darkness covers the land like in Egypt. It's probably the kind that people feel. This judgment is the last of the trumpet judgments that affect the physical state of man. The remaining three trumpet judgments bring spiritual darkness upon the earth's inhabitants. Again, this is called forth from heaven, reminding us to repent and turn to God through Jesus Christ. Things are not going as usual; God calls all too immediately repent and turn to him for life. If they harden their hearts, they will perish.

The debilitating effect this will have is phenomenal, and people may be afraid to move from their locations. When Egypt was judged by God with the plague of darkness through Moses's hand, the people got struck in one spot for three days and nights, and still they hardened their hearts. Wake up and give your life to God. Let us not be those who harden our hearts when God brings certain consolation opportunities of repentance between his judgments. These judgments God designed for us to get right rather than harden our hearts.

One-third of the day disappears, and the night is prolonged.

Not only was the day one-third less time but one-third less light. The night draws on with one-third less light. This situation is extreme darkness. This condition will elevate the cooling temperatures, and however long this goes on, it will bring tough times upon earth's inhabitants. Again, this is divine judgments we need to get out of then fix it and go one mentality. This judgment is to bring repentance. This divine warning points to the helplessness and frailty of man in crises because of judgment. Humankind hardens their hearts by cursing God and trying to compensate and go on. No, this is designed to get the world to stop and pray.

This darkness halts business as usual and forces the earth's inhabitants to be stationary. This plague happens so that they might contemplate, pray, repent, change their hearts, and call on God. No, they don't do that. Instead, they try to adapt, compensate, and ignore the warning, and they harden their hearts and go one. The arrogance of man is astounding. Let us acknowledge our Creator and give full attention to him so he will spare us.

A warning comes to earth's inhabitants.

"And I beheld, and heard an angel flying through the midst of heaven, saying with a loud voice, Woe, woe, woe, to the inhabiters of the earth because of the other voices of the trumpet of the three angels, which are yet to sound!" (Revelation 8:13, KJV).

The people of earth repented not because of the first four trumpet judgments. So now an angel visible to all humanity flies in midair, giving warning to the planet's inhabitants of what is to come. Perhaps some will repent and call on God. Maybe some will be spared. Now heaven manifests and warns humanity that spiritual judgment is coming on men. More darkness is coming, but this time, it is a spiritual darkness. Men will grow dark within themselves.

As God turns out the light physically, he also turns out the light spiritually so that the good old days and ways get lost to the grave spiritual darkness. The environment on earth turns to gross darkness. The environment, as socialists have noted, affects how people act. As this darkness settles in men's hearts, their deeds of evil are unrestrained. We, as believers, must excel not in darkness but the light if Christ is in us.

So let's hold fast our place in Jesus Christ so we don't partake in the coming physical and spiritual darkness.

CHAPTER 9

[handwritten note: 5th Trumpet - men smitten]

There comes a day of manifest evil.

Will there come a time that evil will manifest itself? Will nature and evil join? What will be the effect of this union on humankind? Revelation shows how evil will manifest upon a God-rejecting world.

In Revelation 9:1–2, we see how spiritual darkness comes upon the earth in an unparalleled fashion. How does spiritual darkness come upon the earth in an unprecedented way? Let's spend some time on that.

This darkness starts with a supernatural being falling to the earth.

[handwritten note: 5th trumpet]

"And the fifth angel sounded, and I saw a star fall from heaven unto the earth: and to him was given the key of the bottomless pit" *[handwritten note: Abyss / from the Abyss]* (Revelation 9:1, KJV).

It can be debated whether the angel having the key is a good or bad angel. What we note is that God is in control, and he sends this angel. Note then the word *fall* (haven fallen) indicates a being that fell from God's will. The verse tells us a star fell and then calls the star *he* (personage). Why would God send a fallen angel to bring forth the terrible spiritual darkness such as not yet been seen? God does this because men have rejected the truth and gospel for the lies of Satan, so now the depths of nature pour forth their evil.

This satanic messenger will unleash the smoke of the abyss, which comes out fully charged with all wickedness. We have seen the rated R movies entitled *Pure Evil*. Well, humankind will get what they have longed for all along. For anyone who hears the good news and rejects Jesus Christ has sealed his fate to the abyss. Also after the Great White Throne Judgment, they go to eternal fire in hell. What are you doing with the good news?

This supernatural being has the key to the bottomless pit.

Now again, this angel could be either an evil angel or a good one who is carrying out his mission. He is only doing what God has given him the power to do, meaning God is in control. Even within these trumpet judgments, God is calling men to himself. The call is to repent and turn to Jesus Christ. But they hardened their hearts. The verse tells us a key is given to this angel. He is assigned this role—to open the abyss and allow the filthy and defiled spirits to bring their corruption upon humankind and nature. These last three trumpet judgments bring great darkness upon humanity, such that they co-labor in all evil.

These will accelerate the judgments of God, bringing the end quicker. This process happens because the martyrs cry out, "How long, O God?" Therefore, in response to them, God accelerates the process of judgment. Remember that these judgments are in answer to the prayers of the saints of God so that those who reject truth, salvation, and righteousness through Jesus Christ will speedily enter judgment. Have you made up your mind? Believe the good news.

The supernatural being opens the bottomless pit.

"And he opened the bottomless pit; and there arose a smoke out of the pit, as the smoke of a great furnace; and the sun and the air were darkened by reason of the smoke of the pit" (Revelation 9:2, KJV).

This smoke comes charged with all kinds of filthy defiling demonic spirits and activity. It blots out again the light of the sun, moon, and stars. It represents the earth's natural life intermingling with all the hosts of evil. Can you imagine the fearful sights, smells, and horror this brings upon men? The verse says that there arose the smoke of the pit; this is a holding place for the worse of spiritual villains. This wrath is a worldwide judgment. We need to know by now that all humanity is affected in these judgments. There is no place to escape. Some people think they will build houses in the mountains and escape the wrath of God. Not So! Wherever people assemble, the choice of God or Satan will come to them. Those who reject God will have evil manifest among them. There will be no escape whatsoever.

Again, wherever men congregate, they experience these judgments simply because they have rejected the gospel of peace. The gospel opens heaven for the believer and opens hell to the God-rejecters. That simple! The gospel seals the unbeliever's fate. It is pertinent we respond to the invitation of the gospel to receive Jesus Christ as our Lord and Savior! Pray and ask Jesus into your heart and life if you have not yet done so. If you reject the good news, then realize the consequences of that choice.

Immediately there are consequences upon the earth.

Here is a judgment upon man as the air gets polluted and charged with evil. Air is essential to life. Remember within the trumpet judgments, one-third of humanity dies. This judgment is not just a physical manifestation of death and evil but spiritual. The hearts of the sinners who reject the truth accelerate in all manner of evil of both old and new kinds. The verse tells us the sun and air become darkened—the physical manifestation of the newly corrupted spiritual darkness that now becomes present on earth at this time. The smoke is a spiritual evil and corruption of natural air.

This manifestation will usher in the way for evil to corrupt all natural ways on earth. It's an open door for evil to happen at that time. The door flings open for the kinetic manifestation of evil. The angel warned of these woes so great that man would gnaw at their pain. These are souls reeling in inner pain and darkness. Jesus said it is going to be a snare which catches the entire world. Are you ready to meet God? I believe I'm not writing the part of it; it will be terrible. Are you prepared for this? The only rational solution is to get saved and escape this time by preparing for the rapture. Let the blessed hope stir you to serve God now.

So know how spiritual darkness penetrates all the earth so you will pray that you might escape this wrath and to stand before the Son of God.

As the abyss (the bottomless pit) gets opened, we observe in the book of Revelation speaks of locusts coming out of the abyss that are soldiers of torment.

Will men suffer in the masses during the tribulation? The tribulation wrath of God brings great torment to men who won't repent such as the fifth trumpet judgment. This opening of the abyss in verses 1–2 brings some powerful forces of suffering to men.

In Revelation 9:3–6, we can know that particular torments shall befall men on earth. Let's examine the sufferings that shall befall men on earth.

Demonic forces (which I call soldiers) come out of the bottomless pit to torcher men.

"And there came out of the smoke locusts upon the earth: and unto them was given power, as the scorpions of the earth have power" (Revelation 9:3, KJV).

Note the power given to the locusts. This power is from God, and it means that he is in charge and not evil. Yet he uses this torment to bring to the lives of all unbelievers the need to repent and believe the good news. For if they refuse to repent, it will only get worse day after day. The verse tells us that locusts came out of the smoke. These locusts are demonic forces set to torcher men. God gave them power. They can hurt but not to kill. They are limited. Their bites are like scorpions. They shall hunt man down and torcher them.

You might ask why should such agonizing pain be allowed by God? But the real question is why man continues in rebellion, unbelief, and sin when God can deal with it if they would come to God through his Son. Man has rejected reconciliation with God because they refuse to believe in Jesus Christ. Jesus has made reconciliation possible. Jesus told us that men wouldn't repent because they love darkness over the light. Let us witness to men. If they don't believe, let's go to praying for them.

These demonic soldiers target the unbelievers for torcher.

"And it was commanded them that they should not hurt the grass of the earth, neither any green thing, neither any tree; but only those men which have not the seal of God in their foreheads" (Revelation 9:4, KJV).

God here differentiates between his own and Satan's followers like the plagues that happened in Egypt. What we see is that those who refuse to turn to God are punished or severely tormented such that they long for death. These demonic forces are limited so that they can only hurt men. What men will they hurt those who rejected the gospel of Jesus Christ? These locusts were commanded not to harm anything but unbelieving men. They do not have unlimited power. These soldiers of torment are only here to make men suffer who don't have the seal of God on their foreheads.

This judgment is one of Revelations wake-up calls to humanity, "Repent and you'll come under God's shelter from the suffering; or harden your heart and suffering will get worse." God has used similar judgments throughout earth's history but never on such a grand scale. If you are an unbeliever, let the taunt of the truth of the pain of this future judgment pursued you to repent and turn to Jesus Christ. Spare yourself from coming judgment.

These demonic soldiers shall cause men to suffer for five months.

"And to them it was given that they should not kill them, but that they should be tormented five months: and their torment *was* as the torment of a scorpion, when he strikes a man" (Revelation 9:5, KJV).

These soldiers of torment hunt men down, and they will not miss the mark. It's probable that they will not cease and will not die until the five-month mission is over. Men will suffer much. So God permitted that the locusts shall not kill. Again, God limits the torture, meaning God is in control. But the locusts will torment for five months so they have a span of five months to torcher men. They come unhindered.

Five months is considered a short and limited time. It is an intensely painful time. God gets men's attention and brings them to repentance. Think again about why this is going on. Men reject the good news; therefore, great evil occurs in their lives and upon planet earth. This torture is just a foretaste of the eternal punishment that awaits unbelievers in hell. God is imploring men to settle their sin issues. Ironically torcher cannot do so. Only the power of the gospel can.

God denies man longing for death.

"And in those days, shall men seek death, and shall not find it; and shall desire to die, and death shall flee from them" (Revelation 9:6, KJV).

The torcher will be so great that men by the masses shall attempt suicide, but death shall allude them. God will not allow them to get a way out of suffering. They shall go through it being thoroughly penetrated by it that they might ponder and consider that this wrath is a forewarning for them to get right and escape future pain and suffering. Let's turn to God and live. Many men will seek death. As we get older, we experience the frailty of our lives and how precious life is. The whole goal in this life is to come to know our God. These persons do not have such a concept as having rejected God. Thus, they seek how they can end it all.

The truth is that without God's help, these men or women just don't get it. Yet they won't turn to God upon his interposing. These people won't see the truth because they harden their hearts. Please don't harden your heart. Will you turn to God and settle your sin account?

So know that specific torments shall befall men on earth to pursue them to repentance. If you don't believe, today is a great day to settle your sin account with God and hand your account over to Jesus.

Soldiers of Torture (Demons?)
Part 2

As we take a more in-depth look at these soldiers of torture, let us contemplate the power of the good news as God's means of saving a man. We see in this woe that it won't change men's hearts.

In Revelation 9:7–11, we understand how demonic soldiers are equipped to hurt men. Let's examine how these demonic soldiers are equipped to hurt men.

These soldiers of torture come fully prepared for their battle.

"And the shapes of the locusts *were* like unto horses prepared unto battle; and on their heads *were* as it were crowns like gold, and their faces *were* as the faces of men" (Revelation 9:7, KJV).

These are demonic supernatural enemies of humanity that come from the smoke of the abyss. They are armed, mobilized, and nothing will stop their conquest. These locusts are battle warriors who catch people who are not sealed by God and cause them great suffering. They have crowns on their heads, which denotes for their tenure of five months they will dominate men. Because they have the faces of men, I'm guessing they have intelligence also.

All those attacked are they who have rejected the gospel of peace; therefore, they have no seal of protection. Mobilization means you're geared up and ready to inflict your wounds on the opposing victim.

Imagine how unable a civilization is to stop a mobilized army? Now imagine that no matter where you are, you can't hide. They come and torture you five months. It's time for men to repent.

These soldiers of torture are seductive with a painful bite.

"And they had hair as the hair of women, and their teeth were as *the teeth* of lions" (Revelation 9:8, KJV).

The hair describes that somehow, they will lure and attract men and then entrap them and inflict their wounds. It may also mean that this could bring dishonor to the female gender, causing some great sin to befall the female gender. The hair, like a woman, is attractive and royal; people will look upon them with fascination. But they have "teeth as of the teeth of a lion." There is some restraint used here, but I imagine they will also bite, not just sting with their tails.

I say they will bite, but a bite can heal, but their sting must contain toxic fluids or venom which maims and brings great pain. Usually, a scorpion's tail brings great agony but doesn't kill.

Why such a torture? Well, man has brought it upon himself by rejecting God by his devices. This warning should cause for repentance, its supernatural, but the naturalists will explain it away. Open your heart and believe the good news.

These soldiers of torture are protected with armor and use it to instill fear.

"And they had breastplates, as it were breastplates of iron; and the sound of their wings *was* as the sound of chariots of many horses running to battle" (Revelation 9:9, KJV).

These demonic forces are armed, and when they come, fear will grip the people because the people know that these are soldiers of torture. They cannot be stopped by human ingenuity. Their armor is supernatural, and man cannot penetrate it. Because of the breastplates these soldiers have, whatever vulnerability they have, men do not discover it. The sound of these beings' wings penetrates the evening atmosphere, and woes and cries of men are heard. They will get into people's houses.

Can you imagine these soldiers of torture as they hold the imagination of their victims (by their splendor) while they inflict them and sting them and inject their venom?

Earth has never seen the likes of these. Will you prepare for the rapture and warn others to escape this?

These soldiers of torture will sting and hurt humanity for five months.

"And they had tails like unto scorpions, and there were stings in their tails: and their power *was* to hurt men five months" (Revelation 9:10, KJV).

By the approach of these beings, they hunt down the humans, capture their attention because of their splendor, and inject their venom. People will seek death on account of this. These beings have tails like scorpions that are known to have a talent, gift, and ability for inflicting pain. These things are given power by God to hurt humanity for five months.

Imagine every night upon sundown the noise of these soldiers that come into a person's room and shock them as they look upon them and are fascinated at this beautiful creature that has them trapped, and then it happens, they are bitten and stung again. They cannot stop it and have multiple wounds for five months.

Do you want to go through that? Turn to God, for this is what hell is all about, a continues torture with no rest.

These soldiers of torture have a king ruling over them and leading them.

"And they had a king over them, *which is* the angel of the bottomless pit, whose name in the Hebrew tongue *is* Abaddon, but in the Greek tongue hath *his* name Apollyon" (Revelation 9:11, KJV).

Commentators identify this one as Satan. I don't know, but this fallen angel leads these soldiers of torture in rank and file to hunt men down to torture them. It is the angel of the bottomless pit who leads them. There is the possibility that this may not be Satan, I'm not sure, but he leads these troops to fulfill their campaign against humankind.

They will carry out their job skillfully; they have been practicing it on souls in the pit for years. They are no strangers to hellish torture of their victims.

Ultimately all who rebel against God spurn the good news, attack, and kill God's followers, and they get a foretaste of hell as it opens to earth. That is a warning, yet they don't repent. Soon, no more grace, mercy, or opportunity to make peace with God will be possible. The lie of Satan has hardened their hearts permanently.

We see again through the employment of hell on earth that as men suffer from demons, they cannot repent and turn to God. They reject the only truth that can set them free, which is the gospel of Jesus Christ. *Trumpet 6 = 2nd Woe*

The Woe of Mass Death *2nd woe Op (3)*

Is their more devastation coming? There are two more woes and seven veils of judgment. Satan's system and plan are manifesting.

In Revelation 9:12–15, we see that we must know how the sixth trumpet judgment brings the second woe upon humankind. Let's examine how the sixth judgment brings the second woe upon humanity.

What we see first is that another woe begins.

"One woe is past; *and*, behold, there come two woes more hereafter" (Revelation 9:12, KJV).

We see that the trumpet judgments 1–4 were physical distress on man by disturbing the earth's ecosystem. Then trumpets 5–7 have to do with spiritual darkness unleashed upon humankind! Trumpet 5 brought darkness, now trumpet six ushers in woe 2. It was terrible that woe 1 (trumpet judgment 5) brought the darkness of the abyss, now trumpet 6 judgment (woe 2) brings forth literal angels of doom and an army of two hundred million strong to kill one-third of humankind. Instead of humanity repenting, they harden their hearts in rebellion against God. Whoever fights God is the loser in life. These people foretaste hell and the eternal doom to come, yet they will not open their hearts to the gospel and truth.

Well, we see, even today, how many stands in opposition to God. People opposing biblical truth demand that we keep it to ourselves and don't go public with it.

The opposition we experience today is only a foretaste of the hardness of men's hearts toward God. Imagine the facts: it is a world that will hunt down believers and followers of God and Jews, and they will kill them. Therefore, not only will they refuse to hear the truth, but also the door to salvation and hope will be gone to them. How you treat God's people is how you treat God. Let us believe the truth so we can live it out.

The sixth trumpet summons heaven's command of judgment.

"And the sixth angel sounded, and I heard a voice from the four horns of the golden altar, which is before God" (Revelation 9:13, KJV).

Here we have this judgment again, tied into the prayers of the martyrs and saints calling for justice and God's plans to go forward. Remember, believers are being killed in unprecedented ways at this time. So the appeal is that God avenges those who have rejected Jesus Christ and his work done on humanity's behalf. When the sixth angel sounded, God and heaven are in control, and whether men realize it or not, heaven rules over the kingdom of men. The golden altar represents martyrs and Christ's atoning work, which has been rejected. All the martyrs are crying out for God's vengeance on men because they reject the truth and live ungodly.

God is listening to the prayers of his saints, and he will avenge their blood. Prayer plays a significant, influential role during the tribulation.

I urge you to pray on all occasions for all people. Do not underestimate the power of prayer.

Demonic spirits are unleashed to kill one-third of humankind.

"Saying to the sixth angel which had the trumpet, Loose the four angels which are bound in the great river Euphrates" (Revelation 9:14, KJV).

This heavenly angel unlocks and lets loose four notorious demonic angels. Continue to be held for this time and day and hour. So sinister are these angels that one-third of humankind is killed by their foreboding. Humanity is getting what he wants—life without God. These four angels are released, and sinister forces move upon earth and men to kill them. Why is it men reject God? Why do they blame God for the woes they bring upon themselves? Is it because Satan has blinded them because they would not repent and turn to God through Jesus Christ?

This judgment occurs somewhere in the seven-year tribulation period. It's not merely a coincidence this happens. Daniel said the prince of Persia would do battle again. That somehow relates to this period possibly because this is territory that will be given to Israel in the great millennial kingdom.

Man's primary problem is that they believe Satan's lie and continually rebel against God and harden their hearts. This rejection of God allows hell to penetrate the earth.

God governs the timing of judgment.

"And the four angels were loosed, which were prepared for an hour, and a day, and a month, and a year, for to slay the third part of men" (Revelation 9:15, KJV). *Kill ⅓ mankind*

This is a judgment that means God allows these angels to do their work of devastation; he is in control. Imagine death on such a large scale that possibly governments will have to summons men at sixty years old and younger to go off to war. It will be a mandatory enlistment of all. These angels come prepared for the year, day, and hour. These demons are locked up all this time, now unleashed! They come ready for the destruction of a third of humanity.

Those killed are men who want a life without God, and they are turned into hell. The nation that forgets its God shall be turned into hell. *those & who refused to repent*

It's time for us to have personal revival; individuals turning back to God equals the salvation of a nation. What is your decision today? Will you turn back to God?

So we see how the sixth trumpet judgment brings in a devastating second woe. This judgment is again designed to bring repentance, but humankind will not repent. Instead, men harden their hearts to their destruction.

Soldiers of Doom

One-third of the earth's population or more dies in the trumpet judgment. We see the ecosystem, torture, and now death comes because of the trumpet judgment. Let's see how the sixth trumpet judgment brings soldiers of doom (not soldiers of torture as in the fifth trumpet).

In Revelation 9:16–19, the four evil supernatural beings lead an army of two hundred million to devastate humanity. What can we know about this two-hundred-million army? Let us examine what we can know about this two-hundred-million army.

It is the most massive army that assembles on earth.

"And the number of the army of the horsemen *were* two hundred thousand thousand: and I heard the number of them" (Revelation 9:16, KJV).

The army is a combination of demonic and human forces. Think of it, two hundred million, a vast army covering the land. That is almost as populace as the number of people in the USA. The number was told to John because it is too great to count. John heard the number of them. Probably all of heaven knew how many there was and will be observing what is going on, for heaven is in control over the affairs of men and the kingdom of hell as we are also noticing. God has a say over what these demonic forces can and cannot do.

Because those tortured by the demonic locusts repented not toward God, we have another manifestation of hell more severe and deadly. These soldiers of doom maim and kill their victims.

The soldiers and their weaponry strike fear in the beholder.

"And thus I saw the horses in the vision, and them that sat on them, having breastplates of fire, and of jacinth, and brimstone: and the heads of the horses *were* as the heads of lions; and out of their mouths issued fire and smoke and brimstone" (Revelation 9:17, KJV).

The power of death is in the horses. It is the fire, smoke, and brimstone that comes out of their mouths and the bites that emanate from the heads of their tales. The riders that sat on the horses had special protective gear. The heads of the horses were as if they were lion's heads, and this is either demonic or biologically designed. But the heads and tails speak of demonic forces.

This is God's sixth trumpet judgment, which judges one-third of humankind who are prepared for death and hell. This is part of the smoke of the abyss consuming those who won't turn to God. How can you escape such a deadly snare? Only if you will seek God, repent, and cry out to God to escape this time.

This army is specially set apart to kill one-third of the earth's population, all who are unrepentant and won't turn to God. Is this not enough to convince you?

These soldiers succeed in destroying one-third of humanity.

"By these three was the third part of men killed, by the fire, and by the smoke, and by the brimstone, which issued out of their mouths" (Revelation 9:18, KJV).

The devastation of these demonic and possibly human forces is tremendous. We got to remember that humankind in this time teams up with irregular supernatural forces (forces of evil). With men hardening their hearts and involving themselves with spiritual wickedness, the wicked force control man's fallen nature. By these, there was the third part of men killed. Because of the indulgence into the supernatural in the occult and black arts and black science, men are judged and die, and men team up with evil forces to destroy themselves.

It's as if they look at their satanic rituals as communicating with pagan gods. Then when they connect with Satan's forces, they follow his lies to their deaths. The only solution for this is the blood of Jesus Christ, which they reject. Therefore, their darkness waxes gross.

Somehow these forces are led by the four demonic angels. Humanity's hope is by the prayers of the saints, but the saints disappear because of the rapture. Now the saints in heaven pray the judgment of God in.

The power of the weaponry of these soldiers has a fierce intelligent of its own.

"For their power is in their mouth, and in their tails: for their tails *were* like unto serpents, and had heads, and with them they do hurt" (Revelation 9:19, KJV).

Somehow the heads of the horses and the heads in their tails are knowledgeable and know how to seek out and kill their victims. The intelligence is demonic control, which cooperates with the four angelic demons to destroy their victims. The power to kill is in their mouths. Also, their tails bite and maim men, probably doing significant damage and paralyzing their victims.

These are not nice guys, and you cannot reason or bargain with them. They come just to kill unbelievers.

Are you an unbeliever or a skeptic, atheist, unrepentant, or unsaved? Now is your chance to make your amends with Jesus Christ. Please repent and receive Jesus Christ as your Lord and Savior today.

So understand that another army, fiercer than the locusts that tortured in Egypt, will come, and they come to kill the unbelievers. Because these unrepentant and unbelievers want eternity without God, so he will appear and destroys them. Verse 19 is the sixth trumpet, which claims one-third of humankind.

The Remaining Unbelievers

What happens to the rest of the earth's population after the sixth trumpet judgment? God's followers are divinely protected, but the unrepentant permanently harden their heart and side up with Satan against God.

What we see in Revelation 9:20–21 is that the remaining unbelieving population refuses to repent. Let's see how the remaining skeptical community refuses to repent.

The remaining populations on earth, who lived through the plagues and have not believed yet, continue in the works of sin and unbelief.

"And the rest of the men which were not killed by these plagues yet repented not of the works of their hands, that they should not worship devils, and idols of gold, and silver, and brass, and stone, and of wood: which neither can see, nor hear, nor walk" (Revelation 9:20, KJV).

We see in the first half of this verse that these people who remain are those who did not get saved and completely harden their hearts. Because of people hardening their hearts, the trumpet judgment number 7 overtakes them. They continue in sins against God and their neighbors. They continue to rebel and do what they want, which is to sin, so much so that they thoroughly take sides with Satan against God. They will go on to receive the mark of the beast and form their alliance against God, his people, and the armies of heaven. It is the unbelievers who have not been killed by the plagues and remain to make a choice again to serve or rebel against God. They repented not of their evil deeds. These persons individually and collectively do deeds in blasphemy against God.

They don't care that they sin against God and do it if they discover it displeases God. It's because they have rejected reconciliation with God and now fight against his coming.

Anyone who won't repent and does deeds against God proclaims that they oppose Christ's Second Coming. Only those who repent and believe the truth will prepare themselves to be ready to meet Jesus Christ. In the book of Mark, Jesus says repent and believe the good news for the kingdom of heaven is at hand.

The group continues idolatry (the worship of demons and objects).

"And the rest of the men which were not killed by these plagues yet repented not of the works of their hands, that they should not worship devils, and idols of gold, and silver, and brass, and stone, and of wood: which neither can see, nor hear, nor walk" (Revelation 9:20, KJV).

Here, in the second part of this verse, are works that are violations against God. These people have gods before Jehovah, which they worship. Any idol worship is worshipping demons, so demon worship and idol worship are at an all-time high, unprecedented at this time. The occult and Satan worship will abound and the worship of intermediary beings and the idols.

People must worship. And since these people turned permanently away from God, they worship demons and idols. The forward movement and prevalence are to assume that men can be gods and give and receive worship at will.

Return to monotheism and its purpose, which is the worship of Jehovah God, Maker of heaven and earth.

This group continues massive commandment breaking.

"Neither repented they of their murders, nor of their sorceries, nor of their fornication, nor of their thefts" (Revelation 9:21, KJV).

These persons not only sin against God, but they sin against with neighbors in unprecedented ways. As murderers, they will be so prominent that it will be something like the time of the days of Noah with mass murderers. Sorceries will abound. Men and women will not repent of their alcohol and drug abuse. All manner of sexual perversions will abound. Thievery on a massive scale will in sew.

As these cut themselves off from God, hell manifests itself through and in their lives. It will be a manifest presence of evil, and God will divinely protect his followers.

Let us seek that which is right in God's eyes. God will preserve his people.

So those after the sixth trumpet judgment, who have not repented, forever harden their hearts so that they must experience God's remaining wrath for aligning themselves with Satan. They are now opposing God outright.

CHAPTER 10

The mystery of God is finished.

What is the mystery of God that is finished? We know that God's purposes in creation and redemption will be complete. But also, the salvation of those who believe the gospel and God will come to its full measure. Therefore, the end of sin and ignorance is complete, and it will soon go on no longer.

In Revelation 10:1–7, an angel announces when the mystery of God is finished. Let's understand what God wants us to know about this scenario.

We see an angel awesome in appearance.

"And I saw another mighty angel come down from heaven, clothed with a cloud: and a rainbow *was* upon his head, and his face *was* as it were the sun, and his feet as pillars of fire" (Revelation 10:1, KJV).

Commentators all express various opinions, whether this is Christ or not. I cannot say if it is or not either, but I think that it's an angel who abides in God's presence. Not Jesus Christ because when Jesus Christ comes, every eye will see him and those who pierced him. His majesty will be so great when he touches the Mount of Olives where the earthquake takes place.

But what a contrast this angel is to the soldiers of torture and doom. This angel comes to announce the victory of Jesus Christ's rule upon the earth. It is not a victory for those who have rejected the truth, for the angel's message seals their doom. Salvation has ended, and they must stand with Satan and perish.

They fill the measure of a fearful expectation of judgment. Satan will advance on every front to quickly kill all followers of Jesus Christ and all Jews if he could. The opportunity to respond to the gospel has a closing date. Don't be too late, respond today.

The angel comes to finish the proclamation of truth.

"And he had in his hand a little book open: and he set his right foot upon the sea, and *his* left *foot* on the earth, And cried with a loud voice, as *when* a lion roareth: and when he had cried, seven thunders uttered their voices" (Revelation 10:2–3, KJV).

Angels are messengers and workers of God. They minister to those who inherit salvation. It is a terrible declaration that angels announce upon the remaining unbelievers that opportunity for God's is over, and that the last trumpet judgment will quickly bring their existence to a close. In that last trumpet judgment, the veils are disclosed, and many things transpire. But it will sum up the end of the mystery of God, concerning the power of the gospel drawing in sinners to God's redemption—it's over.

No unbeliever will experience the opportunity to be saved this point forward. Its scope is covering all. Ironically, angels announce the good news in the gospels; now they announce it's close to the remaining people. This happens because God's plans for his kingdom to rule literally on earth require that all who offend be cut off.

Every man has been given ample opportunity to believe. The question then is, "What did you do with Jesus Christ? Did you receive or reject him?

Things will take place that is not recorded.

"And when the seven thunders had uttered their voices, I was about to write: and I heard a voice from heaven saying unto me, seal up those things which the seven thunders uttered, and write them not" (Revelation 10:4, KJV).

This verse indicates many things will take place that is unknown to us. We must not assume we know all the events of the end dogmatically. When it tells John to seal up those things, it is talking about the judgments or declarations that shall befall the peoples of the earth which we know not.

REVELATION

It is mind-boggling how people try to fight God. Now the people of earth have openly taken Satan's side so that when the remaining judgments happen, they join Satan's economic system. They willingly destroy God's people and attempt to defy God.

They have cut themselves off from heaven's glory and God's will. Look at our own choices. Are you shutting God out of your life? Open the door to him.

God's angels participate in the transformation of earth's kingdoms into Jesus Christ's rule.

"And the angel which I saw stand upon the sea and upon the earth lifted up his hand to heaven, And sware by him that lives for ever and ever, who created heaven, and the things that therein are, and the earth, and the things that therein are, and the sea, and the things which are therein, that there should be time no longer" (Revelation 10:5–6, KJV).

The angel declares that within the days of the seventh trumpet that the end of the possibility of salvation comes, time as earth knows it is over, and the delay of God's plans for his kingdom on earth is finished. The angel swears by the one who created heaven and earth. It is this trademark of God that differentiates him from all other gods. He alone created the heavens and earth. Why? All the other so-called gods cannot create because they are false. God is the Maker of heaven and earth.

Anyone who proclaims themselves as a god or worships strange so-called deities, ask them what solar system they created?

This declaration means that within the days of the remaining judgments, God is going to bring to a close and end all those opposing the one true God.

By the blowing of the seventh trumpet, God will have accomplished his mystery.

"But in the days of the voice of the seventh angel, when he shall begin to sound, the mystery of God should be finished, as he hath declared to his servants the prophets" (Revelation 10:7, KJV).

Think also the testimony of the apostles who were Jesus Christ's witnesses. This passage recaps what we have been saying. That the remaining judgments close life from those who have rejected truth, and this makes way for God's kingdom to come in. It comes through wrath. That is why Jesus said in the book of Mark that we are to repent and believe the good news for the kingdom of heaven is at hand.

Men cannot enter unless they have been born again, so all who those people who refuse Jesus are doomed to hell. Therefore, the prophets and apostles warned people to repent and turn to God.

Even the kingdom of Israel in the Old Testament was disbursed by God so that the sinful gravity would not rule. He disbursed the nation. Is it not also true for the millennial kingdom? Nothing shall enter, which offends and has not been cleansed by Christ's blood.

The angel announces the fulfillment of the mystery of God. That's why those who reject Jehovah, look for their messiah (a false Christ), the Antichrist. A character that they suppose is enlightened who can defeat Jehovah and lead the world to an enlightened age. They are deceived and will perish. Don't join in with their folly.

Have a Working Knowledge of God's Word

Recall this is heaven's analogy of what's taken place on earth. John is in the Spirit on earth in this passage, but to be in the Spirit is still being influenced and guided by heaven and its revelation for earth and humanity. What did heaven impart to John and other apostles and prophets of old? Well, heaven bestowed God's revelation, will, Word, and judgments. We see in this passage that God gives to John his word of prophecy.

We see in Revelation 10:8–11 that it is essential we have a thorough knowledge of God's Word. Let's examine why we must be thoroughly acquainted with God's Word.

We should be thoroughly acquainted with God's Word so that we can take from God that which we are to give to the world.

"And the voice which I heard from heaven spake unto me again, and said, Go *and* take the little book which is open in the hand of the angel which standeth upon the sea and the earth" (Revelation 10:8, KJV).

John received the book, which is an inference to God's word to John, and whoever will hear and receive God's word. They must put effort into acquiring the word so they can proclaim or give forth the counsel of God. God uses those who prepare. John was told to take the little book. We must share the message that is in the Bible. When God gives a word, he will follow up with further instructions.

If you take the time to acquire God's word, to obtain the resources to share his Word, you'll be on your way to being able to give forth what God would tell you.

We must acquire God's word because the thing needed the most in the world is God's counsel. We can obtain and give it.

We should be thoroughly acquainted with God's Word so we can participate in the receiving and proclamation of it.

"And I went unto the angel, and said unto him, Give me the little book. And he said unto me, take *it*, and eat it up, and it shall make thy belly bitter, but it shall be in thy mouth sweet as honey" (Revelation 10:9, KJV).

Like John, we must thoroughly acquaint ourselves with God's message. We must take the time to eat it (read and study) and digest it (understand and apply it). It indeed is sweet to taste, and it helps keep us coming back, but the results of living and sharing the Word are bittersweet. We have good and bad experiences. The angel spoke of it being bitter in John's belly. John's words up to now offered hope to the unbeliever, but now it will unveil only the vast darkness and final judgments which shall end the rebellion against God.

There is bitterness in this because John gave a message which offered hope and salvation, but people refuse to repent, so they now hear the news of their doom. There is sweetness in this because the destruction of those who remain defiant to God brings in the liberation and reward of the saints.

It is our pleasure and sadness to share the message of God's Word to all people we meet. His word addresses people on every level. We must let God impart his word to us to share with others.

We should be thoroughly acquainted with God's word so we can experience the results and opposition to sharing the word.

"And I took the little book out of the angel's hand and ate it up; and it was in my mouth sweet as honey: and as soon as I had eaten it, my belly was bitter" (Revelation 10:10, KJV).

John rejoiced at the taste of God's word, the millennial kingdom, Jesus Christ's reign, the triumph of the saints, the New Jerusalem, etc. But the damage of Satan, the crushing of many Jews, the judgment on the world and earth were a very bitter result of being a partaker of the Word of God. John had taken the book and ate it. The Bible is too graphic and harsh for most people, including born-again believers. As with John, there is a sense the word became part of him as he digested it.

Until we eat the word, circumstances will control us, but once we digest the word, Christ is formed, and the Spirit of God can guide us. Paul fretted over some of his followers when he said, "Oh, that I be in travail until Christ be formed in you."

What kind of Christian are we? Are we a baby or newborn Christian or a worldly Christian or a spiritual Christian? God is longing for Christ's full stature in us. But that cannot happen until we digest the word of God.

We should be thoroughly acquainted with God's word so that we can share the biblical message to all God sends us.

"And he said unto me, thou must prophesy again before many peoples, and nations, and tongues, and kings" (Revelation 10:11, KJV).

John had a thorough understanding of God's Word, having walked with Jesus Christ, and as in chapter 1, he is told to prophesy again. Like John, we have the word of God to share with all people. People are at different places in their spiritual life, yet the word of God meets the soul where they are. The angel told John that he would prophesy again before peoples, nations, and kings. John's message would reach all through the Church age and beyond. To those who receive and heed salvation, to those who hear and reject, it means judgment.

The Bible says that man shall not live by bread alone but by every word that proceeds from the mouth of God. We have been given the full Word of God, the Holy Bible, so that we can be thoroughly equipped to share God's timely word. Only God's word can reach into the deep recesses of the soul. If the people reject God's word, then they lose out.

Do you know, as you study, understand and share the Word of God, that you're imparting God's message of life to people? Why don't you try to share the Bible message with people today?

Therefore, we must have a thorough working knowledge of the Word of God to be his witnesses. The higher your comprehension of God's word, then the higher will be your witness capabilities. So then put in the time and effort to read, hear, study, understand, and apply God's Word.

CHAPTER 11

Understanding John's assignment.
Why would John need to measure God's temple? Was it built correctly? Or is this possibly reference to preserve his elect? Just what is this assignment that God gave to John?

In Revelation 11:1–2, we see that we can understand John's assignment to measure the temple of God. What is this assignment given to John? Let's look at this assignment given to John to measure the temple of God.

John Is Given a Tool

"And there was given me a reed like unto a rod: and the angel stood, saying, Rise, and measure the temple of God, and the altar, and them that worship therein" (Revelation 11:1, KJV).

Here John has given a unique tool with which to measure the temple and altar (things physical), and them who worship therein (things spiritual). Recall that the world would not repent at the seal and trumpet judgments, so God measures those who repented and believed the truth for their preservation, know that there will be some who die for whatever reason, but they die in the Lord or saved. Satan will stir a mighty wave of persecution. John is given a measuring instrument that brings preservation to God's elect even over the centuries. John's vision and work has encouraged and inspired the faithful in Christ.

John is the worker used to put God's boundaries of protection on God's own for this period. If we are willing, God can use us to preserve those who will come to Jesus through faith.

It is expected that a literal temple will be built, but we also see a spiritual temple consisting of those who believe in God. The tool which measures our spiritual life is the Word of God. Study it to stay wise unto salvation.

John is given a task.

Whether this is a literal temple or (and) the people of God, it stands for the habitation of God which consists of all who are his faithful followers. There shall be many at this juncture in the book of Revelation, concerning its timing on earth, possibly at the end of the first half of the seven-year period. Within verse 2, Satan will occupy the outer court for three and a half years (or the gentile nations who have not/ nor will not repent). John is told to rise and measure. These measurements put exact boundaries of protection upon all that pertains to God's inheritance and elect. It also is a measuring tool that differentiates true believers from false believers.

Those who are believers in word only are left to the outer court, out of God's divine protection and in with the judgments he pours upon them. They will team up with Satan. God has always put a difference between his people and Satan's follower in times of judgment.

Again, this is not saying that any of the faithful will not die, but if they should die, they will die saved, being in Jesus Christ. Are you in Jesus Christ?

John is given boundaries.

"But the court, which is without the temple leave out, and measure it not; for it is given unto the Gentiles: and the holy city shall they tread under foot forty *and* two months" (Revelation 11:2, KJV).

Up to the end of the three-and-a-half period mentioned in the second part of this verse, probably the last half of the seven-year tribulation, the Gentile rulership apart from God, for Israel will be the world capital when Jesus Christ sets up his millennial kingdom. The verse talks about the court, which is without that embodies all who refuse to repent and turn to God. They are on the outside of God's plans. These are the militant unbelievers who are cast out of the intention of God's salvation.

These measurements cover the boundaries of judgment versus salvation, which God gave John to measure on behalf of his people.

Throughout the centuries, God has preserved his people; and in the tribulation, God will do the same. What a great hope for those who are in Jesus Christ, who follow God and believe the truth. Even as people die for believing in Jesus during the tribulation, God has a special place in heaven for them. Keep following God and believe in him.

martyrs

Following God doesn't mean everything will be easy, but this is the assurance that God keeps his own. Have you given your heart to Jesus Christ yet? Because if you're willing to see, this battle between Satan and God is being waged over your soul.

John is given understanding.

Here is declared to John that the Gentile nations (all who are outside of Christ) shall trample the holy city, Jerusalem, until the time of her deliverance upon the Messiah's Second Coming. They will be merciless and trample down the people of God, both the followers of God and the Jews. Satan will exercise his full fury to attempt to exterminate all of God's people. The verse tells us that the holy city shall they tread underfoot. For this remaining period, all who have now joined with the Antichrist comes to destroy Israel. They attempt to wipe Israel off the earth. They also try to destroy God's followers wherever on the planet they find them.

The measurement is told to us so that those who believe during this period (last three and a half years), and in the persecution of all the periods of all ages might retain the assurance of their salvation in Jesus Christ, even if they are to suffer or die. John mentioned the patients and suffering of the saints, which means that whoever does the smallest harm to God's people will receive their judgment accordingly. If it doesn't happen immediately, then it will happen in future time. Justice will be done.

Many will die for their faith, especially in this particular period of the tribulation. Because as God pours out his wrath, Satan attempts the same thing on God's people. If you are called to suffer and die for your faith, are you prepared? We must continually carry our cross because it is part of following Jesus Christ.

So understand this critical assignment by God to measure and preserve God's people. Let this be a source of comfort in your trials by knowing God has put his boundary of protection upon his own.

God Has Two Witnesses

What is the mission of these two witnesses? Elijah was a prophet to Israel. We are not told who the other witness is. Let's see what these witnesses do.

In Revelation 11:3–6, we can observe that God gives power to two witnesses in the days of the trumpet and vial judgments. Let's look at the kind of power God gives his two witnesses.

God gives his two witnesses power to prophecy for approximately three and a half years. *2nd half of TRIB*

"And I will give *power* unto my two witnesses, and they shall prophesy a thousand two hundred *and* threescore days, clothed in sackcloth" (Revelation 11:3, KJV).

Here are two witnesses who are expressly appointed to prophesize God's message at the time of the end. God gives power to these two witnesses to confirm and back up his word with judgments and plagues. People speculate who exactly these people will be, so I will not comment here. The power these witnesses have to speak is from God. They are given the ability to speak God's word. We are not sure who they are, possibly Elijah and Enoch (or Moses or John the Apostle, etc.). They will speak 1,230 days or three and a half years in which they will witness for Jesus Christ.

God will have a witness, as he always has, to express his reasons for judgment. In Egypt, God had Moses telling Pharaoh to let God's people go. It was in Ephraim Elijah was the prophet confronting the prophets of Baal.

These further warnings against the path men have chosen to take, yet they don't repent. *Oil = the HS*

God gives his two witnesses the Holy Spirit anointing along with the light of his Word. *Jews = oil, prophets* *witnesses* *Light - the Word*

"These are the two olive trees, and the two candlesticks standing before the God of the earth" (Revelation 11:4, KJV).

An olive tree produces olive oil, and lampstands are to brighten a room. Likewise, God has given oil and the Word to light upon humanity. If men don't repent, then they will be judged. Whoever and wherever these prophets speak God's word, it shall be done as they say it. The verse tells us these two stands before the Lord of the earth. They witness to God's impending and kinetic will and judgments; they are agents to make manifest God's word and bring forth his judgment.

They are the primary sign that Jesus Christ is about to return. Malachi says Elijah will return as a witness before the great day of the Lord, so we know one of them is Elijah.

People will hate these two witnesses because they demand repentance and to do God's will. Persons will experience God's wrath, who refuse to repent.

God gives his two witnesses power to devour their adversaries with fire from their mouths.

"And if any man will hurt them, fire proceeded out of their mouth and devoured their enemies: and if any man hurts them, he must in this manner be killed" (Revelation 11:5, KJV).

Many, I assume, will attempt to destroy these great witnesses, but God will have them witness until their appointed time. They receive the power to kill their adversaries. Fire comes from their mouths and devours them; possibly they can use any plague on the people as well.

If any man attempts to hurt these witnesses, they get killed. You would think that this would be proof enough to repent, but the world hardened their hearts at the trumpet judgments, and they do so here now.

Unbelievers have thoroughly made up their minds to fight God and join Satan. Nothing will stop the mission of the witnesses until finally the end of the time of their witnessing.

You are a witness, so ask God to work his Spirit in and through you so that you will be a ready witness.

God gives his two witnesses power over earth and sea to smite it with any plague as often as they will.

"These have the power to shut heaven that it rains not in the days of their prophecy: and have dominion over waters to turn them to blood, and to smite the earth with all plagues, as often as they will" (Revelation 11:6, KJV).

They will need such power as men continue on a sinning rampage. It will be the worst sinning the earth has ever seen. They can cause crises in the middle of people's sinning. As often as is worthy of their speaking, then it shall be done. They cut off sustenance by stopping the rain. They can counteract a cultic ritual and bring havoc on the violators. They can bring any such judgments as those.

Despite that they verify God's words of judgment with plagues and fearful signs, people won't repent. Judgment will convince only a few because it takes the power of the cross through the person of Jesus Christ and the Holy Spirit to change man's heart.

Is your heart hardened? Open your heart and mind to Jesus Christ, and he will bring a change of heart to you.

So God gives his two witnesses power to back the word he gave them to speak. God will back up our testimony also.

The martyr's testimony remains through death.

What is the purpose of the death of a martyr? Is it that they testify to a living God? Is it that their lives condemn the guilty? There is more as we see in the passage that the martyr's death is judgment to the rebellious.

In Revelation 11:7–10, we can understand how God's witnesses testify through death. Let's examine how God's two witnesses testify through their death.

The death of the two witnesses marks the completion of God's warning and plan to repent.

"And when they shall have finished their testimony, the beast that ascendeth out of the bottomless pit shall make war against them, and shall overcome them, and kill them" (Revelation 11:7, KJV).

Satan tells the beast what to do, which is to make war with the two witnesses and all the saints and the Jews. I genuinely believe the witnesses represent two particular people, not just them. It represents the completion of God's witnessing to a world that has rejected God. And that means Satan attacks all followers of God, including Jews. Millions get killed for their faith, but not all who believe become exterminated, for many will be left to enter the millennial kingdom and repopulate the earth. It is essential to know that the death and overcoming of all those who perish because of their witness, and the

131

two witnesses mean the end of any possible grace to the obstinate of the world. The verse tells us at the time the two witnesses finish their testimony that they die. These witnesses know that to give their testimony means their death, and they are prepared to die. The beast ends up making war against them. This influence empowering the beast is a mighty demonic angel in Satan's ranks who obeys Satan and kills the people of God.

I think that this demonic angel is one in Satan's since, in chapter 12, Satan comes forth as the dragon. He is still busy accusing God's people before God. In Revelation 12:1–9, Satan fights in heaven and then is cast to earth. Coming then with great fury, he sets up his lie and destroys many people. All of Satan's works tie in because all who would not repent and now rejoice over the death of God's saints, and two witnesses follow Satan's lies to death and hell.

When Satan is cast down, they are prepared to join his ranks and attempt to fight God. They will be those who take the mark of the beast, which identifies them as belonging to Satan. Whose side are we on currently? If you take the mark of the beast, you will enter punishment eternally.

The treatment of the witnesses after their death discloses the hardness and obstinacy of the people of the world.

"And their dead bodies *shall lie* in the street of the great city, which spiritually is called Sodom and Egypt, where also our Lord was crucified. And they of the people and kindred's and tongues and nations shall see their dead bodies three days and a half and shall not suffer their dead bodies to be put in graves" (Revelation 11:8–9, KJV).

This ill-treatment that wars against the saints and the witnesses to war against them and kill them and refuse them burial is typical of how Satan has treated the martyrs throughout the Church age. It all culminates the satanic rampage against God's people after the last witnessing goes forth, and God determines that no more witnessing comes to the unbelieving world. The world excludes themselves from God's plan, and Satan instructs his followers to kill as many of the followers of God as they can, including these two witnesses. The people gaze at the dead bodies of those who warned them, whom the beast killed. God allows them to neglect their dead bodies, signifying the doom awaiting the unrepentant of the earth. The city of Sodom and Egypt probably means Jerusalem, but God's followers died all around the world in cities known as Sodom and Egypt (signifying sin and corruption), which will soon be destroyed as Sodom was.

If a person will not respond to God's witness and make an intentional move away from sin, Satan, the world, their flesh, and to God, then they will (no matter what age) seal their fate. Such choices lead to rejecting the hope God offers through Jesus Christ.

How you treat the followers of God matter; there is a judgment explicitly based on that. Do God right by doing his people right.

The two witnesses receiving slander during their decease is another nail in the coffin for the rebellious people.

"And they that dwell upon the earth shall rejoice over them, and make merry, and shall send gifts one to another; because these two prophets tormented them, that lived on the planet" (Revelation 11:10, KJV). *refused to repent*

It seems reasonable that these two prophets are two individuals well-known. The language is specifying in these verses what happens to the persons, yet it relates to all those who witness for God. Remember Revelation has been a source of comfort to the faithful throughout the Church age—all has looked to Christ's triumph as the guarantee of theirs. Again, the people of the earth can go on with their sin unhindered as they always wanted and rejoice over the two dead martyrs. Jesus said people loved darkness rather than light. These two prophets tormented them because of the power that God gave them. It is the truth by all God's witnesses that cause fear, fretting, and fuming in the world; they testify to the unrepentant doom.

These people of the world are beyond business as usual but revel in sin. The occult obstinately opposes God; they are ready for Satan and his antichrist to take charge. They take eternal hell so they can rejoice in wrongdoing a little longer.

We need to open our hearts and minds to Bible truth. The power behind all witnessing is the Holy Spirit and the Word of God. If you want to change, you need to hear and obey God's word.

the 2 witnesses brought back to life after 3½ days

So know that even through their deaths, God's two witnesses speak along with all other martyrs that the end purpose of wickedness is complete. God's plans will go forward.

There are purposes for the catching up of the two witnesses.

What significant is the catching up of the two witnesses? What warning does it mean to those refusing God? How does it encourage believers on earth? Let's examine the meaning and purpose of the catching up of the two witnesses.

In Revelation 11:11–14, we see how God will bring his terror upon earth's inhabitants. Let's examine how God will bring his terror upon earth's inhabitants.

God brings the fear of the Lord upon earth's inhabitants by raising his two witnesses from the dead.

"And after three days and a half the Spirit of life from God entered into them, and they stood upon their feet, and great fear fell upon them which saw them" (Revelation 11:11, KJV).

Here is the difference between those who serve God and those who enlist into the Antichrist's system. God's people will rise to eternal life. The collaborators of Satan, though they flourish for a season, will perish in eternal judgment. Oh, it appears Antichrist overcame them, but the truth is their testimony had ended so the world could again accelerate in their sin and come to their ruin. The spirit of life entered God's witnesses, who demonstrate the difference between God's presence and the world's darkness. The world sees these as bad guys opposing their freedom, but they came to rebuke the abuse of their liberty. We are not allowed to use our freedom for indulgent sin.

Because the soul that sins shall die. This fear comes upon earth's inhabitants because only God can verify their testimony by raising them from the dead. Satan will attempt to copy this.

The resurrection of Jesus Christ from the dead is the guarantee of our transformation. One day, God will raise us from our graves. We must be in Jesus Christ to experience this—a personal radiant relationship with him.

God brings his terror upon his enemies by catching up his two witnesses.

REVELATION

the 2 witnesses by raised over to heaven while watching (CNN)

"And they heard a great voice from heaven saying unto them, Come up hither. And they ascended to heaven in a cloud; and their enemies beheld them" (Revelation 11:12, KJV).

The terror of the Lord falls on all observers as they realize God calls his two witnesses home. They now know that they were from Jehovah God, and that they rejected their witnesses. Now it's too late. All the observers hear a great voice. In front of all the people of the earth, the two witnesses ascend into heaven.

All this affirms the Lord's purpose to his followers. They are commanded to endure to the end.

We must endure in our faith with patient perseverance so that we don't throw in the towel no matter how hard it gets.

God sends an earthquake and strengthens the faith of his remnant. *2nd woe?*

"And the same hour was there a great earthquake, and the tenth part of the city fell and in the earthquake was slain of men seven thousand: and the remnant was affrighted and gave glory to the God of heaven" (Revelation 11:13, KJV).

Here a remnant believed was spared and strengthened their faith in Jehovah God. They persevere in their faith. To verify God's will, he sent a great earthquake that same hour because of the hardened hearts of the unbelievers also. So those who follow Jesus Christ gave glory to God. Some believed, feared God, and acknowledged him.

God's judgments are also designed to strengthen his faithful. This earthquake happens the same hour as the ascension of God's two witnesses. God is verifying his judgment.

We must take warning and believe the truth. Will Jesus find faith in you? And will it produce repentance and obedience?

God sends another woe.

"The second woe is past; *and*, behold, the third woe cometh quickly" (Revelation 11:14, KJV).

We have ended the sixth trumpet judgment here. There will be another that will sound, which ushers in the vial judgments. Satan finds himself cast to the earth, while the people of earth get what they want—pure evil or life led by Satan himself. Now the third woe comes and, with it, sums up the end of the reign of wickedness.

It won't happen all at once but in rapid succession. These coming judgments bring the unrepentant to their end.

All these are signs warning of impending eternal doom to unrepentant people. Man's only hope is to open to the biblical truth.

So God brings terror to the people of the earth because they won't have anything to do with God's ways; therefore, the catching up of the two witnesses is a sign of terrible doom awaiting the unrepentant.

The celebration of the reign of Jesus Christ.

Why must the reign of the kingdoms of earth become the kingdoms of our Lord Jesus Christ? Is it just to put a stop to wickedness or so that the righteous can now rule with Jesus? We will see that in Jesus Christ's reign, God will be vindicated along with his saints, and each will in time occupy their place of responsibilities.

In Revelation 11:15–19, we see that all the saints will join in on the celebration of the reign of Jesus Christ. Let's examine why all the saints join in on the celebration of the reign of Jesus Christ.

There is a celebration over Jesus Christ's reign.

"And the seventh angel sounded; and there were great voices in heaven, saying, the kingdoms of this world are become *the kingdoms* of our Lord, and of his Christ; and he shall reign for ever and ever" (Revelation 11:15, KJV).

The sounding of the last trumpet will include the last woe judgment and the vials or bowls. This blast signifies Jesus Christ's reign, which now moves forth to carry out the death blow judgment over all wickedness. Jesus Christ resumes his rulership over the earth. The verse tells us the kingdoms of this world become our Lords. Jesus's rule is announced.

This verse notes that he wasn't ruling, but he now lays off all self-imposed limitations so that he can fully reveal and end the purpose of wickedness. His final judgments will deal a death blow to sin and rebellion.

We look for the day of the coming of God's kingdom and his good will to be done. Let us hope and long for the rule of heaven upon the earth.

There is worship over Jesus Christ's reign.

"And the four and twenty elders, which sat before God on their seats, fell upon their faces, and worshipped God" (Revelation 11:16, KJV).

Here has been a great pleasure waited for as Jesus Christ takes over the reign of earthly kingdoms. He is revered for his lordship. The twenty-four elders represent the saints in heaven, who bow and worship our Lord and Savior. We also will rejoice and worship God for his reign because he saved us, preserved us, and gave us an inheritance.

Won't it be great to be under the kingship of Jesus Christ? That time is quickly approaching. Can you imagine being under the God whom we have never seen yet? Now he is reigning over all the universe and kingdoms of the earth. We will be taking our place with him; it is worth serving him currently.

Oh, the joy for those who believe and serve God. Will you offer your service to God? It will be remembered.

There will be thanks over Jesus Christ's reign.

"Saying, we give thee thanks, O Lord God Almighty, which art, and was, and art to come; because thou hast taken to thee thy great power, and hast reigned" (Revelation 11:17, KJV).

There is great rejoicing by the martyrs and saints because now justice will rule, saints will be rewarded, and Jesus Christ now takes rulership over the earth. God is no longer going to be sinned against. This verse describes how God will make a short end to the challenge to his rule. It's not over yet, for war in heaven with Satan is about to begin.

Because Jesus Christ's name is our salvation and it will be vindicated, only by Jesus Christ can there be the peace and hope God designed for men to experience.

Let us pray for his reign and pray that God will put a stop to all wickedness and hurt.

There is anticipation over Jesus Christ's reign.

"And the nations were angry, and thy wrath is come, and the time of the dead, that they should be judged, and that thou shouldest give reward unto thy servants the prophets, and to the saints, and them that fear thy name, small and great; and shouldest destroy them which destroy the earth" (Revelation 11:18, KJV).

Here is a time also of silence over the fate of the unrepentant on earth. Even though nations were angry since Jesus Christ's first advent till now, the nations have tried to hinder his rulership. But the dead will be judged. It's now time for wrath to stop the life of the living dead. God will also reward his servants. God's servants will be responsible and have authority.

The wrath now begins to accelerate more. Here is the cosmic battle ending, the end portion that stops Satan and wicked reigns of men.

Do you see why it is so foolish to fight and try to stop or drive God out of your life? The future is all about his reign.

There is activity occurring over Jesus Christ's reign.

"And the temple of God was opened in heaven, and there was seen in his temple the ark of his testament: and there were lightnings, and voices, and thundering's, and an earthquake, and great hail" (Revelation 11:19, KJV).

John gets to see into the holy of holies in heaven. Things are going on that affect earth. John got to see the ark of the testament. This ark is the heavenly one in which the earthly one was a pattern after. Plus, there were earthquakes and great hail. This activity is affecting earth.

Because the truth about Revelation is that what goes on in the spiritual realm affects earth and its inhabitants. John sees this in the holy of holies, and an earthquake takes place.

That is why I say its heaven's perspective on what happens on earth. Will you view this from heaven or earth? You choose to be saved or not—choose today.

So all the saints will join in on the reign of Jesus Christ. Soon each will take their place as rulers under Jesus Christ's kingship.

CHAPTER 12

The travail of Israel.

We must realize Jesus Christ is ruling, so there is a series of battles between Satan and Jesus, Satan and Israel, Satan and the believers, and Satan and heaven. Therefore, Israel will suffer in the tribulation, for Satan is losing his domain.

In Revelation 12:1–2, we see Israel's travail in bringing forth the Messiah. Let's look at some things that point to Israel's travail.

Heaven watches as the drama unfolds over the nation of Israel.

"And there appeared a great wonder in heaven; a woman clothed with the sun and the moon under her feet and upon her head a crown of twelve stars" (Revelation 12:1, KJV).

Israel has undergone great travail over the fact that she was chosen to bring forth the Messiah. She became the center of the cosmic battle between Satan and his forces and God and his plan. Satan will fight you if he learns God is using you for his work. God's angels also view from heaven and minister God's salvation, will, and glad tidings as they participate in this struggle to bring forth God's plans. The great wonder in heaven is the sign of the nation of Israel. It speaks of the travail of all that is good against wickedness, yet God prevails.

This is a sign in heaven and earth, for here again is Israel as a nation, and even today, Satan stirs all kinds of evil forebodings against her. This means the battle rages on. Satan is fighting Israel, but God keeps her alive!

This is a great hope for the followers of God, Jews, and Gentiles because Satan is defeated and will be cast to earth to deliver his last fleeting rebellious attacks. God and his people win.

Israel is identified here along with the twelve patriarchs.

This great wonder shows the woman to be Israel. The twelve stars represent the patriarchs. Israel again appears on earth's scene and will undergo great pain and suffering as never before. This woman represents Israel. Israel is crowned and is royal, God's chosen nation to rule the world. Be sure she will triumph in Christ.

She undergoes pain again because she produced the Messiah, and Satan will vehemently persecute her for this. The mass killings of the Jews by Antichrist are to stop the coming of the Messiah. The reasoning is that if the Jews are dead, then the Messiah won't come. God spoils the plan though.

Satan is enraged with anyone who gives their life to Jesus Christ. Be ready to face suffering for your faith in Jesus Christ.

What we see is Israel has struggled and suffered to bring forth the Messiah, both from within and from outside.

"And she being with child cried, travailing in birth, and pained to be delivered" (Revelation 12:2, KJV).

No other nation has undergone such travail of existence as Israel. Since she was chosen to bring forth the Messiah, Satan has caused her to suffer, and he won't stop until his end and know Jesus Christ has defeated him on the cross. There is only so much time before his end comes. The woman cried in much pain! Satan has caused much suffering to come to the Jews for being God's chosen.

Satan is jealous and is trying to stop God's plan of his rule on the earth, the Millennial Kingdom, because then Satan can't manifest his evil. The course of wickedness is winding down because Christ now has taken the throne and is ruling earth. Satan's time and plans are coming to an end.

We better be on the right side. Join God's team today!

So understand Israel's travail over the multimillennia's concerning her existence, and that she is the instrument of victory by which Christ rules the world.

Satan's Rage against Jesus Christ

Why does Satan rage against God and his people? Satan, since his fall, has been losing his place of power. Therefore, Satan is infuriated with Jesus Christ and his people. So then, Satan takes his rage out on all that is associated with God.

In Revelation 12:3–4, we see we should know how Satan has raged his fight against Jesus Christ. Let's look at how Satan has raged against Jesus Christ.

Heaven witnesses the rise and fall of Satan.

"And there appeared another wonder in heaven; and behold a great red dragon, having seven heads and ten horns, and seven crowns upon his heads" (Revelation 12:3, KJV).

This cosmic battle between Satan and Jesus Christ drew out a third of the angels; it encompasses the persecution of Israel and the Church. Throughout the millennia of humanity's existence, this cosmic battle included the fall of man and man's destruction in hell. Satan was created a perfect being who led the worship hosts in heaven into the worship of God—so it is said. But he sinned by pride, desiring to usurp God, and from that time on, he sought to fight God to his end. The great red dragon identifies this being as Satan. The Antichrist gets his power from Satan.

The ten horns symbolize the ten global federations of the one-world government, given its power by Satan. Why, for our information, does Satan form this last government? Satan set them up to attempt to destroy the possibility of Christ's millennial reign and triumph at his Second Advent. Satan has been involved in the past seven empires as a source of influence in which he uses the governments to resist Israel, Christianity, man's salvation through Christ, and to fight Jesus Christ at all fronts. He has many people employed to do his bidding.

This cosmic battle has been going on millennial after millennial, century after century, decade after decade, and year after year. Only God sees the beginning and end. We must be sure we conform to the Bible's pattern.

Satan Leads a Rebellion

"And his tail drew the third part of the stars of heaven, and did cast them to the earth: and the dragon stood before the woman who was ready to be delivered, for to devour her child as soon as it was born" (Revelation 12:4, KJV).

This wonder is especially noted in heaven because that is where the battle initially began—Satan by his rebellion against Jesus Christ in heaven. He didn't want to worship Christ anymore but usurp him. So he drew a third part of the angels from heaven. Satan duped a third of the angels into following his rebellion. This fallen angelic host is a mighty evil force, which will battle in the heavens in verses 7–9, and Satan and his demonic angels lose the battle. So the scene is being set for Satan's fall.

Therefore, we must determine to continue with Jesus Christ by fighting the good fight. The book of Revelation warns us to endure to the end.

When Satan knocks on your door, you must resist him by staying faithful and loyal to God, continue to walk with God through your wilderness, bear your cross, fight the good fight against Satan, and help others who are struggling in their faith.

Satan Sought to Destroy Jesus Christ

Throughout Israel's existence in the long past, Satan hounded the nation so that she might not bring forth the messiah or savior of the world, not just with Mary and Joseph but all of Israel's history. Satan persecuted her. The verse tells us that Satan stood before the woman. Satan wanted to kill, stop, and hurt God's program through Jesus Christ.

So we see that Satan attacks Jesus, Israel, fellow believers, and heaven. But his end is quickly approaching. Systematically, since Jesus Christ began to rule in heaven, Satan's steps are being removed from under his feet. Jesus went to the cross to demonstrate that God can accomplish all his will through his Son's death. The point of Satan's claim of defeating God becomes his defeat.

142

Jesus wasn't overcome at the cross; he defeated Satan. What will you believe about the cross? Believe in the atoning work of Jesus Christ and live.

So know Satan has raged his fight against Israel, Jesus, fellow believers, and heaven. He has lost his place and is infuriated; therefore, he is taking his wrath against anything that is likened to God and his presence.

God's Preservation

What was God's purpose for the drama of good and evil that has and is occurring in and at the end of the age? We will see how God preserves a believing race to enter the millennia (Jews and Gentiles) and gives victory to saints and rulership. God's preservation of Jesus Christ and Israel is for the benefit of all who have ever trusted God.

In Revelation 12:5–6, we can consider how God preserves Christ's kingdom and the nation of Israel. Let's examine how God protects Christ's kingdom and nation.

God caught Jesus Christ up after his work after his first advent so that preparation for his return at his Second Advent as King of kings and Lord of lords with his saints.

"And she brought forth a man child, who was to rule all nations with a rod of iron: and her child was caught up unto God, and *to* his throne" (Revelation 12:5, KJV).

Satan opposed Israel to stop the Messiah's arrival. Satan killed Jesus to stop God's plan. God raised Jesus from the dead and raptured him to the third heaven, where he awaits God the Father's command to receive his Church and come back as King of kings and Lord of lords. This man-child was Jesus Christ who was to rule the nations. This is what Satan is trying to stop, for he will be locked up during that time. With a rod of iron at Jesus's Second Advent, he will rule mightily and crush all his enemies. It will be the day of the Lord, a great and terrible day, where God smashes the nations that rebelled. We have hope because God rose or caught up Jesus Christ. This will happen with the Church also one day, and those who live faithfully unto Jesus Christ will reign with him.

Our victory is tied into Jesus Christ's victory over Satan at the cross and his catching up into heaven, for we will hear the trumpet and be caught to our heavenly dwelling. The rapture is hope for the pre-tribulation saints. We are inspired to live and stay prepared and staying in a vibrant personal relationship with Jesus.

Christ's appearing could be any moment; thus, we must live in a state of readiness. We must continue in the faith of Jesus being the Son of God and obedient to his lordship over us.

God will prepare a place for the Israelites for three and a half years to preserve them for the millennia kingdom.

"And the woman fled into the wilderness, where she hath a place prepared of God that they should feed her there a thousand two hundred *and* threescore days" (Revelation 12:6, KJV).

We can see that as the battle gets ready to happen in the heavens between Satan and his hosts and Michael and heaven's angels, God prepares a place for the Israelites safety. Those who study the scripture believe the truth of the Messiah (Jesus) and fight against Antichrist's system. These are given a place of refuge. But all the Jews who join Satan and Antichrist's network perish along with all the nations who team up with Antichrist. The verse says that the woman fled into the wilderness; this is all of the Jews who reject Antichrist and believe in Jesus Christ. Here will be a place prepared for them. God divinely provides a home and all she needs.

Those who come to faith are considered worthy by God to be preserved and will become pioneers in the millennial kingdom for Christ's reign on earth. They shall be feed for 1,260 days. God sure knows how to preserve his people. We can take courage in this hope. Have we not seen this through Jesus Christ's work at Calvary and the Holy Spirit cares over us?

Let us not fret and fume over our petty provocations, but let us trust in our God.

So consider how God preserves Christ's kingdom (a kingdom of priests unto God), which includes the faithful saints of all ages. God preserves Israel and his followers through the tribulation. This preservation should give us great hope to endure our challenges and to keep the faith to the end. It is this nation and these saints who rule with Jesus Christ after he smashes the rebellious nations at the great day of the Lord in the millennial state.

Satan continues to lose his grip as he is defeated in the war in the heavenlies.

How does this war cause another blow to Satan? Satan loses his place in the heavens. Satan also loses the heavenly edge. Satan is now confined to time and space, and he knows his time is short.

We see in Revelation 12:7–9 that there is a coming war in the heavens. Let's examine what is significant about this impending war in the heavens.

There will be war in the heavens between Satan and his angels versus Michael and his angels.

"And there was war in heaven: Michael and his angels fought against the dragon; and the dragon fought and his angels" (Revelation 12:7, KJV).

There have been battles in the past such as: (1) Satan cast out of the third heaven; (2) Jesus defeats Satan at the cross; and (3) other actions are Michael and his angels defeat Satan and his angels (which we will look at now), Satan locked in the abyss for a thousand years, and finally, Satan cast into hell.

What we see in this fallen angel called Satan, who has set the universe in rebellion against God, he continues to lose his battles and hold when faced off with God and his angels. He especially loses as Jesus Christ stood to rule when the kingdoms of this earth became the kingdoms of our Lord Jesus Christ. Yet this battle is between angels; those who are loyal to God defeat Satan and his angels. God's angels drive Satan and his cohorts out of heavens 1 and 2 down to earth. This war brings great rejoicing in heaven but utter chaos on earth. This war in heaven brings Satan's defeat out of heaven and causes woe on earth, which probably marks the second half of the tribulation (the great tribulation). This marks Satan's great carnage on the Jews and the Gentiles who follow Jesus Christ.

Again note: This is an angelic war! Jesus already defeated Satan and all his forces on the cross at his very weakest point. Now Michael's heavenly hosts drive Satan and his hosts out of heaven where he will never enter again! Those loyal to God defeat the rebellious angels. Let us take heart at the fact that stage by stage Satan is being defeated! It is a terrible war, but in Jesus Christ, we are assured of the victory.

Michael is the highest angel, and he works for Jesus Christ. Don't you want to be on the winning team? By personally receiving Jesus Christ as your Lord and Savior, you'll join the winning team.

Satan and his forces prevail not and lose their place in heaven.

"And prevailed not; neither was their place found any more in heaven" (Revelation 12:8, KJV).

Again, Satan receives an awful defeat, being driven entirely out of the heaven's domain. Thus he is locked onto planet earth, where he knows his time is short! No more can he destroy God's created order in the heavenlies. He is now subject to earth's time and space, and after three and one half years, he will be locked into the abyss. Satan prevailed not and proved to be no match for Michael. Michael doesn't play around, and he gets the job done. There, therefore, was found no place for Satan anymore. There was no entryway for Satan to enter heaven ever again. No accuser of the brethren anymore; never to do business there again.

We see Satan losing ground, and he is infuriated and takes his wrath out on the people of the earth, particularly the Jews and anyone who follow Jesus Christ. Now rejoicing begins in the heavens because Satan is gone!

Why would people enjoy pleasures for a season by rejecting God and then perish and suffer eternally? Because Satan has blinded them, and they keep saying no to Jesus Christ and God. Revelation is about repentance and faith in Jesus Christ that continues to the end.

Satan and all his forces are to come down to the earth.

"And the great dragon was cast out, that old serpent, called the Devil, and Satan, which deceived the whole world: he was cast out into the earth, and his angels were cast out with him" (Revelation 12:9, KJV).

Woe now to the earth because men will follow Satan's lie, the Antichrist and his economic time bomb system, right to their eternal punishment. Woe to those who follow Jesus Christ because Satan will hunt them down (though they suffer and die, they will be safe in Jesus Christ). Woe because Satan brings suffering to the Jews. Men

he knows

become Satan's pawns who do his business now. Satan is madly infuriated. The verse tells us that the dragon was cast out to the earth. Now Satan stuck in time, and his time is short, and being on earth, he will go to work immediately to destroy valiantly until his end.

Great darkness is coming to Antichrist's system. Can you imagine the madness that comes to the people?

Have you ever been controlled and did a wrong thing under that influence? Well, the whole world will be managed by Satan (all who are not saved). The lost will do things that are great abominations. Let's be ready for the rapture!

So know that a war in heaven is coming which brings liberty to heaven's occupants, but it brings havoc to planet earth. Plan your escape through faith in Jesus Christ!

Satan's Overthrow

Will Satan's accusations be overthrown in the heavenlies? As we will see, Satan loses ground. He is quickly running out of time, and thus, he takes vengeance out on man. Let's see how Satan is overcome by heaven's occupants.

In Revelation 12:10–12, we see how Satan is overcome. Let's see what the Bible says about that in this passage.

Satan is overcome by being cast down from heaven.

"And I heard a loud voice saying in heaven, now is come salvation, and strength, and the kingdom of our God, and the power of his Christ: for the accuser of our brethren is cast down, which accused them before our God day and night" (Revelation 12:10, KJV).

Satan
3rd woe

Now as Satan comes down, this brings the third woe upon mankind. There is hope for the Jews and followers of Christ. That hope is found in Jesus's shed blood. Now Satan's fall from the heavens 1 and 2 to earth means that the greatest slaughter of people (especially the Jews and believers) ever known, and war in Armageddon breaks out where souls will die by the millions. There is great rejoicing in heaven over Satan's overthrow. But now he has come down to earth where he will never have access to heaven or God's thrown again. Woe to

throne
typo

the earth's inhabitants because this accuser has come upon them. The adversary has come down to earth.

Satan is overthrown and removed entirely out of heaven. The heavenly Father and Jesus has prevailed through their heavenly battle warriors, Michael and his angels. The saints of heaven had a part by overcoming Satan through the blood of Christ and the word of their testimony. This defeat of Satan is devastation for all false beliefs and followers of Satan's lies. They end up with no hope of heaven! It was at the cross where Jesus defeated Satan, and this victory, which is ours, is the victor of the past, present, and future overcoming of Satan.

All Christians must confess their faith in Jesus Christ and his victory over Satan. We must own Jesus and his victory as our own before men to be counted as Jesus's own.

Satan is overcome by the blood of Christ and the testimony of his saints.

"And they overcame him by the blood of the Lamb and by the word of their testimony, and they loved not their lives unto the death" (Revelation 12:11, KJV).

It has been the means of victory, Christ and his shed blood, for all saints whoever overcame in life. They drive Satan out of heaven by the shed blood of the Lamb of God. It is not the victory of the saints or their own accomplishments but what Jesus Christ did for all who come to God by faith in him and his work on the cross. The saints overcome Satan, and they revolt against Satan in heaven! Many gave their lives for the Word of God and their testimony of Jesus Christ. These martyred saints offered up their lives.

We must keep winning victories for Jesus Christ or we will be losing them. These saints willingly or not, laid their life on the line to win through their death for Christ's cause. This laying of one's life down is what a martyr does, and Satan will, upon his fall, see to it that every Jew or believer he captures will die. He will attempt to get them to reject their faith in God and kill them anyway.

We have a choice if we are alive and go through the tribulation. One confesses Jesus Christ and dies and, thus, goes to heaven as a martyr, or one recants their testimony die anyway and go to hell. Do not deny Jesus Christ.

Satan is overcome by being forced down to earth.

"Therefore rejoice, *ye* heavens, and ye that dwell in them. Woe to the inhabiters of the earth and the sea! For the devil is come down unto you, having great wrath, because he knows that he hath but a short time" (Revelation 12:12, KJV).

Now Satan loses his domain in the heavens one and two. Therefore, he is furious, so he works and indwells the Antichrist. Satan will attempt to kill Jews, believers of all nationalities, and all men saved or not. Those who are unrepentant will be forced to worship Antichrist and receive his mark. Woe upon the earth's inhabitants! This woe is worse than the plague of the soldiers of torture and doom because now all the heavenly evil hosts are on the ground, manifesting themselves.

I perceive whoever has repented already done so; now it's a battle between evil and good. Satan now has only a short while. Satan knows this, and he goes to work to exterminate God's people.

It is our privilege to accept Jesus Christ as our Lord and Savior before all this takes place. I ask again, have you received Jesus Christ as your Lord and Savior?

Satan is overcome and cast out of the heavens where he never will reside again. But woe to earth's inhabitants because Satan has come with great wrath!

Satan's Wrath against Believers and the Jews

What will Satan do to God's people? He will put them on the run and slaughter them. He will wear them out with all his fury. Satan is going to attempt to wipe out the Jews and believers.

In Revelation 12:13–17, we will see that Satan brings great persecution upon all the followers of God. Let's look at how Satan brings great persecution upon the followers of God.

Upon Satan's removal from heaven he immediately begins his attack on the people who follow God.

"And when the dragon saw that he was cast unto the earth, he persecuted the woman which brought forth the man *child*" (Revelation 12:13, KJV).

Satan is now cast out of heavens one and two and begins the most significant killing the world will ever see. Satan knows he has only three and a half years to destroy the Jewish remnant so that Jesus cannot rule the world at his Second Coming. Satan's reasoning is that there will be no more Jewish people. The verse tells us that the dragon saw that he was cast to the earth. Upon Satan's failure in the heavens, he has now been confined to earth's time and space; therefore, he persecutes the woman. Satan goes immediately to work on destroying the Jews because through them; God brought the Messiah.

We must also see this time as a period where many believers suffer and die for their faith in Jesus Christ around the world. Satan's rage will be intensified upon Israel but also on all who have the testimony of the Lord Jesus Christ.

This persecution is the time that Israel must flee. Israel must preserve herself.

God provides a place of shelter for the Jews to take refuge.

"And to the woman were given two wings of a great eagle, that she might fly into the wilderness, into her place, where she is nourished for a time, and times, and half a time, from the face of the serpent" (Revelation 12:14, KJV).

Upon the abomination that makes desolate, the Jewish people acknowledge Jesus Christ's warning and flee. God supernaturally provides transportation and provision for the Jews. We need to note the time, three and a half years. It's this last half of the tribulation (the great tribulation) where Satan will attack and wreak havoc on the Jews. The woman flies with two wings. Somehow God provides transportation for Israel as flying into the wilderness. It's as if Israel is again fleeing her Egypt.

God will have a remnant of a third of the Jews, which will be saved. Those who do not leave (two-thirds) die and will not be saved. They must hear and respond to Jesus Christ's prophecy. Those who do will live. These Jews who die want to remain in the world.

This persecution will also be a hard time for all believers, especially Jewish believers. Now they will begin to say, "Blessed is He (Jesus) who comes in the name of the Lord."

Satan sends supernatural vomit to wipe away Israel.

"And the serpent cast out of his mouth water as a flood after the woman, that he might cause her to be carried away of the flood" (Revelation 12:15, KJV).

Satan attempts to sweep away the fleeing remnant of Israel. Those who would not leave before the flood came to an end in the flood; those who trusted in their God are preserved and saved from the flood. The wave that is sent might be vast armies to wipe out the Jews. The surge is likened to water. Again, I speculate that this flood is vast armies come to destroy Israel. The serpent intends to carry the woman away or kill her.

Why are the armies of the world cooperating with Antichrist against Israel? Somehow Satan convinces them that if the Jews live, then they will ultimately become Israel's slaves. The Jews must die to prevent Jewish domination.

The remnant must flee and call on God's salvation. Those who harden their hearts perish.

God allows the earth to stop Satan's supernatural rampage against the Jews.

"And the earth helped the woman, and the earth opened her mouth, and swallowed up the flood which the dragon cast out of his mouth" (Revelation 12:16, KJV).

God, as with Pharaoh's army, opens the earth and swallows them up like the Red Sea. Note again those who would not leave Jerusalem are caught and destroyed in flood. Those who fled Jerusalem are the ones who get saved. We see that the earth helped the woman. This help reminded me of the account when Joshua was fighting Israel's enemy, and he told the sun to stand still, and it did for the space of about a day! The earth swallows up the entire army or vomit or whatever it is.

Moses also had a situation where a group of rebels rebelled against him, and God opened the earth and swallowed them. God will destroy Satan's rage and pursuit against God's remnant.

God's salvation is again conditional: they must obey and flee to the wilderness, and God will provide salvation.

Satan seeks out to kill all who have the testimony of Jesus Christ.

"And the dragon was wroth with the woman and went to make war with the remnant of her seed, which keep the commandments of God, and have the testimony of Jesus Christ" (Revelation 12:17, KJV).

The dragon takes up a case against the remnant of the woman. This attack could mean those who stayed behind or those still scattered around the world or any believer in Jesus Christ. I say that because (Jews and Gentiles) they come to faith and hold the testimony during that time, and most likely, Satan will hunt them down because they are offspring of the graces God gave the world through the Jews.

The dragon makes war with the remnant. Satan starts a worldwide holocaust against the Jews and believers of all nations. The Bible says those who keep God's commandments and have the testimony of Jesus Christ are the very ones that Satan attacks. The believer lives out their testimony, so it sets them apart; they have godly behavior. Their behavior is how they are identified; lawlessness will characterize all other people who reject Jesus Christ.

All tribulation saints must be prepared to give their testimony and die for it; their lives were always on the line for Jesus.

So Satan brings great persecution to believers in all the earth because his time is short. So be forewarned so you can be prepared to stand for the faith.

CHAPTER 13

A ntichrist's influence.

What kind of influence will Antichrist have? He will command the life and death of his subjects, and he will pick up and put down nations. Antichrist will be the world's most powerful leader outside of Jesus Christ.

In Revelation 13:1–4, we see why we should understand the great influence of the beast or Antichrist. Let's look at why the Antichrist has significant power.

The Antichrist has great influence because he commands the world government.

"And I stood upon the sand of the sea, and saw a beast rise up out of the sea, having seven heads and ten horns, and upon his horns ten crowns, and upon his heads the name of blasphemy" (Revelation 13:1, KJV).

During the tribulation, Satan stands with anticipation for the Antichrist to come to power. Satan will empower this monster to rule the last world government. He will divide the world into ten regions (ten horns or the leaders of the areas), and somehow the names are blasphemies against God. This beast that comes out of the sea is the Antichrist and his world empire which comes to power and takes the scene of world affairs. The ten horns are the rulers under the dictator. The seven heads represent all human power, including the Antichrist, under the control of Satan, in the form of world governments.

This control of Satan over man happens after the rapture because men reject Jesus Christ. Antichrist will wield his power by lifting collaborators and putting down resisters.

Do Not Be Led to Accept Satan's Deception
Choose Jesus over Satan's Lie!

The Antichrist has great influence because he represents the height of man's power under Satan's rule.

"And the beast which I saw was like unto a leopard, and his feet were as *the feet* of a bear, and his mouth as the mouth of a lion: and the dragon gave him his power, and his seat, and great authority" (Revelation 13:2, KJV).

This Antichrist sums up the pomp and dignity of all former authorities who lead apart from God's leading. He has human genius empowered by Satan and representing all past powers. He represents all men could be without God. Satan gave him his power and authority. Satan empowers this demonic human.

Men follow this monster as their highest idol and god. Satan brings a false sense of security through this man.

It is a folly to live our lives as if God had no say so in our lives. If we will not let, God rule over us, the only other alternative is to be Satan's subjects. Do not follow the path of the crowd, which exalts man as the highest authority. God is the highest authority.

The Antichrist has great influence because he deceives the world into thinking he is god.

"And I saw one of his heads as it were wounded to death, and his deadly wound was healed, and all the world wondered after the beast."

After some world crises, the Antichrist is either the healer or healed of a significant wound. He then causes all unbelievers to worship him as a god by penalty of death. Rejecters will be killed. One head was wounded means that a blow occurs to the Antichrist or his kingdom. The Bible declares the wound is healed. False miracles happen, and the crisis is resolved. From this point on, the entire world wondered after the beast. The world is led to worship Antichrist.

Because the deceived do not know the truth, they follow the Antichrist (Satan's lie). How easy it is to lead people astray who don't know the truth?

All the world will hail this satanic-led man because they rejected *Jesus*
the truth of the good news. Therefore, God sends them a strong
delusion, so they believe the lie.

The Antichrist has great influence because he pulls in the worship of all unbelievers by satanic might. *Satan influences all to follow antic*

"And they worshipped the dragon which gave power unto the
beast: and they worshipped the beast, saying, who *is* like unto the
beast? Who can make war with him? (Revelation 13:4, KJV)

The unbelievers, who reject Jesus Christ, receive and embrace
the lie of Satan. They worship Antichrist and give all their allegiance
to him. They even worship Satan, who gave such a man so high
authority. Satan is behind all this blasphemy. The people go on and
worship the beast and proclaim him as the great god. They declare,
"Who can make war with him?"

The Antichrist seems to have all the answers. He feeds and
guides all who submit to him.

All who give their allegiance to Antichrist lose their eternal life.
Choose to give your allegiance to Jesus Christ. Do not join Satan.

So know why Antichrist has such influence; the power of evil
leads him. God will reject all who give their allegiance to him.

The Rebellion of Antichrist

Have you considered that your choosing who sides you're going
to be on, either God's or Satan's? To rebel against God is to serve the
self, the world, and Satan. To repent and believe the good news is to
join God's side. As we will see, the Antichrist wages a harsh warfare
against God.

In Revelation 13:4–6, we examine how Antichrist slanders with
his mouth. Let's examine how Antichrist vilifies. *repeat*

The Antichrist slanders through being worshiped.

"and they worshipped the dragon which gave power unto the
beast: and they worshipped the beast, saying, who *is* like unto the
beast? Who is able to make war with him?" (Revelation 13:4, KJV).

These persons on earth who reject the good news give their allegiance to the leader, the Antichrist. Antichrist has the idea of being

155

either against or standing in the place of another. He is empowered by Satan; thus, those who give their allegiance to the Antichrist are giving it to Satan. They attribute God's power to Antichrist and believe he is more potent than anything called god. Satan is behind this as he draws the multitudes to worship him and the beast. Satan misleads the world into thinking the Antichrist is the real god, and they give consent. They begin to reason and express that no one can make war with the beast.

All who are deceived worship the Antichrist and reject the true God. This reciprocating deception between Antichrist and his followers fueled by lies, stirs him to great blasphemies.

This is the great deception—Antichrist embodies all the lies and destructive habits of all former blasphemies. Don't give him your allegiance.

The Antichrist speaks blasphemies for forty-two months.

"And there was given unto him a mouth speaking great things and blasphemies; and power was given unto him to continue forty *and* two months" (Revelation 13:5, KJV).

God allows Antichrist to blaspheme until the time of his faithful martyrs have come in. The great things Antichrist speaks are fueled by Satan promising false power and prosperity to his followers and contempt upon God, heaven, and his people. He goes on in this way for three and a half years while he and the world fall under the judgment of God. There is no escaping the judgment of God for the Antichrist and his followers. God permits Satan to give Antichrist a mouth that is enabled to speak great deception and lies. He blasts the god of heaven and his people and things.

This time is at the beginning of the second three-and-a-half-year period marked by Satan's fall and the deadly wound of Antichrist and the abomination of desolation. It is at this time millions will be killed for their allegiance to God and their rejection of Antichrist headship.

I want to ask you, "Whose side are you on?" If you blow off these truths, then you're in danger. Repent and believe in Jesus Christ or you'll go through this deception.

The Antichrist Slanders God and Heaven

"And he opened his mouth in blasphemy against God, to blaspheme his name, and his tabernacle, and them that dwell in heaven" (Revelation 13:6, KJV).

This speech is a mark of infidelity, apostasy, reprobation, and Anti-faith. The Antichrist blasphemes God, heaven, and his people. Those worshiping Antichrist have joined him in assuming he conquered Jehovah and his people, so there never has to be obedience to the one true God again. They can make up their own rules and do whatever they want like Cain's line, a heritage of rebellion and violence.

This rebellion is Satan's and the world's outright attack at God and is their final rebellion against God. God allows it and comes through judgment to destroy them.

The application is clear—choose whose side your one. You have the choice of choosing either the kingdom of light (God's) or the kingdom of darkness (Satan's lie). If you serve self, the world, or Satan, your choice is to be destroyed by the wrath of God. If you repent and turn to Jesus Christ, you live with God eternally.

So consider the slander of Antichrist how he is fueled by Satan and deceives the whole world into rebellion against God. You must choose now who side you're going to be on. If you rebel and reject the good news, then you'll suffer the fate of the Antichrist; but if you obey the gospel, then God will spare your soul. Again, whose side are you on?

Antichrist's War with the Saints

Does the future pose danger for God's followers? Possibly the whole world will turn on them. They may suffer greatly and even die for their faith. Yes, threats are ahead, but take courage in the God of your salvation.

We see in Revelation 13:7–10 that we ought to know that Antichrist will make war against the saints of the highest God. Let's examine how Antichrist wars against God's people.

Antichrist Kills God's People

"And it was given unto him to make war with the saints, and to overcome them: and power was given him over all kindred's, and tongues, and nations" (Revelation 13:7, KJV).

There begins the persecution of all the saints of God in the first three and a half years, but as Antichrist sets his headquarters in Jerusalem, a great wave of persecution overtakes the Jews and saints of all nationalities. Because of this "victory" over the saints of God, the world determines Antichrist won against Jehovah, and they become his complete subjects. They surrender to his reign. All the power he has is allotted to him to fulfill God's will. What is essential then is to have a right standing with God. We are not to seek to escape the responsibilities or the future in facing evil. When the verse describes how the Antichrist overcome the saints, it is not saying he overcomes their faith. Instead, Antichrist kills the saints of God; thus, the world heralds him with their allegiance. Because of this, he is given power over all kindred tongues and nations.

With the whole world now under his control and the people serving him, they work as one in killing the saints. Hitler systematically wore out the saints. The Antichrist will be much worse.

If one is saved after the rapture and lives within the tribulation time frame, he should accept his martyrdom for his faith without retaliating and know that all who harms God's elect will die with the same intentions.

The World Gives Its Allegiance to Antichrist

"And all that dwell upon the earth shall worship him, whose names are not written in the book of life of the Lamb slain from the foundation of the world" (Revelation 13:8, KJV).

We observe truth here. That security is not found in one's needs being met through Satan's system, but that we are in a relationship with Jesus Christ and are in the lamb's book of life. The verse tells us that all people whose names are not in the lamb's book of life will worship the beast. These are they who rejected the gospel of

Jesus Christ. Their names are not in the book of life. These folks forfeit eternal life for temporary alignment and satisfaction with the Antichrist. There is a book called the book of life that has written on it all that repent toward God and believe in the Lord Jesus Christ. It is much better to be in that book and suffer and go hungry so that one can be found in Jesus Christ as the book of life will note. Therefore, to align oneself with the Antichrist and take his provision will end in one's destruction.

The collaborators of Antichrist perish with him after seven years. This rebellion will be occurring throughout the tribulation and judgment of the nations.

Make sure you join the right side and be on God's team. Though Satan appears to be winning, he is defeated.

God determines justice for his people.

"If any man has an ear let him hear. He that leadeth into captivity shall go into captivity: he that killeth with the sword must be killed with the sword. Here is the patience and the faith of the saints" (Revelation 13:9–10, KJV).

As the saints of God face off with the Antichrist, God leaves them with some rules: Wherever they find themselves, they must stand for Jesus Christ's cause and bear the consequences of it (even death) without retaliation. Also, the saints must realize God decreed that whoever harms his saints will, in due time, be overthrown by God's wrath. The verse gives pertinent information for the saints when it tells us to hear. If you find yourself in captivity, it is God allowing you to share your testimony so that the good news goes there, knowing suffering probably awaits you. We, as Christ's saints, bear the consequences of sharing our faith wherever we are; this is part of the patience and faith of the saints.

Justice will come by repaying wrath upon the very ones who have caused the suffering upon the saints. The Bible declares people reap what they sow. No one gets away with harming the saints of God. In time, they will be judged.

So stay on God's side and take your suffering. It's better to suffer from evil than to have your name blotted out of the Lamb's book of life.

Understand that Antichrist will make war to destroy real follow-ers of God so that you won't lose hope and press on in faith.

The False Prophet's Agenda

Is the false prophet a nice guy or not? Will he go around in a humanitarian campaign? Will he unleash deception this world has not seen yet? Let us examine the kind of influence this serpent exercises.

Revelation 13:11–14 help us to understand how the false prophet exercises his power. Let's see how this man will use his authority.

The false prophet exercises his power in appearance as a savior but in words as Satan.

"And I beheld another beast coming up out of the earth; and he had two horns like a lamb, and he spake as a dragon" (Revelation 13:11, KJV).

Here comes another man on the scene that completes what is called the tribulations unholy trinity. He is the false prophet who acts like or imitates the functioning of the Holy Spirit. He does this by causing all peoples to accept and worship Antichrist just like how the Holy Spirit points to Jesus Christ. This false prophet acts as if he is a gentle, concerned person who has the best interests of the people at heart in his diplomacies, but as he speaks every time, the message he brings is as if it was a dragon speaking. He speaks blasphemies and slanders God, for Satan empowers him. He has two horns and imi-tates God's care ridiculously over his people. He speaks as a dragon through his words and deceives and leads people to follow Antichrist and deny the real God by the punishment of death.

This is the false prophet's ploy to deceive men into false worship and to their eternal doom. He uses powerful words and exercises unimaginable supernatural powers of deception so that he awes all people into compliance. Because of this false prophet's big mouth and Satan's supernatural powers, he deceives the entire world and, through spiritual bullying, forces them to join Antichrist's side as his followers. Read Deuteronomy 13:1–3 which clearly says if a prophet does miracles and yet leads you to abandon the worship of the true God, then he is a false prophet.

I beg you not to be deceived any longer. The spirit of Antichrist (the unclean spirit) and the spirit of the false prophet (deception) are already manifesting in all places. Choose you this day who you will serve, either the god of this world or the one true God of the Bible. If you don't choose, then you have already made up your choice to serve Satan.

The false prophet exercises his power to deceive the world into worshipping Antichrist.

"And he exercises all the power of the first beast before him and causes the earth and them which dwell therein to worship the first beast, who's deadly wound was healed" (Revelation 13:12, KJV).

Here, the nice false prophet exercises satanic powers and causes all the peoples of the earth to worship Antichrist. Who seemingly had been fatally wounded, but healed? This nice guy points to Satan's lie (son) as the hope of the world. This false prophet exercises all the power of the first beast. In other words, Satan empowers him for his unholy witness to the lie, the Antichrist. Because the false prophet gets the entire world to worship the Antichrist, now the whole world is engaged in heretical idolatry against God.

He does this by persuading and forcing all people to worship the coming Antichrist by penalty of death. Here is the manifest of the hope of the evil the world so craved.

When Antichrist is worshipped, then great evil will manifest such as the killing of all decanters and those that oppose doing so.

Will the false prophet be your guiding light in the future? If you refuse the Holy Spirit's invitation to repent and believe upon Jesus Christ, then you'll become a deceived follower of the false prophet's agenda. Decide today to take your stand for the gospel truth.

The false prophet exercises deceiving wonders to woe earth's inhabitants to set up an image unto the Antichrist.

"And he doeth great wonders, so that he makes fire come down from heaven on the earth in the sight of men, And deceives them that dwell on the earth by *the means of* those miracles which he had power to do in the sight of the beast; saying to them that dwell on the earth, that they should make an image to the beast, which had the wound by a sword, and did live" (Revelation 13:13–14, KJV).

Here is earth's inhabitant's buddy using satanic powers to persuade and mesmerizes the people so that he convinces them that they need to set up idols or images upon the Antichrist in all towns. So he causes all to worship or die upon refusal, especially in Jerusalem. He is such a nice fellow that he does great wonders to persuade the people to accept that all dissenters should be executed. He declares that all peoples set up their images and demand their people come to worship upon the death penalty. Isn't that nice? The image is placed in Jerusalem. The false prophet even gives the image power to talk.

Do you see why you must make your decision now? If you don't, your friend, the false prophet, will persuade you. Do not think you'll resist him if you had a chance to know Jesus Christ before the rapture. You'll succumb.

Your choice is to either listen to the Bible's testimony or the unholy trinity. You will decide either now for Jesus Christ or later for Antichrist or suffer death—you choose.

So don't think the false prophet is gentle; he is a serpent who will bite you with death and hell. He will exercise that kind of power. You choose who you will serve today.

The false prophet's work

Do you like being forced into agendas? What about being forced into an argument that you don't want to be in? How about being forced into a problem that was not of your doing? The false prophet will force all people to choose Satan's lie or die.

We read in Revelation 13:15–18 how the false prophet forces all people to depend on Antichrist by the punishment of death if they are dissenters. Let's see how the false prophet forces all people to depend (join sides) on Antichrist.

The false prophet forces all peoples to worship Antichrist or die.

"And he had power to give life unto the image of the beast, that the image of the beast should both speak, and cause that as many as would not worship the image of the beast should be killed" (Revelation 13:15, KJV).

Here is our friend and helper who cause all peoples of the earth, who have not yet decided to worship Satan through allegiance to Antichrist, to worship him by sheer force. The choice is to either worship Satan's son or die by execution. What a friend and helper this false prophet imposter is, bringing religion to bear on the pressing issues of his day. If I have fun, pray for me. Maybe I'll get saved. This false prophet gave life to the image of the beast. This demonstration is evil power or a human-made process of life assimilation because this image of the beast speaks and recognizes true allegiance to the Antichrist and will condemn men to death upon the recognition of a lack of heartfelt devotion to Satan's lie. This image comes to life is the working of the friend of humanity, the deceiving false prophet.

He coerces the multitudes into this doomsday scenario because Satan knows his time is short. He must damn the souls of men as fast and quantitatively as possible with the least amount of resistance. This is the secret agenda working from the unholy trinity: Satan sets up the Antichrist as his son and draws the world to worship him through his unholy false prophet, through alignment in an economic system that damns the souls of all who receive the mark.

Now are you persuaded to give your life to Jesus Christ or not? If these messages don't persuade you, I feel you may become a full-blown candidate for the worship of Satan and his lie in the future.

The false prophet forces all peoples to enter the Antichrist's economic control system.

"And he causes all, both small and great, rich and poor, free and bond, to receive a mark in their right hand, or in their foreheads: And that no man might buy or sell, save he that had the mark, or the name of the beast, or the number of his name" (Revelation 13:16–17, KJV).

Here is where the false prophet forces all the earth's inhabitants to give their allegiance to Satan. How does the false prophet do this? He causes them to receive an economic identification mark which marks them as belonging to Antichrist. They become by default the Antichrist's loyal subjects or Satan worshippers because they took his mark, which makes them his. He causes all to receive this mark who refuse the gospel of Jesus Christ. No one during this time, when the mark is enforced, can escape their fate. This mark is the infamous mark of the beast or Satan's id system. No man can buy or sell. If you miss the rapture, and you reject the Antichrist's mark, you will likely die for refusing to take the mark, either by execution or starvation. But stay true to the one true God, and you will live in heaven upon your death. Don't you love Satan's spirit of gluttony? He will be telling men and women how hungry they are and to get his mark to live.

Take note, I will not sugarcoat this. Those who come to faith in the tribulation will most likely die for their faith. In the tribulation, the cost of salvation in Jesus Christ is martyrdom. Please be ready to die for your testimony! If you do, you will live with God forever.

I feel sorry for America; they are the fattest people in the world, so consequently will take the mark.

How is your appetite? Do you feel the need to feed when you get hungry? If you can't fast months at a time and live on grubs, you'll probably give in to Satan's system. Who will you serve today?

The false prophet forces all people to receive a mark that identifies them as Antichrist's subjects.

"Here is wisdom. Let him that hath understanding count the number of the beast: for it is the number of a man; and his number *is* Six hundred three score *and* six" (Revelation 13:18, KJV).

This mark is the mark of man, and the fact it is repeated three times means it is man acting as a god in an unholy trinity. This is blasphemy against the One and only God, Jehovah. Those who receive the mark are now identified as belonging to Satan. They were warned by angels not to accept the mark but willingly did so. This is wisdom to know that Satan marks his collaborators to protect and nurture them for works of evil. This mark is the mark of a man and is the 666 number aligning people with Satan through the unholy trinity by people who hate God. The whole world is in rebellion against God and his people.

This rebellion occurs after the rapture when millions fight God. Psalms chapter 2 speaks of this rebellion and how God puts the nations in derision.

One more time, do you choose to follow and worship Jesus Christ? If not, you have chosen to follow another path that will manifest in serving Satan and hell.

So realize the purpose of the unholy trinity is to make you a slave of Satan and the candidate of death and hell. Choose you this day who you will serve!

CHAPTER 14

The singing choir of heaven.
Who are these 144,000 in heaven singing? Are these Jews or are they saints of all ages? Let's consider what God says in Revelation about them.

In Revelation 14:1–5, we can consider heaven's select singing choir. Let us examine who this select singing choir in heaven is.

This singing choir represents saints who have faithfully served God.

"And I looked, and, lo, a Lamb stood on the mount Sion, and with him a hundred forty *and* four thousand, having his Father's name written in their foreheads" (Revelation 14:1, KJV).

This verse probably represents faithful saints of all ages. Commentator debate who this group is, are they Jews, believers of all ages, etc.? But in contrast to those who team with Antichrist, these 144,000 believers refuse to be polluted by Satan's false religious system, nor do they worship his image. These persons have the Father's name written upon their foreheads.

This group also represents the difference between those who succumb to Satan's lie and false religions and those who endure to the end. It was promised to overcomers that God's name would be written on them. But to those who succumb, they would be destroyed.

This warning should spark vigilance in our readiness to serve, follow, and meet our Lord and Savior Jesus Christ. Anyhow if you be found faithful, God will reward you also.

This singing choir sings songs that are uniquely assigned to them to sing only.

> And I heard a voice from heaven, as the voice of many waters, and as the voice of a great thunder: and I heard the voice of harpers harping with their harps: And they sung as it were a new song before the throne, and before the four beasts, and the elders: and no man could learn that song but the hundred *and* forty *and* four thousand, which were redeemed from the earth. (Revelation 14:2–3, KJV)

As noted about the 144,000 which were redeemed from the earth, this indicates that these represent believers of all ages. A new song represents the saved within the new covenant salvation. This is a multitude joining in singing a new song of God's grace. Only these 144,000 could learn and sing this song. Since they were the redeemed from all the earth, they represent the entire saved saints.

Why this group? I believe it is because they were particularly vigilant as not to be deceived and defiled by any manner of Satan's perverted religions. They practiced being separated unto God.

There is a song to be singing for those who have been redeemed and stay faithful. You will be singing God's praises also.

This singing choir represents the first fruits of each age of believers.

"These are they which were not defiled with women; for they are virgins. These are they which follow the Lamb whithersoever he goes. These were redeemed from among men, *being* the first fruits unto God and to the Lamb" (Revelation 14:4, KJV).

The satanic religions of their day did not defile these believers; they were pure unto God. Now in their heavenly state, they follow Jesus Christ wherever he goes. Redeemed and are the first fruits or choicest. They are virgins that indicate that Satan's lie and false worship do not corrupt them. They follow the Lamb or have accustomed themselves to pursue Jesus Christ and go with him wherever he goes.

In each age, Satan attempted to deceive. These now sing also to mock Satan's lie on earth and mock all who bowed to Satan's deception. The whole unsaved world gives in to the great lie.

Let us then consider the end of both the faithful and unfaithful. Let this stir you to make the right choices in following Jesus Christ.

This singing choir represents the power of God's saving ability.

"And in their mouth was found no guile: for they are without fault before the throne of God" (Revelation 14:5, KJV).

Here, only the redeemed can be without fault because of the work of Jesus Christ on Calvary. These representatives of Jesus Christ and his work in all the saints demonstrate the power of Jesus Christ's blood to save and change persons. There was no guile in these persons. God cleaned them up, and in their gratefulness, they, by God's help, maintained their testimony. They were without fault.

This elite group is a demonstration of God's power of salvation and renewal to convert a sinner into a faithful saint.

Do not write off the born-again experience as fanaticism. God does regenerate the heart and saves the soul and saves those who call on him. He exercises power to change their lives.

So consider this select heavenly choir as a testimony to God's saving power and to those who wholeheartedly follow Jesus Christ. So you know that God faithfully carries out his work of redemption in the lives of men.

The Message of Angels

Will angels proclaim the good news in the tribulation? How will they participate in witnessing? What will it mean to those who reject the good news? Let's examine what kind of messages these angels pronounce.

In Revelation 14:6–13, we see that we can know what messages the angels will give to the world in the seven years of tribulation. Let's see what words that angles will provide during the tribulation hour.

Angels preach the everlasting gospel.

> And I saw another angel fly in the midst of
> heaven, having the everlasting gospel to preach
> unto them that dwell on the earth, and to every
> nation, and kindred, and tongue, and people,
> Saying with a loud voice, Fear God, and give
> glory to him; for the hour of his judgment is
> come: and worship him that made heaven, and
> earth, and the sea, and the fountains of waters.
> (Revelation 14:6–7, KJV)

In contrast to what's going in the earth, where the false prophet
encourages worship of Antichrist and to receive his mark, God sends
angels to warn them not to do so but to repent and turn to the one
true God and give him their allegiance. The angels preach the everlasting gospel. The gospel in the tribulation hour is the same as now
with the exceptions (it announces judgment is now and is ushering
in at the Second Advent). They tell people to fear God. The angel's
message is designed to turn people back to the true God.

This broadcast in midair will be worldwide and will probably be
only one time, then no more gospel light. There will be no excuses.
Again, if we hear the gospel, we must repent and believe.

We must repent (change) and let God have his way in our lives.
Revelation is a book designed by God to cause us to get right.

Angels pronounce judgment.

"And there followed another angel, saying, Babylon is fallen, is
fallen, that great city, because she made all nations drink of the wine
of the wrath of her fornication" (Revelation 14:8, KJV).

Babylon is destroyed because she promoted a worldwide move
to destroy the Jews and Israel and believers. They drank of her wrath,
so Babylon will have to drink of God's wrath (political, economic,
and religious). This Babylon probably refers to a metropolitan region
in Iraq that will dominate during the tribulation, and its influence
will likely be worldwide. The wrath of her fornication is her intense

hatred and punishment for God's people; she causes all nations to drink of it.

Thus, her punishment will be on her metropolitan area and the end-time economic, political, and religious powers of the tribulation period. This pronouncement causes all who contemplate the worship of Antichrist and the receiving of the mark to possibly repent and return to God. This will be an announcement that proceeds ahead of time, Babylon's fall. This announcement is to give warning and guidance to those who will be loyal to God.

Why must some people wait until such turmoil before repenting? To assume you can put off your choice now is ludicrous. You won't do it then either. I beg you to repent, change, turn to God, and seek him who made you.

Angels warn of the eternal punishment for those who receive the mark (of the end-time economic system) of the beast and those who worship the Antichrist.

> And the third angel followed them, saying with a loud voice, If any man worship the beast and his image, and receive *his* mark in his forehead, or in his hand, The same shall drink of the wine of the wrath of God, which is poured out without mixture into the cup of his indignation; and he shall be tormented with fire and brimstone in the presence of the holy angels, and in the presence of the Lamb: And the smoke of their torment ascendeth up for ever and ever: and they have no rest day nor night, who worship the beast and his image, and whosoever receives the mark of his name. Revelation 14:9–11, KJV)

Jesus

Angels announce or warn that anyone who follows the false prophet's admonition to worship the Antichrist or receive his mark or name will eternally suffer for their rebellion against God. The verse tells us that any man who follows this deception damns his soul forever. The same shall incur the wrath of God. Immediately God will pour out his anger on them. Eternal torment awaits these satanic idolaters.

Because this warning goes out, they will reject it and give their allegiance to Antichrist or Satan in rebellion against God. All idolaters will have their place in the lake of fire. I know of areas I need to change. Think about such areas in your life and get it right before God. You'll spare your soul.

Angels announce the blessings on those who stand in faith (and die) for the Lord.

"Here is the patience of the saints: here *are* they that keep the commandments of God, and the faith of Jesus. And I heard a voice from heaven saying unto me, Write, blessed *are* the dead who die in the Lord from henceforth: Yea, saith the Spirit that they may rest from their labors; and their works do follow them" (Revelation 14:12–13, KJV). TRIB martyrs

Here, saints are admonished to stay faithful to God, and eventually their enemies would be punished; they will die for their faith, and that rest and reward awaited them. So it appears that Satan attacks the followers of God with the economic, political, and religious system that he has set up. Satan's time is short. The verse mentions the faithful of the saints, which have the meaning to be reliable, waiting for God's retribution. Rest for you will come. Then the verse goes on to tell us that those who die in the Lord will be blessed. From this announcement on, all believers found will be put to death. Do not deny your faith; they will kill you anyway.

God has a unique rest and rewards for such tribulation saints. Again, Jesus admonished saints in his letter to the churches to endure to the end.

Tribulation saints mustn't compromise by altering their testimony to fit their circumstances; that type of person cannot inherit the salvation God has planned for them.

Now you have discovered the messages of the angels. But know that this same gospel goes to you today. What are you doing with this good news? Will you repent and believe the good news today? You may not be able to tomorrow.

The End-Time Harvest

How will the end-time harvest occur? Men will be the thing harvested, some for good and some for evil. Men will be harvested for heaven, and men will be harvested for hell. Let us be sure we have believed and repented.

In Revelation 14:14–20, we see how angels harvest the earth. Let's see how these angels will participate in the harvest of the earth.

Angels participate.

> And I looked, and behold a white cloud, and upon the cloud *one* sat like unto the Son of man, having on his head a golden crown, and in his hand a sharp sickle. And another angel came out of the temple, crying with a loud voice to him that sat on the cloud, thrust in thy sickle, and reap: for the time is come for thee to reap; for the harvest of the earth is ripe. (Revelation 14:14–15, KJV)

At the end of the age, when the earth's peoples have entirely rejected God's goodness, God will give the command to his angels who, in turn, announce the reaping to begin. This will be God's wrath bringing in the harvest of souls. Those who rejected Christ will go to eternal damnation and those who believed (and might or might not have been killed by Satan and his collaborators) will go to eternal life. But it is also, at Christ's coming, that a judgment of nations occurs, where the goats on the left go to everlasting punishment, and the sheep on Jesus' right get to enter the millennial state. The Lord Jesus gathers the people to be judged. There is an illusion to a grain and grape harvest, where those who do God's will enter the millennial state. All others go to eternal doom.

This announcement for reaping is after the angels announced the good news in the air for the world to believe and to reject the number of the beast. Time has transpired and people made their decision. Now their eternal destinies are set. Therefore, there is no more life going forth unto the unrepentant. The time for reaping has come. The people now rot and need to be harvested for judgment! That is those who took the mark. It's a scene of a vineyard field when the fruit withers because there is no more moisture; the fruit stinks and is rotten. Such will be unrepentant, and they will have no opportunity to repent, picked for the winepress and destroyed.

The result of the eternal destinies of the peoples of the earth all correlates to how they responded to the ones God sent into their lives, warning them to repent. Is there a change in your life?

Angels participate in the judgment of the nations.

> And another angel came out of the temple, which is in heaven, he also having a sharp sickle. And another angel came out from the altar, which had power over fire; and cried with a loud cry to him that had the sharp sickle, saying, thrust in thy sharp sickle, and gather the clusters of the vine of the earth; for her grapes are fully ripe. And the angel thrust in his sickle into the earth, and gathered the vine of the earth, and cast *it* into the great winepress of the wrath of God. (Revelation 14:17–19, KJV)

Here God uses angels also with the son of man to judge the people of the earth. This scene alludes to the Day of Judgment in the valley of decision, in the Armageddon battle where God decides to judge all the earth. The angels thrust in their sickle. The armies of the earth gather together and are destroyed at this valley; actually over all Israel and the dead cover the land.

The people had their chance to repent; now Satan rounds up his people to this valley to fight with God. He knows he is defeated, and yet the people are deceived and follow Satan to their deaths there. Angels announced the good news with warnings, and the peoples of the earth made their choice of who they would follow.

We must repent of any rebellious attitudes we have toward God. We must repent and get our lives right, or this could be our fate.

Armageddon

The crush of the nation's dead will cover the land.

"And the winepress was trodden without the city, and blood came out of the winepress, even unto the horse bridles, by the space of a thousand *and* six hundred furlongs" (Revelation 14:20, KJV).

The devastation is horrendous. Millions lie obliterated on the land of Israel. As God decides, this is the harvest, all wicked who took the mark parish. There is more to this; those who did God's people wrong will be judged, etc. The winepress is trodden down. Wave upon wave of armies come and are wiped out all the way until the carnage is as high as a horse's bridle.

Do not blame God. This is the action of Satan and how he led multitudes to follow his Antichrist to rebel against the one true God, leading people to their doom. Satan did this, and those who died willingly followed him. If anyone would act wisely, it's better to suffer and die in a denial of Satan having his way than to perish fighting with Satan. One dies and goes to heaven; the other dies and goes to hell. Fear God and not Satan.

You choose whose side you on. Will you be crushed along with the rest of the world who follows Satan?

So note well that angels will participate with Jesus Christ in the end-time harvest. Let's, therefore, heed the good news by believing and repenting.

CHAPTER 15

The song of the tribulation overcomers.

Why do heaven's tribulation overcomers sing? They sing because God vindicates them of their offenders. They also sing because of God ushering in his millennial kingdom through judgment. These overcomers declare God's manifest judgments.

In Revelation 15:1–4, we observe that it will come to pass, that God's tribulation overcomers will declare the righteous judgment of the Lord. Let's watch how God's tribulation overcomers affirm God's righteous judgments.

God's overcomers are they that overcame in Jesus Christ during the tribulation.

> And I saw another sign in heaven, great and marvelous, seven angels having the seven last plagues; for in them is filled up the wrath of God. And I saw as it were a sea of glass mingled with fire: and them that had gotten the victory over the beast, and his image, and his mark, *and* the number of his name, stand on the sea of glass, having the harps of God. (Revelation 15:1–2, KJV)

These that are depicted in this contextual setting have overcome and passed through the tribulation. They defeated the beast not by avoiding his rhetorical hellish attacks and folly but by going through the fire and passing into eternity in Jesus Christ. They overcame by prayer, the Word, the blood of the Lamb, and the word of their tes-

Bible   Jesus' precious blood

timony. These martyrs passed through the sea of Satan's wrath, but God will recompense their enemies, and now they have got the victory. They endured to the end, not loving their lives over death for Jesus Christ.

These came to faith during the tribulation hour; now must suffer and die. Thus, they overcame because they did not give their allegiance to the Antichrist. Our stand must be just like that, and we must determine our loyalty is to God alone.

How can you or I declare the righteous judgments of God if we won't stand for our God? If we don't stand, there can be no participation in the joyful victory they enjoy in Jesus Christ.

God's overcomers sing a unique song.

"And they sing the song of Moses the servant of God, and the song of the Lamb, saying, Great and marvelous *are* thy works, Lord God Almighty; just and true *are* thy ways, thou King of saints" (Revelation 15:3, KJV).

So like the Israelites passed through the sea and sang their victory song to God, so does this group praise God for delivering them out of Satan's influence for all eternity. To rest in Jesus Christ forever. The song of Moses was Israel's victory song. They sang of God's great and marvelous works, but now they begin to sing and anticipate God's full victory on earth and over nations.

All heaven is now anticipating what the martyrs have been crying for all along; God's total reign is no more questioned. Right now, God restrains his dominion, but then he won't.

God is still allowing his ambassadors in his Church to win the lost so that he will have called out many to himself. Soon this opportunity will be gone.

God's overcomers praise God for his judgments.

"Who shall not fear thee, O Lord, and glorify thy name? for *thou* only *art* holy: for all nations shall come and worship before thee; for thy judgments are made manifest" (Revelation 15:4, KJV).

Soon God's judgments will manifest, and those who have rejected God by receiving Antichrist, his name, or the mark will perish.

All nations shall come, the Bible tells us. This looks at Christ and his victory during the millennial reign. The judgments of God are made manifest. These saints declare that the judgments of God are transpiring.

During the tribulation, all those things will take place and all the horrors in previous chapters and upcoming chapters.

This will be the song of those martyrs who had cried for God's vengeance for so long, whom the Lord told to be patient till their number had come in, and now they rejoice in Jesus's judgment.

So the tribulation overcomers rejoice in God's judgment over the nations in praise of God, and so God's righteous rule will bring in a kingdom where his saints will reign with him.

Angels Carry Out God's Wrath

How do angels play a part in the end-times? They announce the good news. They participate in the functions of heaven. Let's see how angels will join in heaven's judgment.

In Revelation 15:5–8, we see that it is necessary to know that angels will help carry out the wrath of God. Let's see how angels assist in carrying out the wrath of God.

Angels proceed out of heaven's tabernacle to complete the wrath of God.

"And after that I looked, and, behold, the temple of the tabernacle of the testimony in heaven was opened: And the seven angels came out of the temple, having the seven plagues, clothed in pure and white linen, and having their breasts girded with golden girdles" (Revelation 15:5–6, KJV).

Here are special angels set apart to fulfill God's plan for judging the earth. They proceed out of God's tabernacle and thrown room. These angels have the seven plagues or are given vials (in verse 7) to pour upon unrepentant humanity. Their clothing is majestic, and they are grand in appearance, having direct access to God. They are enthusiastic about fulfilling God's good plan, having a zeal for that which is right, holiness! The verse tells us the temple in heaven was open. The temple was open and out of the tabernacle, proceed with these great angels to carry out the judgments of God. As they come out, the smoke arises, which prevents all heaven's and earth's inhabitants from hindering the wrath of God. Grace and mercy are over for the unrepentant.

Because men refused to repent and hated righteousness and closed the door to truth, these angels carry God's last plagues by which God brings in his kingdom through final victory over them. Angels are swift messengers, not only for good but to carry out the judgments of God. That is what these angels will do.

There is ultimately coming zero hope for those who will not repent and serve God. It is not unreasonable to offer ourselves to God. He made you, and I serve him in accord with his will and Word and the Spirit's leading.

Angels are given the seven vials full of God's wrath to pour upon unrepentant humanity.

"And one of the four beasts gave unto the seven angels seven golden vials full of the wrath of God, who lives for ever and ever" (Revelation 15:7, KJV).

Now the vials are given the angels to pour out upon humanity; that is those who sided with Satan. The four beasts are (seemingly) chosen because they represent God's created order, and since the portion of earth's inhabitants rebelled against God (in an active rebellion), they must be judged. So the seven angels receive from the beast the vials for pouring out God's judgment. The beast gave them the vials. Again, it is a representative of the created order who gives or hands out the vials. Golden vials contain the wrath of God and will be administered to the unrepentant.

So we see that angels participate in the administration of the wrath of God. All of heaven now watches as these angels administer the vials, probably during the whole last three and one half years.

Here again is a warning for repentance because upon this time on, no more opportunity for repentance is available.

Angels administer the seven last plagues while all heaven watches.

"And the temple was filled with smoke from the glory of God, and from his power; and no man was able to enter the temple, till the seven plagues of the seven angels were fulfilled" (Revelation 15:8, KJV).

Here now, no more clemency can be offered. No amnesty now! Only prayers of judgment; actually now no one is permitted to direct their prayers to the sanctuary. Thus, for an allotted time, judgment will fall unhindered. The verse tells us that the temple was filled with the smoke of the glory of God. The glory of God keeps out the patron and their prayers until the wrath is complete. No man can enter. Nobody is permitted to stop the judgment: this says sin has an ending time.

God will, in time, determine when judgment will fall. Our job is to be ready to repent and believe by turning to God through Jesus Christ. This will be like a movie to watch for heaven's citizens. Unable to enter heaven's tabernacle, they watch until God's judgment is poured out fully and consumes the enemies of God.

This specific time in heaven is a powerful motivating point to escape from the wrath to come. If we admit our need, we must respond.

Therefore, know that angels will carry out God's will in judging the unrepentant, so be quick to see your need for Jesus Christ and turn from your wicked ways.

CHAPTER 16

G rievous sores.
    What begins to take place when the vials are poured out upon the earth? It's God's judgment for the rebellious. People break out in terrible sores. Let's be sure our lives are not lived outside of Jesus Christ.

As we read Revelation 16:1–2, we should know that grievous sores will come upon those who take the mark of the beast. Let's examine why painful wounds come upon those who take the mark of the beast.

Heaven commands the outbreak.

"And I heard a great voice out of the temple saying to the seven angels, go your ways, and pour out the vials of the wrath of God upon the earth" (Revelation 16:1, KJV).

Since no one was allowed in the temple, the voice is probably God's, and he commands the vial judgments to begin with a loud voice. This again is heaven's decrees upon a godless world. Still, the voice was probably God's based on the assumption that only God was in the temple.

This happens because heaven is judging the earth and bringing forth Jesus Christ's kingdom. The kingdom comes in literally through judgment.

This coming of the kingdom is causing or cautioning us to examine our own lives to make sure we better be in the faith.

This sore is from God's wrath.

It is God's wrath that is poured out from heaven. This is a grievous and offensive and disgusting boil that breaks out upon the beasts and adherents in the land. The angel pours out his vial, and it is just one judgment upon another, and at this time, it's a dangerous grievous sore. It is unbearable to bear. This judgment comes on those who took the mark of the beast. It is for all those who rebel and receive this identification as belonging to Satan.

This judgment is a worldwide phenomenon, and none will escape it who took the mark. The Bible says that God knows how to reserve the wicked for judgment and preserve his own from wrath.

This judgment comes because they have heard the message preached but rejected it, so they are now rejected or lost forever.

This sore is worldwide.

"And the first went, and poured out his vial upon the earth; and there fell a noisome and grievous sore upon the men which had the mark of the beast and *upon* them which worshipped his image" (Revelation 16:2, KJV).

All the inhabitants of the earth will experience this judgment from God. No one can hide. Once the angels pour their judgments out, they vanish off the scene. The decision is universal in scope. Everybody who received the mark and hardened their hearts against God receives this judgment.

There will be no place to run; it will come upon them.

Is your heart right with God?

This sore is very grievous.

All those Antichrist pushers and supporters will now be judged. Each man and woman will be like Job with great pain and disgust, and the people will be in agony. The Bible says that there fell a great sore. This judgment consumes their ability to function.

All those with allegiance to Satan are, thus, judged for their participation in following him. Anyone who receives Satan's mark, name, and worships him will be destroyed.

Determine now to avoid the error of what will take place. Avoid the whole scenario by being born again and in a vibrant walk with God.

Those who give their allegiance to Satan will be judged. Take steps to avoid the whole end-time scenario through knowing Jesus Christ.

The Water Becomes Polluted

How does all water become corrupt? We see oil spills pollute water. We have also seen toxicity in streams, but could all waters of the earth become polluted?

In Revelation 16:3–7, we find that we must know how God punishes the inhabitants of the earth. Let's examine how God punishes the inhabitants of the planet.

God punishes men by destroying life in the sea.

"And the second angel poured out his vial upon the sea; and it became as the blood of a dead *man*: and every living soul died in the sea" (Revelation 16:3, KJV).

Not all persons die from this plague, but it dramatically affects how men live. What is interesting is that as God is dealing with the armies of the nations at Armageddon, he is also dealing with all other God-rejecters through his plagues and judgments. There is no rest or place to hide for those who took the mark of the beast. God deals with all his enemies through his plagues. As the angel poured out his vial, he acted as God's agent pouring out God's wrath. We see that the waters turn foul and cause all things to die in the sea.

God uses these plagues to gain victory over his enemies so when he returns, much of his work is done. The people of the earth, at this time, have already rejected God and received the Antichrist's lie, yet the food of the planet was still sustaining them; now that will all change.

I have a personal lesson for all of us to learn. When I was a boy, I cut grass for an old doctor. I wanted him to get saved and asked if he knew Jesus as his Lord and savior. He told me he did not believe in a God who could hear all our prayers, and he would not receive Jesus Christ. This is the God we see in the book of Revelation coming back and dealing with all humanity. My friends, he is real and deals with all men in his time. Live out the purpose he made you for instead of denial and rejecting him because if you do, you will be rejected. That man is burning in hell right now for rejecting the gospel of Jesus Christ.

It does not pay to reject God and demand that he still takes care of you. That will also come to an end as well.

God punishes man by stop-gapping the drinking water.

"And the third angel poured out his vial upon the rivers and fountains of waters; and they became blood" (Revelation 16:4, KJV).

Now men not only lack food within the sea, but they cannot drink water anywhere. The sources of water have become corrupt. No water or any source is edible anymore. All sources become bitter, the rivers and fountains. The water all becomes like blood and unfit to drink, and those who made God's people suffer now suffer.

This is a worldwide plague that affects all people. No doubt men will be cursing God as they die.

You probably could not store up enough water for this time, so you also better make your peace with God before it's too late.

God punishes man by forcing them to drink blood.

> And I heard the angel of the waters say, thou art righteous, O Lord, which art, and was, and shall be, because thou hast judged thus. For they have shed the blood of saints and prophets, and thou hast given them blood to drink; for they are worthy. And I heard another out of the altar say, even so, Lord God Almighty, true and righteous *are* thy judgments. (Revelation 16:5–7, KJV)

Here, the people are forced to drink bitter water, polluted and deadly. The chemicals cannot be boiled out of it. Since these people supported and participated in shedding the blood of the saints, they now drink blood. The heavenly hosts declare God is righteous in all the judgments. This is God's divine judgment. The host says these persons have shed blood and are worthy of drinking it. God righteously judges the people for their sin, and he is right.

I couldn't imagine this world being thoroughly polluted, yet people will grope for water as helpless and lost because they hardened their hearts and bitterly fought God as they suffer wrath.

Do not harden your heart, instead repent and believe the good news today. Spare your soul from what's coming.

So know that God punishes the inhabitants of the earth by taking away their drinking water; if you cannot stand under that, then it's time for you to repent and believe in Jesus Christ.

A Scorching Terror

Will the sun's heat kill people? Can this earth's natural order change that drastically? Can it be impossible to go outside? Let's see what happens to people when the sun rages.

In Revelation 16:8–9, we see we can know that in the tribulation, the sun becomes a scorching terror. Let's examine two ways the sun becomes a scorching terror.

The sun scorches men with fire.

"And the fourth angel poured out his vial upon the sun; and power was given unto him to scorch men with fire" (Revelation 16:8, KJV).

It's important to note that God, by His sovereign will, gives this angel the power to scorch men in this way. Not only is there nothing to drink or scarcity of fluids, but now the sun burns men. Men will then get infuriated and not repent. Seeing that it is God who does this and not Satan or Antichrist, they blaspheme God. Somehow there will grow an increase in heat and light, so much so that if people go outside, they burn. This power was given to scorch men. Most people think things will be business as usual. What do you do when you can't go out?

The Bible says these days will be shortened or no flesh shall be saved; that is for the elect's sake. This judgment is for those who kept their allegiance to Jehovah; therefore, he shortens the sunlight hours in the day. Something blocks the rays of the sun so that the people will be spared.

Do not think to yourself that if you don't repent now, you will do so in the tribulation. Because unless you respond to God's grace that enables you to repent, you won't repent. In the tribulation, the

Could they still repent? I certainly hope so

people wouldn't repent. Don't get in this trap, repent now or perish then.

Men blasphemed God because of the Sun's heat.

"And men were scorched with great heat, and blasphemed the name of God, which hath power over these plagues: and they repented not to give him glory" (Revelation 16:9, KJV).

The Antichrist will be polytheistic and will believe that the OT God was a bad God who emanated from the gods' above. Through secret knowledge, the Antichrist believes he defeats Jehovah. In these last days of the tribulation, they won't turn to Jehovah. They were scorched! Many will die because of the heat. They blaspheme the name of God! Where is Antichrist to hold back God's judgment? No repentance is going on. It can't, for they already made their pact with Satan's lie and will ride it to the end and perish. They would not acknowledge or recognize Jehovah, though they knew he did it by his hand.

Ironically Jehovah causes nature to go crazy on the unbelievers, but they harden their hearts. Only God can cause a heart to become tender and repent. When God calls and people reject him, the door immediately closes.

Do not harden your heart as you hear these messages, make the decision, move to change, and believe in Jesus Christ. Do change in your life what God is showing you. Refusing to do so is not acceptable to him. Do not harden your heart to him.

So understand that in the tribulation, the sun becomes a scorching terror. But the earth's fruit is spoiled and worthy to perish. Repentance will not come out of those who serve Antichrist and have given allegiance to him. Therefore, through these last seven vials, God gains victory to sweep in his kingdom through judgment. No one can intercede for the unrepentant at this time.

Exceeding Wickedness and Blasphemy

What will happen to Antichrist's reign? Jesus Christ will waste it away. Jesus Christ will destroy it with the brightness of his coming. Ultimately that is the end of Antichrist's rule.

It is critical as we read Revelation 16:10–11, for us to consider that the kingdom of the Antichrist becomes a thing of disdain. Let's find why the territory of the Antichrist becomes a thing of contempt.

The seat (authority) of the Antichrist becomes exceeding wicked.

"And the fifth angel poured out his vial upon the seat of the beast; and his kingdom was full of darkness; and they gnawed their tongues for pain" (Revelation 16:10, KJV).

Darkness and wickedness come upon the capital of the Antichrist's authority because wickedness dominates his cabinet. There becomes no rest for the subjects under his reign! It gets so bad they are being consumed in their pain. There is no relief for those who turned and gave their allegiance to the Antichrist. They are overwhelmed and are on the brink of extinction because their trust and compact are with Satan and his lie! Satanic demonism is at its height, and great wickedness is abounding and destroying people. As the vial is poured on the seat of the beast, the evil of Antichrist engulfs all his helpers. Darkness overtakes his kingdom. Probably meaning both darkness as a plague and the exceeding sinfulness of the nature of his kingdom: he has slaughtered millions of people (especially followers of God) and he usurps God's authority and breaks all God's commandments. Therefore, the people gnawed their tongues in pain. The subjects of the Antichrist are inundated by torture and plagues, and Antichrist tyranny, etc.

This vial is primarily the source of this darkness. It—like Egypt's plague by the hand of Moses—brings literal darkness and acceleration of Antichrist's wickedness. Remember Antichrist is the personification of that which is evil, Satan in human form. Is it any wonder that the earth's inhabitants' rail in pain and lives in great darkness?

We must consent to the attitude that we will oppose and reject the spirit of Antichrist today. That attitude will grow and preserve those who reject Satan and his lie and build up the wall of righteousness.

The subjects of the Antichrist blaspheme exceedingly.

"And blasphemed the God of heaven because of their pains and their sores and repented not of their deeds" (Revelation 16:11, KJV).

The subjects of Antichrist will not turn to God and repent! They cannot after becoming dependent on this polytheistic tyrant and a false god. They, thus, attack Jehovah for their pains and sores and continue sinning to their end. In their view, the flesh can be indulged in any way they want, and they don't care. They blaspheme God. Their blaspheming is accelerated because of the darkness of the Antichrist's kingdom. They have pains and sores. For the unrepentant, this will be their end. And they repented not of all their evil. There is no hope for repentance or the life of God for them.

These people refuse to repent even in their complete duress because they love their sinning more than turning to God and living. People today won't receive Jesus Christ because as Jesus said himself, "They love darkness rather than light."

We cannot turn to the light unless we habitually are doing so. Why don't you begin to daily turn to God for what you need and the holiness of God that you need to be imparted into your life?

So Antichrist's kingdom will become a thing of disdain. Let us, therefore, consider and hear to avoid and oppose Satan and his lie. So if Satan's kingdom manifests in your community before the time, you won't be his victim. Therefore, take your stand for Jesus Christ.

Preparation for Armageddon

How does God initiate the battle of Armageddon? We see Satan thinks he can win against God. We understand the people of earth believe Satan's lies, so they send their armies. This preparation ensnares all the earth.

In Revelation 16:12–16, we learn that we must understand how the Lord gathers all the earth's armies to the valley of decision (the time when God decides to judge the people of the planet). Let's examine how God gathers the troops of the earth for this decision to judge them.

The Lord dries up the way to the east.

"And the sixth angel poured out his vial upon the great river Euphrates; and the water thereof was dried up, that the way of the kings of the east might be prepared" (Revelation 16:12, KJV).

God sets in motion the final preparations to assemble earth's armies for judgment. God dries up the Euphrates River, so all the kings of the east will also join in on the world's worst and most devastating war to be fought, Armageddon! The sixth angel pours his vial on the river Euphrates, and this prepares the way for the kings of the east to come. God initiates the preparation. God is going to allow Satan and his unclean helpers to gather all armies for this war.

God is bringing these God-rejecters to their doom, for they have renounced God completely. This place called Armageddon is the gathering place where God renders the decision to judge and send his Son back at the Second Advent. Satan assumes he can stop God by killing the Jews and fighting God.

The problem is all the peoples of earth join in on Satan's lies and rampage and get destroyed. We must take our stand for Jesus Christ and suffer for it. God gives us boldness to do this.

The Lord draws all armies of the earth because of Satan's lies.

"And I saw three unclean spirits like frogs *come* out of the mouth of the dragon, and out of the mouth of the beast, and out of the mouth of the false prophet. For they are the spirits of devils, working miracles, *which* go forth unto the kings of the earth and of the whole world, to gather them to the battle of that great day of God Almighty" (Revelation 16:13–14, KJV).

These spirits are a stench in God's nostrils and gather all armies to fight with God. They are unclean spirits. They are sent to the kings of the earth and convince them to go to battle. They came out of the mouth of Satan, the dragon. These unclean spirits proceed from the unholy trinity. These unclean spirits are devils working various miracles to cause the world to rebel against God to their destruction.

God uses the unholy trinity to accomplish his will, which is to gather the grapes for the wrath of Almighty God to judge as the Second Advent approaches.

Be prepared to escape what shall occur for those who miss the rapture. Make sure you're saved and walking with Jesus

The Lord admonishes you to stay ready.

"Behold, I come as a thief. Blessed *is* he that watches, and keeps his garments, lest he walk naked, and they see his shame" (Revelation 16:15, KJV).

Jesus admonishes us to be continually clothed with Jesus Christ and his righteousness and be ever ready for his coming, or we will be treated as an infidel. We don't want to be found naked! He who stays unprepared will lose out with God.

God has given all the means necessary for us to be prepared. Our job is to take that means and apply ourselves to it.

Even before the rapture, great admonition and exhortation are given for you to be and stay prepared. To remain ready is your job!

The Lord gathers the armies at Armageddon for judgment.

"And he gathered them together into a place called in the Hebrew tongue Armageddon" (Revelation 16:16, KJV).

Here is where God brings these rebels to their end in the valley of decision when God decides to render judgment. This war is terrible news for the world. The nations gather their armies together, and ultimately it was God who brought in this Armageddon. It is the staging place for the war: it carries out over all Israel.

Israel is to be cast off the earth by some. Those who so treat Israel will suffer the same fate they gave her.

Renounce Satan and serve Jesus Christ for eternal life.

So we see God purposes the way for the armies of the earth to gather where God renders the decision to judge them.

Avoid the Wrath to Come

Will wrath continue? We see today all kinds of increase in disasters, etc. Men are growing exceedingly wicked also. It is coming! The wrath of God is coming. Let us flee the coming wrath!

In Revelation 16:17–21, we come to understand how the seventh vial brings in the final devastation. Let's see how the seventh vial brings in the eventual destruction.

The seventh vial ushers in the final judgments.

"And the seventh angel poured out his vial into the air; and there came a great voice out of the temple of heaven, from the throne, saying, it is done" (Revelation 16:17, KJV).

God's wrath is poured out by the seventh angel into the air, and the atmosphere is charged with wrath. After this judgment, God's wrath is completed, changing the world as we know it. Just like the plagues of Egypt, yet this will reshape the earth and societies. When the angel poured his vail into the air, a supercharge of wrath comes against Satan's forces. They are all uprooted. Jesus said that it was finished on the cross. Now God says that it is done to the purpose of his wrath which comes to destroy evil and usher in the coming of Jesus Christ. Recall that evil is a state of living without God. That is ungodliness. That is going to be destroyed.

With this judgment, God's final blow wins the total victory. It must come to the complete removal of evil—that's what this judgment does.

Either we choose to repent now or we accept being destroyed by the brightness of Jesus Christ's coming. Today is the day you must choose.

The seventh vial ushers in a great earthquake.

"And there were voices, and thunders, and lightnings; and there was a great earthquake, such as was not since men were upon the earth, so mighty an earthquake, *and* so great.

So the atmosphere is charged with wrath like the plagues that devastated Egypt. And an earthquake happens that levels all mountains and cities. So great is this earthquake that it reshapes the landscapes. The world changes from how we know it, and there are voices and bolts of lightning; These strange phenomena signify wrath, and the earthquake affects the whole world.

God is closing the times of the unrepentant (yet they repent not). They curse and sneer at God; wrath will not draw them.

Let us humble ourselves before God and examine our hearts. If you are in the wrong, seek God for the help you need.

The Seventh vial ushers in judgment on Babylon.

And the great city was divided into three parts, and the cities of the nation's fell: and great Babylon came in remembrance before

God, to give unto her the cup of the wine of the fierceness of his wrath. And every island fled away, and the mountains were not found" (Revelation 16:19–20, KJV).   *Rome*

Because of Babylon's persecution of God's followers, God visits Babylon with destruction. She is paid for the mistreatment she gave to God's people. Jerusalem may also be judged. The judgment also comes on all cities of the earth, and they are leveled, and mountains removed. Babylon falls by the fierce wrath of God, and he changes the way the land looks because every island flees away. This tells me the surface of the earth changes.

This judgment is the final blow to societies as we know them. I believe internationalism will be gone. The last satanic strongholds come crashing down. Those who trust in nature are destroyed.

If you're a naturalist (someone who lives life with no reference of God in it), you will be devastated when God takes his hand off nature, and you become a victim of nature. You'll curse God to your death. Repent!

The seventh vial ushers in a great hailstorm.

"And there fell upon men a great hail out of heaven, *every stone* about the weight of a talent: and men blasphemed God because of the plague of the hail; for the plague thereof was exceeding great" (Revelation 16:21, KJV).

These stones are approximately a hundred pounds. There is no escape from this devastation. Governments will already be decimated, and the world government will not be able to fix the problems. They will agree to blame God, determine to fight God and his people instead of repenting. It's their sin, not God.

The hail is great. No one can escape God's wrath. They blaspheme God by sneering at God. The plague will be exceedingly high. How can an unbeliever escape; they cannot for God will make Jesus Christ revelation clear to these rebellious.

It will be too late to repent, too late for salvation, and too late for healing. Today we can sense this Spirit on us. Repentance is ending. After three and one half years or the last three and one half years, no prayers are offered for men. Judgment quickly destroys the people.

Do not miss the rapture for any pleasure or sin. Stay on guard to avoid the wrath to come.

We still can avoid the wrath to come in our pre-rapture state if we will repent and turn to Jesus Christ for our salvation and God's order.

CHAPTER 17

Introduction to the great whore.

What is the great whore? She is the apostate religion of the world. She serves Satan's purposes. Let's see why God judges her.

In Revelation 17:1–2, we see it is critical to know why the great whore is judged. Let's examine the information given to John that explains why the great whore is judged.

John is given specific insight into the great whore.

"And there came one of the seven angels which had the seven vials, and talked with me, saying unto me, come hither; I will shew unto thee the judgment of the great whore that sits upon many waters" (Revelation 17:1, KJV).

An angel approaches John the apostle and explains who the great whore is and the punishment that shall befall this whore. There came one of the seven angels who poured out one of the vials and told John to go with him, and he would show John the mystery and explain it and give him insight.

John must be told about the whore because of the great whore's influence and how God will bring her to an end. This great whore is both the sophisticated religious system under Satan and a city called Babylon located somewhere in Mesopotamia area, or could it be a region unknown?

As this chapter unfolds, let us consider whether we serve the living God or a sophisticated religious system. Make sure you belong to God doctrinally, morally, and socially.

John is told that the great whore shall be judged.

The reason the angel pulls John aside is to show him of the coming judgment upon the sophisticated religious system serving Antichrist. How it has become celebrated, yet God causes Antichrist to turn on it and destroy it. The angel tells John he would show him the judgment of how the great whore will be judged because she is the religious system that worships Antichrist and serves him. This religious system is connected to all peoples and governments and is interconnected to all people.

This great whore is judged because she worships Antichrist, she causes nations and people to be defiled by her cult, and she has been killing saints. This religious woman is also the conglomeration of all cults and occults and apostate Christianity, whereby from old Babylon up to our present-day false satanic religion flourished but shall now come to its end. There will be no more satanic religions.

Let us stay true to the one true God, Jehovah! Anyone who veers off course will become part of this church and come under God's wrath.

John is shown that the kings of the earth have committed abominations with the great whore.

"With whom the kings of the earth have committed fornication, and the inhabitants of the earth have been made drunk with the wine of her fornication" (Revelation 17:2, KJV).

Whatever this wine is false religious rituals, oil, fornications, etc. She causes all to become stumbled and maddened by her wine. She defiles the entire world by her intoxicating brew and causes the people of the world to participate in her acts against God. The people of the world join her in her worship of Antichrist and satanic rituals. The leaders of nations engage in her filthy conduct to defy God, kill saints, and worship Satan.

This is Satan's religious system for the world, and it culminates into this whore that is centralized with the governmental leaders. They will turn and destroy her in time.

Make sure you don't turn from your allegiance to Jesus Christ, or you could be counted as one of Satan's ministers.

John is made to know of how the earth's inhabitants drink the wine of the great whore's fornication.

So the inhabitants participate in her unholy religion—that is, she worships Satan, kills the saints, and abandons from the true faith and the worship of the true God. So does those of the world who drink her wine. The verse tells us that the earth's inhabitants are affected by this whore. I don't know what happens to the false prophet in all of this accept he is cast into hell with the beast. But he leads the way in this false worship. But all are made drunk by the whore. The world's people are prepared to participate in such a false religion and probably immorality as well.

This fornication can mean all types of ways this church abandons from biblical truth and sins against the true God. They, no doubt, will practice abominations against Jehovah.

We are told to come out from among her, or we will be judged with her in her sins. Let's stay true to the biblical apostolic faith. In time, if it is a real place, we will know and should come out of this place.

So know why the great whore is judged. She worships Satan, abandons the true faith, and kills the saints, so you will not do likewise. Thus, stay faithful to God through a walk with Jesus Christ and biblical teaching.

Who is the great whore?

Let's look at who the great whore is again. She is the culmination of world religion into an end-time monstrosity. She gives birth from her inception at Babel four millennia ago until now. She is Satan's counterfeit against God's true believers.

In Revelation 17:3–7, we learn that we can know who the great whore is. Let's examine this passage to discover who the great whore is.

The woman is the one world religion of the last days who rides upon the kings of the earth in the past and present and future.

"So he carried me away in the spirit into the wilderness: and I saw a woman sit upon a scarlet colored beast, full of names of blasphemy, having seven heads and ten horns" (Revelation 17:3, KJV)."

Here is John getting a full picture of what has been Satan's counterfeit religion throughout the ages. Being in the wilderness gives John a view in truth: the whore is a false religion who is now riding upon the beast (Antichrist) and his last day's government. The real color signifies great bloodshed. The woman sat upon the scarlet-colored beast; for a time, the false religion will be part of Antichrist's agenda, but God will bring an end to the wrong belief. Names of blasphemy, this is the beast's trademark, yet the false religion very much is a part of that.

This false religion has been around since Babel now is part of the abominable last world gentile empire. Religion has always sought to usurp the government.

You need to realize God is going to use Antichrist to overthrow this end-time world religion. All who join are destroyed.

The woman has an appeal of grandeur but is full of abominations

"And the woman was arrayed in purple and scarlet color, and decked with gold and precious stones and pearls, having a golden cup in her hand full of abominations and filthiness of her fornication" (Revelation 17:4, KJV).

So by interacting with the governmental leaders of the last days, this woman becomes adorned with beautiful things, dressed in scarlet (she partook and is drunk on), signifying her participation in the death of the martyrs. The golden cup is the brew of her involvement in the death of martyrs and her abominable practices against God. This woman is dressed to entice the adherents of Antichrist. The vessel (golden cup) she drinks from, which she is delighted in, which are the martyrs of the saints abominations and gathering others into her practices. She is a woman who bears heretical children.

These abominations are all things designed by Satan that are repulsive to God.

We must be right doctrinally, ethically, and socially, or we will have participated in the abominations of this false religion. Make sure your walk honors God.

The woman is known for her defiling promiscuity.

"And upon her forehead *was* a name written, MYSTERY, BABYLON THE GREAT, THE MOTHER OF HARLOTS AND ABOMINATIONS OF THE EARTH" (Revelation 17:5, KJV).

This false religion has been around for millenniums. Satan has had his antitheses of the followers of God. This woman has been producing offspring over and over through the years. Both the end-time religion in her final form and a local city (or nation) somewhere as a base of her operation. As a mockery to Jerusalem, this is what is meant by Babylon the great. Mother of harlots may say the begetter of false religions and the murderer of saints.

Through her grandeur, she entices world leaders into her abominations. So great is her last day's promiscuity that all earth participates.

Avoid false religions and false belief systems as much as you can. You preserve your soul through your obedience.

The woman is drunk by the constant killing of the people of God.

"And I saw the woman drunken with the blood of the saints, and with the blood of the martyrs of Jesus: and when I saw her, I wondered with great admiration" (Revelation 17:6, KJV).

This woman revels in the drunkenness of the blood of the saints of God. John probably was astounded at this abomination. It is a continual intoxication on killing regularly the followers of Jehovah. The martyrs of Jesus are those who took their stand for Jesus Christ.

She plays well in Antichrist's scheme in killing the saints. She is in the world government headquarters probably.

Come out from among her and them and be ye separate. Do not take up her ways. We are called to love the servants of God and not kill them. This may be a literal call to depart from her land.

The woman's mystery had to be explained to John.

"And the angel said unto me, wherefore didst thou marvel? I will tell thee the mystery of the woman, and of the beast that carried her, which hath the seven heads and ten horns" (Revelation 17:7, KJV).

This woman is not obtusely seen today because people go on with their lives paying no attention, but false beliefs abound. This false religion of the end-times was forced upon all the people of the earth and now comes to her end.

This only goes on the first three and one half years, and then Antichrist tears the woman to pieces. God has a time frame for everything.

This time we are in before all this takes place is the time of grace, and our responsibility is to side up with Jesus Christ by receiving him as our Lord and Savior. Have you done so?

So know who the great whore is, and you'll avoid her offspring the false religions.

Unbeliever's Admiration of Antichrist

Will unbelievers admire Antichrist? Many will applaud the Antichrist because he is a man of grandeur and power or because he is keen on deep sayings and answers. But mainly people will admire him because Satan works through him.

In Revelation 17:8–11, we learn to know why the earth dwellers marvel at the beast. Let's examine why earth dwellers wonder at the creature.

The earth dwellers wonder at the beast because the beast fools the world through a miraculous comeback.

"The beast that thou saw was, and is not; and shall ascend out of the bottomless pit, and go into perdition: and they that dwell on the earth shall wonder, whose names were not written in the book of life from the foundation of the world, when they behold the beast that was, and is not, and yet is" (Revelation 17:8, KJV).

The world marvels at the beast that died and revived and his kingdom, the revived Roman Empire. And the world wonders knowing, outside of God, no power can withstand the beast. The power of this one world government was is currently not present and shall ascend. We see it coming alive today before us. The end place for Antichrist, his kingdom, and his followers is the Lake of Fire.

Therefore, because of the marvelous comeback of the beast from his deadly wound, all the unsaved of the world marvel at the monstrosity. World powers arise from time to time, but this is both God's doing and Satan's scheming.

The comeback is that now Satan indwells Antichrist and works his garbage in the last world kingdom. Let us beware not to miss Christ's appearing, so we don't get caught with Satan's crowd.

The earth dwellers wonder at the beast because the beast and woman share in the headquarters area.

"And here *is* the mind which hath wisdom. The seven heads are seven mountains, on which the woman sits" (Revelation 17:9, KJV). *Rome*

John helps us to see that the seven mountains, which is probably literally Rome, also signifies the world's great empires past, present, and future in which the woman relied upon to do her lusts and contriving's against God's people. A conglomeration of all the natives under this world power influences who aided false religions and promoted discouragement and death of the saints. The seven mountains indicate that the last Roman empire will be strategically located. The verse tells us the woman sits upon this location, signifying that the world religion will have its headquarters in the same place. *7 Hills* *7 nations too*

There will be again a world religion in which all belief systems worship Antichrist. If a person serves in a false belief, he serves Satan. Now in the Tribulation, the people outright worship Satan. *Rome*

We must avoid false beliefs because this is the result and why Satan has his false religions and cults to destroy people. The Bible says to come out from among them. Remember that it is better to die serving God in genuine faith than to live in a false religion.

The earth dwellers wonder at the beast because the beast is one of the seven kings with his kingdom on earth.

"And there are seven kings: five are fallen, and one is, *and* the other is not yet come; and when he cometh, he must continue a short space" (Revelation 17:10, KJV).

At the time of the writing of Revelation, five kings with their kingdoms already fell. One was presently ruling Rome, and one was to come, which is the Antichrist over the last world kingdom. He will rule for seven years upon the rapture taking place. There would be seven kings over seven world empires. The last one is yet to come over this last vast empire forming. He will continue a short time meaning that he will rule for seven years until Jesus Christ returns at his Second Advent and throws the false prophet and Antichrist into hell!

1 Assyria *2 Egypt* *3* *4 Greece* *5 Greece* *fuller* *(6) Rome = at that time* *(7 Antichrist or ??? revived Roman Empire*

This again shows God is in control. He puts people in power and removes people out of power. The book of Daniel explains how the kingdom of God rules the kingdom of men.

We should rely on God for all our needs; when people trust in governments, the governments turn into monsters.

The earth dwellers wonder at the beast because he died and came back to life. Also, the beast is the eighth king.

"And the beast that was, and is not, even he is the eighth, and is of the seven, and goes into perdition" (Revelation 17:11, KJV).

This king either is fatally wounded and comes back to life or comes out of perdition. Most likely, his death and recovery are staged by Satan, who makes him the eighth king. The Antichrist is one of the kings and becomes an eighth.

Satan can perform spiritual deceptions. Satan's deceptions will cause the whole world to marvel.

Make sure your experience aligns with God's Word so that Satan won't deceive you.

So the beast captures the earth's dweller's imaginations so that they admire and marvel at him. Be sure you escape this lie by repenting and putting your trust in Jesus Christ.

The Kings of the Earth Team Up with the Antichrist

Do the earth's kings submit to Antichrist? They give their whole reason for being to the Antichrist. They also do his bidding in their lands. The kings make themselves subject to the Antichrist.

You can know how the kings will submit to Antichrist, according to Revelation 17:12–14. Let's see how the kings submit to Antichrist.

The kings are appointed by Antichrist.

"And the ten horns which thou saw are ten kings, which have received no kingdom yet; but receive power as kings one hour with the beast" (Revelation 17:12, KJV).

Here are ten kings who have never yet been a kingdom. For it says, they have not yet received a country. But they will! Ten kings shall arise, and at the time of the end, they shall be appointed to rule under the guidance of Antichrist. They shall do all the beasts

Armageddon

bidding for him in their lands. They shall presume to join Antichrist in a battle against the Son of God. Ten kings with their kingdoms which have not yet arrived. Could this be a reordered world with ten kings reigning over regions? They receive power with the beast. This is God's plan to bring an end to gentile rulership.

This is the end-setting for the times of the Gentiles. It's a shame that it closes with all nations fighting God; it closes with total failure on man's part! We heard of favorable beginnings with lousy endings or failure. That describes these ten kings with their kingdoms as they destroy God's people with Antichrist and fight, God-God will win!

We should pray for our nations not to support such monstrosities. Pray, our countries will not become a goat nation!

These kings give their total allegiance to the Antichrist.

"These have one mind and shall give their power and strength unto the beast" (Revelation 17:13, KJV).

Can you imagine that the world will become so utterly evil that its world leaders give all their power to the Antichrist? Yet, Revelation says that very thing will happen. The kings of the earth give themselves to Satan's lie-Antichrist. I assume by immediate penalty of death for dissenters. These kings had one mind! Their only purpose is to serve the Antichrist's ambitions throughout their kingdoms. They give all to the beast's desire. No point in resisting; I think those who oppose are taken out—all shall be subject.

In other words, these kings have one mind and force all in their kingdoms to comply with Antichrist or die. Can you imagine the world's ten kingdom division all uniting to support Satan's plans? Just think of the devastation to man that will cause.

This means there will be no place for safety for a believer. It is better you take your stand and die for it; because if you deny Jesus Christ, they will kill you anyways upon recanting Christ.

These kings join Antichrist in making war against Jesus Christ (who defeats them). *Armageddon*

"These shall make war with the Lamb, and the Lamb shall overcome them: for he is Lord of lords, and King of kings: and they that are with him *are* called, and chosen, and faithful" (Revelation 17:14, KJV).

Armageddon?

How imbecilic that these empires choose to unite to fight off Jesus Christ's return and to destroy his people. They go out to make war with Jesus Christ! These take up the presumption of fighting off the coming of Jesus Christ. It's hard to kick against the pricks. The Lamb will overcome and defeat them!

At the time of Armageddon, these shall come together and fight and be annihilated. This is called the multitudes in the valley of decision and is where God decides to judge the nations of the earth.

Do you see how, whether you're in the army or outside of it, that if you rebel against God, his judgments will overtake you? Get right with God today!

So we see how the kings of the earth submit to Antichrist and are destroyed. No doubt there will be no age limit to the draft that Antichrist will demand to get the people to fight for him. Men and women equally will be required to go. Do not be one of them!

How the World Religions Will End

Can it be possible that the world religions will end? Does God have a plan to end world religions? Will Antichrist annihilate all beliefs? Let's see how God will bring all religions to an end.

We must see in Revelation 17:15–18 how God will end the religious whore. Let's see how God will end this whore.

Take note of how the whore influences all the earth.

"And he saith unto me, the waters which thou saw, where the whore sits, are peoples, and multitudes, and nations, and tongues" (Revelation 17:15, KJV).

Just as Antichrist rules the vast multitude, his end-time religion also rules with him. Her tentacles spread throughout the whole earth. She has reigned on the earth since Babylon, moving her seat of influence from city to city as a counterfeit to the true religion of faith in God. Antichrist's rule from Satan has had his religions too and the great whore, Babylon the religion; mother of harlots (her offspring religions and those who kill the saints) has spread her venomous tentacles throughout the whole earth. She who murdered the prophets dies a horrible death. She is religious Babylon, the city is economic

Rome = economic Babylon

Babylon, and the Antichrist is political Babylon. All of them come to their end in their own time. Waters means the Babylon cult religions spread themselves over all the earth yet centralize in a location in the end times. The meaning behind the idea of the whore sitting is that the false religions of the world go from one place to another, relocating over decades to fulfill Satan's purposes. Again they centralize in a specific location in the last days.

This influence again has begun years (millennia) ago at the Tower of Babel and has grown and spread with the changes of the nations and peoples. All of that is about to end; she will be destroyed. God is going to cause such hatred between the leaders of the ten nations and the whore that they kill her.

We are commanded to come out from the false and cultic religions and serve the God of the Bible; that includes the land of this cult. If we refuse to believe in God, Satan will force you to worship Antichrist and then be destroyed for your hesitation.

The nations destroy the whore.

"And the ten horns which thou saw upon the beast, these shall hate the whore, and shall make her desolate and naked, and shall eat her flesh, and burn her with fire. For God hath put in their hearts to fulfil his will, and to agree, and give their kingdom unto the beast, until the words of God shall be fulfilled" (Revelation 17:16–17, KJV).

The rulers of the earth will rise and brutally pursue and destroy all traces of false religion, as well as followers of God. God causes these kings and their kingdoms to be in sympathy with Antichrist. The people of these kingdoms shall hate any religion outside worship of Antichrist and shall eradicate it. The kings of the nations shall strip her of all her riches, buildings, and annihilate her, make her desolate. They will kill her followers. God is the one who puts this in the king's hearts to do. These kings still carry out the will of God, even though they serve Antichrist.

These nations decide these false cults do not serve the purpose of furthering Antichrists agenda, so they kill off the whore. Nations have risen against religions before; many battles have been fought over who has supremacy.

eat first by false religions?

Get rid of all religions — Just worship Anti

It's best if you make the rapture by being in Jesus Christ. Avoid the vices of any wind of doctrine (false religion) and then serve Jesus Christ.

The whore is a city (perhaps a nation), as well as a religion, political and economic Babylon.   Rome ?

"And the woman which thou saw is that great city, which reigns over the kings of the earth" (Revelation 17:18, KJV).

There are these aspects to Babylon such as: religious Babylon, which will be destroyed here; economic Babylon, which is a city (or nation) destroyed; and political Babylon, which is destroyed by Jesus Christ's Second Coming. But before chapter 18, the capital of Babylon shall be destroyed. Let's examine this. Religious Babylon has ruled from towns from the beginning of false religions. The woman is all false religions combined in one. The verse talks about the great city since there was no great city which reigned over the kings of the earth. It's talking about religious cults dominating nations over the history of man. It culminates in a last one world religion that is in a future city (or country).

This is the religious city which shall be destroyed by Antichrist in chapter 18. It is Babylon, the literal economic city.

Again, hold fast to the truth that you were taught. This will help you keep your position in Christ.

So we see how the religious whore is destroyed, and that's why there is no place to hide—serve God today and live.

CHAPTER 18

Rome

Babylon's economic end. How will this world's commercial Babylon end? The power of evil will strike commercial Babylon down. Let us look more closely at the world's economic ways coming to an end.

It is necessary to know how economic Babylon will be a desolation. As we read Revelation 18:1–3, let's consider what will happen to Babylon.

An angel comes to announce Babylon's fall.

"And after these things I saw another angel come down from heaven, having great power; and the earth was lightened with his glory" (Revelation 18:1, KJV).

It's not clear if this was an angel of a previous chapter or an angel who is new to the scene. But his glory radiated the earth; no doubt that glory signifies how that economic Babylon will be destroyed. This is commercial Babylon. The religious, economic, and political Babylon are each covered in separate chapters. The forces of evil destroy religious Babylon in chapter 17. In chapter 18, evil forces are part of economic Babylon's destruction. In chapter 19, political Babylon will be destroyed with her armies by the brightness of Jesus Christ's return. After John has seen the destruction of religious Babylon, the angel shows him the destruction of economic Babylon. The angel's light lightened the earth.

This city represents the whole world economic system and every town that has not separated itself from her. It is a real place as well that causes all the earth to partake of the economic system. It represents the economies of all the past as well. It's not hard for God to wipe out a city. Have you ever seen a small anthill made from sand? Swipe your foot across it, and it's wiped out. It's just that easy for God to do likewise.

We are commanded to come out, not only out of wicked Babylon but also the sins that we commit. Let's get rid of it. That way, we won't share in the judgment of those sins.

Babylon becomes a place of desolation.

"And he cried mightily with a strong voice, saying, Babylon the great is fallen, is fallen, and is become the habitation of devils, and the hold of every foul spirit, and a cage of every unclean and hateful bird" (Revelation 18:2, KJV).

The angel announces that this great city and her world influence and dominance are gone. She shall be the desolate roaming place of unclean spirits. Things that offend will be made to live there. It's Babylon's time to be judged. This great city will be no more. Babylon's dwellings are desolate, except for foul spirits.

Such will be the end of all cities or nations who forget their God. God's judgments and Satan's wrath destroys everything. Remember that Babylon incorporates religious, economic, and political apostasy around the world. Whoever harbors sin will be judged, and sin removed in the seven years of tribulation.

Our part is to separate ourselves from all that defiles; this will be the preservation of our souls.

Babylon's world influence comes to nothing.

"For all nations have drunk of the wine of the wrath of her fornication, and the kings of the earth have committed fornication with her, and the merchants of the earth are waxed rich through the abundance of her delicacies" (Revelation 18:3, KJV).

Babylon so influenced the nations into the intoxicating mixture of her wrath on the saints and innocent people that all who have drunk will suffer in her destruction. All the countries will participate in this wrath. She is angry with the saints and so made the kings of the earth mad at the saints. The merchants became rich through her, but judgment has come to give her two times what she did to others and double the punishment for the lavishness she gave herself.

God is repaying her for the sins she had committed in her rejection of God and murdered the saints. Do not share in her sins by repenting and obeying God. Come out of the crimes and do God's Will. Come out of her and live.

So know that Babylon and her influence come to an end. Praise God and rejoice.

Removing ourselves from defilement.

Is removing ourselves from evil necessary? Once we are saved, we need to guard that salvation by removing ourselves from sin. If we escape the tribulation hour, we must be born again and remove ourselves from evil (ungodliness—living in a state of being without God directing us). We will see how we must remove ourselves from sin.

In Revelation 18:4–6, we see that we must remove ourselves from evil. Let's examine why we must remove ourselves from sin.

We are urged to withdraw from all sin.

"And I heard another voice from heaven, saying, come out of her, my people, that ye be not partakers of her sins, and that ye receive not of her plagues" (Revelation 18:4, KJV).

We are commanded to put the sin out of our lives and separate ourselves for the Lord's work. This word is explicitly telling us to remove ourselves from this territory. We need to avoid even the condition of entering temptation because we are so prone to sin. All this is so we won't be partakers of the judgment that falls on all of Babylon soon. I realize this is dealing with future events, but all scripture is given for our admonition. Come out of her means to be removed from the power, influence, and association of her and sin. Through Jesus Christ's atoning work, we have the strength to say no to sin, and we must act on our faith and remove ourselves from her land. The Bible makes it clear why we do this, so we don't partake of her sins!

It is expedient to withdraw from sin, so we are not judged with the abominable. The Bible makes it clear that we must say no to sin and to go to God to remove our evil.

What do you got to do to overcome sin in your life? Seek God for what it is you need that will help you overcome the sin that easily besets you.

We are told that God will visit the sin of Babylon.

"For her sins has reached unto heaven, and God hath remembered her iniquities" (Revelation 18:5, KJV).

We must, with God's help, let go of habitual sin and serve God, or we to will be visited with judgment. The Bible declares that her sins reached to heaven. God now shall remember her sin. God will punish her crimes. Leave her now!

This includes all who follow in her ways. If we reject Jesus Christ and serve idols and commit immorality, then we will be judged.

We must make sure our walk with God is up to speed. If we are not in Jesus Christ, we won't make the rapture and will undergo all this. There is a reason why the rapture causes us to live for God while we wait for him to call us home. We want to be caught doing God's will, working for God, loving God and others, living in the Holy Spirit, and always living ready for the unannounced day!

We are warned of the exceeding wrath poured upon the wickedness of the world.

"Reward her even as she rewarded you, and double unto her double according to her works: in the cup which she hath filled fill to her double" (Revelation 18:6, KJV).

God is telling us judgment will be paid double unto those who did severely unto God's people, and for good, they gave themselves there will be double wrath upon them for that. Babylon will be punished (all the people who are the heart of her). It will be in the same way she used her ability to mistreat the saints.

This is the heritage of the saints; that people will be given double for how they treated the saints.

Why join in the world's careless ways? Repent and turn to God for the remission of sins and live.

So remove yourself from evil so you will be spared from going through the seven years of judgment.

Judgment on Economic Babylonian Attitude

Is there an attitude we must avoid? How about inordinate self-preservation or living for the sake of pleasure? As we will see, it is this precise attitude that God will judge.

In Revelation 18:7–8, we can know how God will judge economic Babylon's attitude. Let's examine how God will judge commercial Babylon's attitude.

God will judge economic Babylon's attitude of self-indulgence.

"How much she hath glorified herself, and lived deliciously, so much torment and sorrow give her: for she says in her heart, I sit a queen, and am no widow, and shall see no sorrow" (Revelation 18:7, KJV).

arrogance

Ironically, the dominating worldview, including Christian circles, is if it feels good, do it! People don't know that it is precisely this attitude that will be judged by God on economic Babylon. That is the world financial system of the last days. Economic Babylon has risen herself up for self-glorification. This attitude and its actions will bring judgment by God. To be rich toward self and not God will be judged. This is self-preservation taken to extremes, where there is no concern to do God's will. Economic Babylon glorified herself; therefore, the measure she used to care for herself will be used to destroy her. Sorrow will be given her, and her world will crash on her. She will sit desolate and ruined.

God has a purpose for all governments and peoples; his good intent is that he prospers them, and they serve him in it. Not so with the last day's one world government. It is devoid of godliness; therefore, God uses it to end gentile world dominance. We must accept that God is in control, and it is his sovereign to set up his kingdom and rule from Jerusalem, not any other nation.

We, as well as any repentant people, must correct this arrogant attitude of inordinate self-preservation. By which we lay no building toward the cause of Jesus Christ, thereby forfeiting any reward.

God will judge economic Babylon's attitude of ease.

When nations remain at ease, idle, and with no contention, they get arrogant and think their prosperity is because of things they have done. God will judge the attitude of superiority. The economic side of Babylon thinks she sits as queen and presumes to acquire blessings with no accountability to God. God will judge this system and destroy it.

No people, government, or system will remain that is ungodly and unaccountable to God, for it is self-serving rather than God serving.

Be sure you are faithful to God in the use of your life and goods and your participation in the world. We will all give an account to God.

God will judge economic Babylon's attitude by various plagues all at once.

"Therefore shall her plagues come in/one day,/ death, and mourning, and famine; and she shall be utterly burned with fire: for strong *is* the Lord God who judges her" (Revelation 18:8, KJV).

Because of economic Babylon's attitude, do it if it feels good and living with no accountability to God, God will destroy this global financial system. It does not serve God but evil and wicked men. In one day shall the end come upon this system. The plagues, etc., will come all at once (death, morning, and famine). She shall be burned. Some worldwide catastrophe, possibly nuclear war, will consume her wealth of goods.

Because the God she mocked by her unjust trade is the most powerful God (indeed the only God) and will bring her to an end. The rock is smiting the feet of the gentile kingdoms, bringing their end upon them.

Please get your affairs in order and pray about your account-ability and faithfulness to God. And as you see areas that need to be changed, please make the adjustments.

We see that this prevailing attitude of economic Babylon is present in the world and the Laodicean Church of today; we must repent and avoid the coming wrath.

Economic Babylon's Destruction

Why will the businesspeople cry over Babylon's destruction? They cannot participate in her corruption anymore. They lose the ability to acquire riches. These and other reasons are why merchants cry over Babylon's destruction.

In Revelation 18:9–13, we see it is necessary to know why the world will cry over the destruction of economic Babylon. Let's see why the world will cry over the destruction of commercial Babylon.

The world will cry over the destruction of economic Babylon because the hope of worldly prosperity dies, for the kings of the earth, along with commercial Babylon's destruction.

"And the kings of the earth, who have committed fornication and lived deliciously with her, shall bewail her, and lament for her when they shall see the smoke of her burning, Standing afar off for the fear of her torment, saying, Alas, alas, that great city Babylon, that mighty city! for in one hour is thy judgment come" (Revelation 18:9–10, KJV).

The destruction of economic Babylon destroys all the world's hope of becoming fluent materially. Now there is no one to buy their goods. Her destruction is seen for days. Now their standard of living goes goodbye. They have lived for earth's treasures and missed heavens. The verse tells us that the kings committed fornication and lived deliciously with her. She enriched them. Now her flow of prosperity ends. They cry that the great city is lost. This city and its world economic dominance end. The great city is reduced to zero.

When people put all their hope in the world, they end up being swallowed in worldly sorrow. Since creation (the world) is their chief reason for being, God disappoints them.

If all your hope is in the world, you will go through disappointing moments to get you to strengthen your reliance on God.

The world will cry over the destruction of economic Babylon because the hope of worldly commerce dies for the merchants of the earth, along with commercial Babylon's destruction.

> And the merchants of the earth shall weep and
> mourn over her; for no man buys their merchan-
> dise any more: The merchandise of gold, and sil-
> ver, and precious stones, and of pearls, and fine
> linen, and purple, and silk, and scarlet, and all
> thy wood, and all manner vessels of ivory, and all
> manner vessels of most precious wood, and brass,

and iron, and marble, And cinnamon, and odors, and ointments, and frankincense, and wine, and oil, and fine flour, and wheat, and beasts, and sheep, and horses, and chariots, and slaves, and souls of men. (Revelation 18:11–13, KJV)

All businesspeople who did business through or by Babylon become distraught because she was the one who purchased their goods or sold them products. They mourn bitterly for their economic poverty. Now they have no way to increase wealth, and they cannot do business with Babylon's financial system no more. A furious cry goes forth for their loss over Babylon's financial system. Now they cannot buy or sell their merchandise, so they are impoverished. All the souls that did business in Babylon cannot be reached.

They put all they had in economic Babylon instead of Jesus Christ and his kingdom; therefore, they lost out. If you build your financial house on selfish interests only and you're not rich toward God, you'll be full of sorrow too.

Who do you do business with? Make sure that in some way, you promote Jesus Christ cause, and you'll have no reason to fear destruction (that is of course unless you live in this Babylon.)

So know that the world will cry over economic Babylon's destruction because she lived presumptuously for herself with no regard for God.

The End of the Good Life

What would happen if the good life were no longer possible? People would weep and wail over being poverty-stricken. People would become frustrated with life. The end of the good life is precisely what will happen in a future time with the fall of Babylon.

In Revelation 18:14–19, we see we can understand how all the merchants of the earth will cry over the end of their riches. Let's see how all the merchants of the earth will cry because, in one hour, their fortune is gone.

All the goods (commodities) that the merchants lusted after are gone.

"And the fruits that thy soul lusted after are departed from thee, and all things which were dainty and goodly are departed from thee, and thou shalt find them no more at all. The merchants of these things, which were made rich by her, shall stand afar off for the fear of her torment, weeping and wailing" (Revelation 18:14–15, KJV).

When the world's economic system and the place of commercial Babylon fall, thus, it will end the merchants' supply of goods, whereby they never again shall buy or sell or taste or enjoy them. Great horror will befall the world because economic Babylon has come crashing down, and now there is no one to do business with them. There will be no more goods available to spice up people's lives. The people will be weeping and wailing. These are not concerned over economic Babylon but the loss of their goods. They have no regard of attachment for Babylon but to mourn their own loss.

Can you imagine the end of the grocery and outlet store? Major panic would erupt.

There is no more substance to work with that will cause people to have employment. Their days become idle and stupefied. Be sure to thank God for his resources in your life.

All the merchants cry because the one world economic system has been wiped out along with all their riches.

"And saying, Alas, alas, that great city, that was clothed in fine linen, and purple, and scarlet, and decked with gold, and precious stones, and pearls! For in one hour so great riches are come to naught. And every shipmaster, and all the company in ships, and sailors, and as many as trade by sea, stood afar off" (Revelation 18:16–17, KJV).

The system that supported the wicked works of the world is now destroyed. All its riches have come to nothing in one hour. That great city will be an actual place as a global economic system. It is judged and wiped out in one hour! Just gone!

They (the merchants) weep because they are now impoverished. When the economic system goes, so does society.

Place your trust in God and build up your Christian network. God will sustain you in it unless you get destroyed for not coming out of her.

All the merchants' hope of ever having anything dies with economic Babylon.

"And cried when they saw the smoke of her burning, saying, what *city is* like unto this great city! And they cast dust on their heads, and cried, weeping and wailing, saying, Alas, alas, that great city, wherein were made rich all that had ships in the sea by reason of her costliness! For in one hour is she made desolate" (Revelation 18:18–19, KJV).

The prospect of business, riches, and lavish lifestyles of rich and famous persons come to their end when their economic god collapses. Babylon economically falls and crashes the dreams of the good life. The people cry, oh, what great city was like unto this one! Is this just a city? Could it be a metropolitan area or is it a nation? Could it be several cities in an area? Is it a nation? I don't know. It encompasses the whole world system, and all mourn because they are now poverty-stricken. This city made everyone rich. They wail not for the people destroyed in the city, but their hopes of the good life are gone.

People complain more today over their fear of economic ruin then social justice. The great depression of 1929–1930s left many hopeless and destitute, and they committed suicide. This is what happens when your hope is not in God. Make sure your hope remains in God and not the economic system.

So know the wailing that will occur over the fall of economic Babylon so that you can make God your refuge instead of the world or materials.

The End of Economic Babylon

Can or will this world's financial system be destroyed? If God is all-powerful, then he can destroy this quickly. If this system is Antichrist, then God will destroy this system soon. The end-time tribulation economic system is a corrupt system that God ends.

We can see in Revelation 18:20–24 how God will avenge his faithful martyr's blood on the world by destroying economic Babylon. Let's see how the destruction of commercial Babylon is God's way of avenging the blood of all martyrs.

God avenges the blood of his martyrs on economic Babylon by destroying her.

"Rejoice over her, *thou* heaven, and *ye* holy apostles and prophets; for God hath avenged you on her" (Revelation 18:20, KJV).

Finally, what heaven's martyrs have been praying for has come namely that for God's righteous rule to be on earth, also for saints to rule with Jesus in glory, the unrighteous system and wicked men who rejected the Messiah, and God's people have to be removed through judgment. The heritage of the saints is that whatever people do to the saints will be repaid to them. This may mean patient suffering of the saints. The Bible says that all are to rejoice over Babylon's destruction. Now the martyrs in heaven can begin to rejoice over the progression of God's program on earth. Economic Babylon is getting repaid for all she has done to God's saints. Babylon will do tremendous damage to the followers of God. Do you understand that picture?

This probably happens during the Armageddon campaign as Satan attempts to destroy Jerusalem and all the Jews. God destroys Satan's capital in one hour. By what means, I cannot tell, but God's hand is against her. You cannot mess with God's people and get away with it.

This again is a statement to all the earth to repent and turn to God through his appointed Messiah. There is no other way.

God avenges the blood of his martyrs on economic Babylon by making her destruction last forever.

"And a mighty angel took up a stone like a great millstone, and cast *it* into the sea, saying, thus with violence shall that great city Babylon be thrown down, and shall be found no more at all" (Revelation 18:21, KJV).

Not only did God avenge his saints, but Babylon's judgment is a judgment in which she shall never arise from again. Violently the complete and total destruction of Babylon will happen. The world's dreams of living without God are removed forever. There will be found no more Babylon for men to use to acquire goods.

Such is the fate of any national system that disregards God. It's like the rich fool; such is the fate for those who are rich toward themselves but not God.

Are you accustomed to doing your business without God? If you choose independence from God, then such will be your fate.

God avenges the blood of his martyrs on economic Babylon by putting out its flame of life.

> And the voice of harpers, and musicians, and of pipers, and trumpeters, shall be heard no more at all in thee; and no craftsman, of whatsoever craft *he be*, shall be found any more in thee; and the sound of a millstone shall be heard no more at all in thee; And the light of a candle shall shine no more at all in thee; and the voice of the bridegroom and of the bride shall be heard no more at all in thee: for thy merchants were the great men of the earth; for by thy sorceries were all nations deceived. (Revelation 18:22–23, KJV).

No more will life's flow go through Babylon again. There will be no music or work or occupying there or marriages. Babylon's spells over people are broken. No one will inhabit this region again. There will be no business there again.

Just as Babylon used her spell to exclude and destroy God's people over the centuries, God removes her life.

Come out from among them. Don't be so caught in the world's system that your swept away with it.

God avenges the blood of his martyrs on economic Babylon by imputing the guilt of the blood of his martyrs upon economic Babylon.

"And in her was found the blood of prophets, and of saints, and of all that were slain upon the earth" (Revelation 18:24, KJV).

It was economic Babylon's love of money that caused her to kill the saints. Now she is killed. The Bible says that in her was found the blood of the saints. She has been responsible for destroying Christ's people.

She didn't view Christ's followers or Jews as an asset to her. The guilt is now judged on her, and heaven rejoices.

Religious and economic Babylon is destroyed, and we had better make sure we are not caught up in her, or we will be judged with her.

So know that this world's economic system (like her religious system) will be destroyed, so we don't partake of these judgments. Repent and turn to Jesus Christ.

a turn/change

CHAPTER 19

❧❦

The martyrs praise.

Will praise be going on over God's judgments? Will praise be going on when evil is stopped? Will praise be going on when the blood of the saints is avenged? When those things happen, there will be praise in heaven.

In Revelation 19:1–5, we see that it is necessary to comprehend the praise that is going on in heaven for the judgment God brings on Babylon (when he avenges the blood of his servants.) Let's observe why there is much praise going on in heaven.

A great host rises to praise God.

"And after these things I heard a great voice of much people in heaven, saying, Alleluia; Salvation, and glory, and honor, and power, unto the Lord our God" (Revelation 19:1, KJV).

All the martyrs and Church and all the hosts of heaven (created order) rejoices over God's salvation and vengeance on his enemies because he avenged the blood of the martyrs on Babylon. This sounded like a great voice! All of heaven stands now rejoicing because wickedness has been dealt with and is coming to an end, the blood of the martyrs is avenged, and the saints can now reign with Jesus Christ according to their appointed positions. For all this, the people shout salvation, glory, and honor to the Lord. Great attributes are acknowledged and accredited to our God!

The created order attributes to God the due praise to him who has done all this. Men never could right what Satan has damaged, but God's plan was in motion. This is God's plan of redemption and salvation, to restore the lost.

It is God's desire for us to be a part of this celebration in heaven, but for us to participate, we must personally receive Jesus Christ today.

The host of heaven praises God's judgments over the Babylonian whore.

"For true and righteous *is* his judgments: for he hath judged the great whore, which did corrupt the earth with her fornication, and hath avenged the blood of his servants at her hand" (Revelation 19:2, KJV).

So God receives praise and is praised by all of heaven for judging the whore for corrupting the earth and for the shed blood of his saints that were committed by the whore's hand. True and righteous are God's judgments. God told the crying martyrs to wait a season, and now the season is fulfilled, and they rejoice! This city (or nation perhaps) is the world's ungodly system.

If you have ever been persecuted and hurt drastically for faith in Jesus Christ, then you would cry for God's intervention too. You would cry because that suffering hinders you from doing God's will.

If you're a Christian now, then at that time, you too will be in heaven praising God for his righteous judgment. You will be thanking God for ending the ungodly world system.

The host of heaven praises God for the whore's everlasting destruction.

"And again they said, Alleluia. And her smoke rose up for ever and ever" (Revelation 19:3, KJV).

Forever heaven will view the smoke of the torment of Babylon, and praise will go forth because in its destruction, God brought his plan of rulership of his Messiah and his saints to bear on the millennial and future reigns. There is continued rejoicing over God's salvation. Babylon's smoke of torment never dies out.

It forever stands as a reminder of the end of the rebellion. Hell's everlasting torment lasts as long as heaven's eternal life.

Make sure your friends and loved ones and yourselves are on the winning side. Share the gospel with them.

The elders in heaven affirm God's actions in worship.

"And the four and twenty elders and the four beasts fell down and worshipped God that sat on the throne, saying, Amen; Alleluia" (Revelation 19:4, KJV).

Here is the high counsel in heaven affirming the righteousness of God's judgments and the approval of worship to God by joining in the praise. The four and twenty elders and the beasts are those who have high council offices in heaven. They are affirming and giving their approval to God.

The high council recognizes the good of God's intervention. Heaven acknowledges that God's intervention allows his plans to go forward on earth.

By praying for God's intervention, we speed on the time of God's appointment of a thousand-year rulership, which includes his saints.

All of heaven is summoned to worship God.

"And a voice came out of the throne, saying, praise our God, all ye his servants, and ye that fear him, both small and great" (Revelation 19:5, KJV).

From the throne, a voice proceeds to call all of heaven to come and worship God for his acts on his creations behalf and to fear and worship him. It could be an angelic voice calling all heaven to praise the Lord. If we can think and speak, then all are invited to praise the Lord.

In heaven, we will gather regularly to worship God.

Take time to praise God in your busy schedule. Don't let this become a life of ungratefulness, worship God.

So praise God for his future judgment of Babylon, and we will be participating in the hope of creation.

The prepared believer is blessed.

How can you prepare to meet your Maker and be blessed in it? You can put Jesus Christ first in your priorities in life. You can bear your cross as you live for Jesus Christ. You are the determiner of the blessings you'll have in Jesus Christ.

In Revelation 19:6–10, we can know how the believers who prepare to meet their Maker are blessed. Let's see how the prepared believer is blessed.

The prepared believer is blessed because they based their life on God's sovereign reign.

"And I heard as it were the voice of a great multitude, and as the voice of many waters, and as the voice of mighty thundering, saying, Alleluia: for the Lord God omnipotent reigns" (Revelation 19:6, KJV).

The believer today may be mocked for his/her testimony, but a great day of pure joy is coming because they lived under God's sovereign reign over them. They received Jesus Christ as their Lord and Savior and continued in a personal relationship with him. There was a voice of a great multitude, a glorious shout, and praise of the bride of Christ, the Church at the marriage supper of the Lamb. These believers based their life on the truth that the Lord God omnipotent reigns.

When you are born again and experience the joy of living for the Lord Jesus Christ, you are a chosen one for shouting at this time in heaven. Why? You prepared by living for Jesus Christ. It's a matter of godliness (living for God) or worldliness (living for self).

It is your option to be saved and continue in Jesus Christ and to serve and live for him or not. But a future time, if we prepared, we will receive a reward.

The prepared believer is blessed for living for their Lord and Savior.

"Let us be glad and rejoice, and give honor to him: for the marriage of the Lamb is come and his wife hath made herself ready" (Revelation 19:7, KJV).

Glory to God because one day, his church will be given her robes, given her place at his banquet, and the bride will be ready. Why will she be ready? Well, she lived for Jesus Christ in contrast to the whore Babylon who murdered believers. The true bride of Christ is clothed with righteous deeds done unto Jesus Christ. So the verse tells us to let us be glad. All heaven rejoices over the bride's position as Jesus Christ's companion. Heaven honors Jesus Christ who gave his life to purchase the bride. The bride has made herself ready! She was given the invitation, and she came to God through faith in Jesus Christ.

The process of living for Jesus Christ starts with rebirth and submission to the lordship of Christ, then patient endurance in growing up and becoming useful in Jesus Christ. There will be different degrees of joy here. For those who caught the vision and lived for God, it will be a great joy. But those who supposed equal status with no laboring for Jesus, there will be less joy.

I don't believe I am complicating this because the fine linen represents deeds done unto Jesus Christ by the individual. Do not be found scantly clothed in heaven. Serve God while in your earthly probationary period.

The prepared believer is blessed by honoring their God by the Holy Spirit inspired deeds.

"And to her was granted that she should be arrayed in fine linen, clean and white: for the fine linen is the righteousness of saints" (Revelation 19:8, KJV).

As we yield to the Holy Spirit's leading on a day-to-day bases, we become vessels that God is pleased to do his work through. Such fine linens will adorn the believer in heaven. The being arrayed by the bride is not with the imputed righteousness of Jesus in this verse but according to the individual's deeds done unto God in response to the salvation God gave them. The verse tells us that the fine linen is the righteousness of the saints. Our acts are what we wear in honor of Jesus Christ. Don't be scantly clothed there.

These righteous deeds may indicate your place and rank at Jesus Christ's banquet table and eternity's roles of responsibilities. This goes along with Jesus's description of greatness equals servant of all.

How have you, are you, or will you honor God in testimony and deeds because according to this verse and in keeping with salvation by faith, it matters how we build on the gospel.

The prepared believers are blessed because they are given the right to partake of the marriage supper of the Lamb.

"And he saith unto me, Write, blessed *are* they which are called unto the marriage supper of the Lamb. And he saith unto me, these are the true sayings of God" (Revelation 19:9, KJV).

A privilege for the believers who are continuing in a relationship with Jesus Christ is that, in the future, they will enter the banquet of Jesus Christ or marriage supper of the Lamb. The verse tells us they are blessed. Oh, rejoice if you are born again. Let that inspire your faithfulness to Christ. The verse says that these are the true sayings of God, meaning that this surely will come to pass.

This is said because the world hates the believer; Jesus Christ has something special for them. If you've ever been to a wedding, there is anticipation. This is a wedding made in heaven.

If you enter, you must respond to God's invitation by personally receiving Jesus Christ as your Lord and Savior.

The prepared believer is blessed because they worship God, who gave them the testimony of Jesus Christ.

"And I fell at his feet to worship him. And he said unto me, see *thou do it* not: I am thy fellow servant, and of thy brethren that have the testimony of Jesus: worship God: for the testimony of Jesus is the spirit of prophecy" (Revelation 19:10, KJV).

The message of Revelation and any Christian message is a testimony of Jesus Christ if it's of God. As Jesus Christ's ambassadors, we point to him and not ourselves. All prophecy must have Jesus as the object of its message. We are to serve and worship God because we all are his servants. He alone purchased our salvation. We don't serve and worship the created order.

It has always been Satan's objective to cause God's creation to worship something other than God. Satan in Eden caused our parents to worship self and caused the fall.

Let's stop putting ourselves before salvation in Jesus Christ. Let's believe in Jesus Christ and be saved.

You can be prepared and blessed by responding to God's invitation to participate in his salvation and learn to yield to the supremacy of Jesus Christ while you have the opportunity.

A Literal Second Advent

Do you believe in Jesus Christ's Second Advent, or are you a scorner? Either you adhere to the Second Advent teaching and live appropriately and in faith, or you reject it and scorn or mock it, so you don't have to change. The fact of a literal Second Coming of Jesus Christ should change our lives.

According to Revelation 19:11–13, we can understand how Jesus Christ's Second Coming will happen. Let's look at how Jesus Christ's Second Advent will occur.

Jesus Christ comes through heaven's open door to judge and make war!

"And I saw heaven opened, and behold a white horse; and he that sat upon him *was* called Faithful and true, and in righteousness he doth judge and make war" (Revelation 19:11, KJV).

As this time period opened (called the seven-year tribulation), it began with Satan's man, the Antichrist coming to rule. He blasphemes God and leads a rebellion against him. Now at the close of this period, God the Son makes war against the enemies of God. Satan is overthrown, and Antichrist and the false prophet are cast into hell. When heaven opens, that is when God reveals the great Messiah. When Jesus Christ comes, he judges all the wicked, unrepentant and unbelievers. This is not a good time for God rejectors. Jesus Christ's true nature is faithful and true. This is made known at that time. The eternal Son of God, who makes war against God's enemies prevails.

Jesus Christ makes war and judges in righteousness because these cannot, nor will not repent, and they must be put out of the way for God's program to go forward. Such will be the fate of all who have rejected Jesus Christ as their Lord and Savior.

Jesus will be admired and worshiped, and his Church ruling with him. Do you want to be with his body of followers or standing in rebellion with Satan's lie (Antichrist)? Choose today who you will serve.

Jesus Christ comes in with majestic authority and dignity.

"His eyes *were* as flames of fire and on his head were many crowns; and he had a name written, that no man knew, but he himself" (Revelation 19:12, KJV).

When Jesus comes, the entire world weeps (nonbelievers) because their fate has come. Jesus sees with his penetrating eyes; they are judged and cast into Hades. The correct thinking is that they are killed and held in prison for judgment. He has a name that no one knows, meaning there are depths of Christ we don't know. Jesus has many crowns on his head. He is the undisputed King of kings, and quickly this will be revealed to the world when he throws in the sickle, and the sinners perish. Jesus has a name no one knows. This again shows that we apprehend some things about God but cannot comprehend him.

His splendor penetrates every heart of man. The Jews and Gentiles who follow Jesus Christ and survive the tribulation will enter, in the flesh, the millennial state. Yes, some will survive and be procreators of the millennial period.

Are you in denial? Do you think that the Second Coming is a fairy tale? You must repent of this scorner's attitude and purpose yourself to meet the King.

Jesus Christ comes as the one who suffered and yet now dips his vesture with the blood of his enemies.

"And he *was* clothed with a vesture dipped in blood: and his name is called The Word of God" (Revelation 19:13, KJV).

This one, who suffered at men's hands to redeem them from the fall, now comes in war and kills all who rejected his redemption and is splattered with their blood on his clothing. He is the Word of God, who made man, not for men to die and go to hell but for a godly and eternal purpose of life, love, and happiness. Despite all attempts to reconcile Christ's enemies to himself, they refuse to repent and turn to God by faith in Jesus. Jesus vesture is dipped in blood. Jesus suffered to save these unrepentant unbelievers and now kills them with his sword, and their blood spatters on his clothing. For two millennia, God's Word has gone out compelling and warning the unrepentant and unbelievers to repent and come to God through Jesus Christ. He told them to come unto him! They wouldn't, so the Word goes forth and kills them and says depart from me!

This departure is for all who reject Jesus and the good news. His spoken word and sheer brilliance will make this happen. No flesh can stand in God's presence. Those who are saved have God's seal of protection on them.

Will you be able to stand before Christ's presence to give account? You will indeed give account to God.

So know how the Second Coming of Jesus, which was anticipated in all ages, will happen. And let us prepare our hearts to meet our Maker.

Jesus has no equal.

Why do I say that Jesus has no equal? He alone leads the heavenly army. He alone defeats sin, wickedness, and all evildoers by his Word. He alone is worthy to open the scroll which determines earth's future. He alone can lock Satan up to stop his evil influence.

As we read Revelation 19:14–16, let us see how Jesus Christ leads his heavenly army to victory. Let's look at how this great victory comes about.

Jesus Christ's armies follow him to war.

"And the armies *which were* in heaven followed him upon white horses, clothed in fine linen, white and clean" (Revelation 19:14, KJV).

This army following Jesus Christ probably consists of both angels and saints. Saints are included according to Revelation 17:14 and have linen white and clean through Jesus Christ's sacrifice. The saints probably have multiple changes of clothes for various occasions. No one in Jesus Christ army lifts a finger; Jesus Christ does all the battling himself. The verse tells us the armies of heaven follow Jesus. Those, his saints, will come to rule with him on his behalf in different regions on earth. These saints were clothed in fine linen. They are radiant and clean, white! These are the garments given to those who believe in Jesus Christ. They wear the righteousness of Jesus Christ and are radiant with him at the Second Coming.

Can Jesus Christ do all the warfare himself, you might ask? He made all the heavens by his Word. It is by that same powerful Word that he shall speak against his enemies, and they will be struck down. A doctor laughed and argued with me saying to me that God cannot hear all the prayers of all people as they pray. As far as I know, he died an unbeliever. I bet in hell that he is attempting to pray to God now. We must make our peace with God in this life.

Why don't you pray to God while he can still be found? There might come a time he will no longer listen.

Jesus Christ strikes all the nations with the Word of his mouth.

"And out of his mouth goes a sharp sword, that with it he should smite the nations: and he shall rule them with a rod of iron: and he treads the winepress of the fierceness and wrath of Almighty God" (Revelation 19:15, KJV).

Jesus smites all people who rebelled against God so that they die. He also takes control of all nations. He kills countless ungodly persons. Jesus speaks with the sharp sword which comes out of his mouth, and the war is over. Jesus quickly gains control over all governments and rules them. Jesus also kills all who teamed up with the Antichrist.

We have been warned and told of God's coming kingdom and the destruction of the ungodly. It's up to us to repent and believe the good news. If you have heard the good news and have downplayed it, then who is at fault? God has been doing all that is possible to secure your salvation, but your response is no!

I urge you to receive Jesus Christ as your Lord and Savior personally. How shall you escape if you neglect so great a salvation?

Jesus Christ is proven the uncontested King of kings and Lord of lords.

"And he hath on *his* vesture and on his thigh a name written, KING OF KINGS, AND LORD OF LORDS" (Revelation 19:16, KJV).

John makes it clear that Jesus Christ stands alone with no equal. The Antichrist and the false prophet are no match and destroyed. Satan is locked up, and the Antichrist and false prophet are cast into eternal fire. All the best and most potent evil forces crumble and are blown away at Jesus Christ's presence. Jesus's name, King of kings and Lord of lords, is written on his thigh. This name speaks of Jesus having no equal or rival.

At this time, all evil has been adequately dealt with, and now God's plan goes ahead. God had intended good for his creation; the problem is that the creation has loved sin above God. It is at this time Jesus puts a stop to sins movement forward.

Know, therefore, that Jesus Christ shall break forth and set all affairs on earth in order. And he will destroy all who have rejected his redemptive work on their behalf. You should see to it that you take steps beyond salvation that allows Jesus Christ to be your Lord also so that you fulfill his will for your life.

Jesus Christ versus Antichrist

Who is going to win between Jesus and the lie (Antichrist)? The lie is Satan's infamous Antichrist. Jesus is the Son of God, who came from heaven. Let's see how Jesus Christ will destroy Antichrist.

We should know after reading Revelation 19:17–21, how the war goes between Jesus Christ and Antichrist. Let's see how the battle goes between Jesus Christ and Antichrist.

There is a call for the fowls to come to the supper of the great God.

> And I saw an angel standing in the sun; and he cried with a loud voice, saying to all the fowls that fly in the midst of heaven, Come and gather yourselves together unto the supper of the great God; That ye may eat the flesh of kings, and the flesh of captains, and the flesh of mighty men, and the flesh of horses, and of them that sit on them, and the flesh of all *men, both* free and bond, both small and great. (Revelation 19:17–18, KJV)

An angel summons the birds to gather from all the earth to eat the flesh of the destroyed army of Antichrist and of all the troops that came, which sought to make war against the Lamb of God. Angels go and summon the birds and beasts before the Antichrist's destruction. The supper of the great God is one of the suppers you don't want to be at. The animals will eat the flesh of the people who are led by Antichrist, who go forth to their death.

God's cleanup crew is summoned to clean up this refuge. Somehow all that blood and guts need to be purged. Birds and beasts will do it.

God prepares ahead of time the crew to clean up the earth after the battle with Antichrist occurs. They eat the flesh of captains, etc.; Antichrist's army will be destroyed.

The armies of the nations gather to fight against God.

"And I saw the beast, and the kings of the earth, and their armies, gathered together to make war against him that sat on the horse and against his army" (Revelation 19:19, KJV).

As Jesus Christ's coming in glory breaks forth; Antichrist turns with all the armies to make war on Jesus Christ. Picture the arrogance of this defeated deceiver leading millions out to their deaths. He knows they will all be destroyed, yet he leads them valiantly to their destruction. The opposition is the beast and the kings of the earth. The leaders of the planet don't want to hand over their authorities to their creator, nor Jerusalem. Gathered to make war against Jesus, these imbeciles are toast.

We are just as foolish, telling God to bug off and let us live our lives any way we see fit or choose to do.

Are you resisting God? Do you tell him off and to leave you alone? We must change this attitude and accept God's gift of life through Christ and his guidance for our lives through faith in him.

The beast and the false prophet are cast alive into eternal fire.

"And the beast was taken, and with him the false prophet that wrought miracles before him, with which he deceived them that had received the mark of the beast, and them that worshipped his image. These both were cast alive into a lake of fire burning with brimstone" (Revelation 19:20, KJV).

So what happens? Old Antichrist and the heroic false idiot or prophet were caught and cast alive into the lake of fire? The Antichrist and false prophet were castes into hell and never will they deceive again. Those who took the mark of the beast and worshiped him were killed.

Those who received the mark chose Satan permanently over God. That mark was Satan's permanent stamp of ownership over those persons. I believe they were cast into the lake of fire at Jesus Christ's Second Coming to.

It does not pay to join in Satan's rebellion against God. If you are rebelling against God, you're on Satan's side, whether you realize it or not.

The fowls become filled with the flesh of the remnant armies.

"And the remnant were slain with the sword of him that sat upon the horse, which *sword* proceeded out of his mouth: and all the fowls were filled with their flesh" (Revelation 19:21, KJV).

This defeat of all the nations' armies and of all persons who resist God and who rejected the gospel and who refused to repent was their deaths—all birds and animals gorge on their flesh. The remnant refers to all the unbelievers who made it through the tribulation and would not believe in Jesus Christ; they will be killed. Jesus will speak one word, and with the sword of his mouth, it will be over for those.

That's all it will take for Jesus to win. Jesus first came as a meek and humble suffering servant. Next time, he comes as the conquering King.

So contemplate whether it is worth you continually turning down opportunities to serve God and believe in Jesus Christ. Why don't you give Jesus your life since we are not guaranteed tomorrow?

Therefore, know what the outcome is going to be so that you and others can choose to repent and place your faith in Jesus Christ today.

CHAPTER 20

S atan's lockup.
    What is the purpose of locking Satan for a thousand years? Hasn't he done enough to warrant eternal fire? God must demonstrate to a man one more time how, even after a perfect environment. Without being born again, men will rebel against God.

In Revelation 20:1–3, we consider why Satan is locked up for a thousand years. It is necessary to understand Satan's thousand-year lockup and how it reflects men in a fallen state.

Man cannot make it if Satan is around.

"And I saw an angel come down from heaven, having the key of the bottomless pit and a great chain in his hand" (Revelation 20:1, KJV).

Jesus binds Satan to prove now that even after Satan is bound and man lives under complete social justice, depraved man will rebel given a chance to do so at a later time. It is the depravity of the heart. God sends an angel to lock up Satan. Man could not ward off Satan, and he needs God's intervention. For a thousand years, Satan will be locked up and not be able to lead men astray.

It has and will be proven that unless men let Jesus Christ change them from within, they will eventually turn on God and allow evil to dominate.

Each person must have a born-again experience. We must exercise a real walk with God.

Man will be given a thousand years to test his loyalty to God.

"And he laid hold on the dragon, that old serpent, which is the Devil, and Satan, and bound him a thousand years" (Revelation 20:2, KJV).

Satan is a real created being, the demonic foe of God, and his followers. He will pursue those who thought that they didn't need God in their hearts to rebel in a final battle with God. During the millennial period, many will not become born again who are physically born. At that time, Satan will deceive them, and they will perish. While the devil is locked up, men will have a period that will be uninfluenced by Satan to make up their minds who will be their god for eternity.

Men will fail because apart from Jesus living inside their hearts, it will be like the fall. No power inherent in man can stop Satan's wicked leading.

We see the same problem today and desperately need God to intervene. Call on him and seek out his will for your eternal security and power to say no to Satan.

Man will be kept from Satan's deception for a thousand years.

"And cast him into the bottomless pit, and shut him up, and set a seal upon him, that he should deceive the nations no more, till the thousand years should be fulfilled: and after that, he must be loosed a little season" (Revelation 20:3, KJV).

A thousand years, man will have the opportunity to be led by Jesus Christ and make up their mind to cleave to him; they fail. Satan is put out of the way for a utopian environment to demonstrate that even with that environment without the regenerating work of the Holy Spirit, men will live out their sin, unbelief, and rebellion.

Satan won't be there to deceive men; they deceived themselves by failing to believe and trust in Jesus Christ for their salvation and to live for him. This goes to show that man cannot direct his life and destiny apart from God or without God's help.

Let us turn our hearts to God for salvation and the help we need. God wants our loyalty to be to him.

Man will be led to rebel against God again.

Satan will be loosed one final time to lead astray those who wouldn't love the truth. They follow him to hell. After a thousand years have passed, Satan is set free again to lead souls to destruction. You better believe they are warned throughout the thousand years. It only takes a short time for Satan to raise a massive rebellion. All the unconverted will rebel against God to fight him to their deaths. A final rebellion is going to occur after a thousand years of peace.

You cannot know or serve God without a rebirth of Jesus Christ Spirit within you.

So know why Satan is bound for a thousand years. So men can be tested to determine who their allegiance is to and make a choice either for God's eternal reign through Jesus Christ or to reject him and suffer forever. Make the right choice today.

The saints will be ruling with Jesus Christ.

Can you accept that saints will rule with Jesus Christ? Jesus will exercise his authority through his ambassadors. He will accomplish his work through priests. Yes, Jesus will work through his faithful followers to keep the peace.

Revelation 20:4–6 shows us how saints will rule with Jesus Christ during his millennial reign. Let's see how saints come to rule and reign with Jesus Christ for a thousand years.

The Church is assigned positions of authority.

> And I saw thrones, and they sat upon them, and judgment was given unto them: and *I saw* the souls of them that were beheaded for the witness of Jesus, and the word of God, and which had not worshipped the beast, neither his image, neither had received *his* mark upon their foreheads or in their hands; and they lived and reigned with Christ a thousand years. (Revelation 20:4, KJV)

John seems to be expressing the authority and positions that the followers of Jesus Christ will be given in the millennium. This includes the Church age and saints of the tribulation. Thrones indicate power and areas given. It is my opinion that they that sat upon the thrones are the redeemed saints. They exercise authority and judgment.

One might ask, "Is this all there is?" No says the apostle, John. The saints have a great future! The reign and rule with Jesus Christ. Jesus is going to assign responsibilities to his faithful. This is a grand thought to rule God's creation with and for Jesus Christ.

If we would aspire to be usable in a significant way, then let us put God's work first in our lives now! We must do so before we give an account of ourselves. This will impact our influence then.

The tribulation saints and Old Testament saints reign after the tribulation with Jesus Christ also.

After the tribulation, if I'm correct, Old Testament saints and tribulation saints are resurrected to join with Jesus and his spiritual hosts to reign in the millennial kingdom. These are those who rejected Antichrist's mark and refused to worship Antichrist. Many of these saints were beheaded. A key knowledge about the tribulation is that to consummate your salvation; you may have to die for your faith. These saints had not worshiped the beast. These tribulation saints were martyred because they refused to worship Antichrist.

They would not cooperate with the notorious false prophet; therefore, they were slaughtered by the thousands or millions. Know, therefore, to acquire salvation in the tribulation requires often one to die for their faith.

Don't wait for the tribulation before you make your decision. Choose today and escape this time of horror!

Woe to those who die in their sin.

"But the rest of the dead lived not again until the thousand years were finished. This *is* the first resurrection" (Revelation 20:5, KJV).

Unbelievers that die in their sin, having rejected the good news, will miss out on the first resurrection. Thus, they stay in the grave in torment until the great white throne judgment where they are consigned to the great lake of fire. They have been postponed until sentenced to the second death. The great white throne judgment is a resurrection unto continues death.

Those who refused to believe the good news in this probationary period are eternally separated from God because of rejecting God's offer of reconciliation. Jesus did the work necessary to reconcile us to

God. They said no to it by rejecting their need for Jesus Christ and his atoning work at Calvary on their behalf.

Do not put off making your choice for Jesus Christ. It will not get easier in the tribulation but harder to make this choice.

God blesses anyone who takes part in the first resurrection.

"Blessed and holy *is* he that hath part in the first resurrection: on such the second death hath no power, but they shall be priests of God and of Christ, and shall reign with him a thousand years" (Revelation 20:6, KJV).

The second death is where unbelievers are resurrected and consigned to the lake of fire eternally. It is a blessing to be part of the first resurrection where those saints get to forever be part of God's plan. They will be priests unto God. They will do the bidding or work of God on behalf of other people. They will be instruments in the millennial kingdom to woe people to God.

Those who take part in the first resurrection are corulers with Christ in the millennial kingdom. They shall reign with Christ a thousand years. There is going to be a kingdom of righteousness coming.

Do you want to reign with Christ in this coming kingdom? I encourage you to lay down your life for Christ's cause now!

Know, therefore, that saints will rule with Jesus Christ in the millennial kingdom; you are choosing whether you'll be a part of this kingdom.

Consider Satan's End

How will it fair for Satan and those who follow him? Do you want to go where Satan goes? Do you want to end your way as he does? Consider then how it ends for Satan and his followers.

In Revelation 20:7–10, we consider how it ends with Satan and those who follow him. Let's look at how it ends for Satan and his followers.

At the end of the millennial dispensation, multitudes will rise in revolt against God (Jesus Christ) after they allow Satan to deceive and lead them.

"And when the thousand years are expired, Satan shall be loosed out of his prison, And shall go out to deceive the nations which are in the four quarters of the earth, Gog and Magog, to gather them together to battle: the number of whom *is* as the sand of the sea" (Revelation 20:7–8, KJV).

It is after a thousand years, God releases Satan to prove the prevalence of the depraved human heart, which, even after Jesus Christ rules, decides that they want existence without God or his control over them. They allow Satan to deceive them and join in revolt with him against God. Satan will be locked up to prove that even a change of environment can't solve man's sinful tendencies. To deceive the nations, Satan goes forth again. We are not in the millennial reign at this time, but what you do concerning Jesus and Satan, right and wrong, good and evil, will be examined one day.

These millions of people revolt because they do not heed the warning that God had given them. Stay close to God and continue in his Word. A child's natural tendency is to walk away from his or her parent and to fall into all manner of mischief. God will show that that is the case with all men.

We must guard our heart and take ourselves by the nape of the neck and make ourselves follow God.

The end of those who follow Satan is a tragedy to their souls.

"And they went up on the breadth of the earth and compassed the camp of the saints about, and the beloved city: and fire came down from God out of heaven and devoured them" (Revelation 20:9, KJV).

It's the same with all who allow themselves to follow Satan's deception. The lake of fire is their end; that is because of Satan and his fallen demons condition, mold, and fashion satanic collaborators to rebel against God. This is to their eternal destruction. Fire comes down and quickly destroys these dissenters.

Satan is going to hell and is going to take out all he can. In Luke 13:1–5, Jesus tells the people that unless they repent, they will all likewise perish.

Who have you decided to follow? If you follow yourself, flesh, world, or a false spirit, then you will die and go to hell. You must turn to God through faith in Jesus Christ.

Satan, along with all who follow him, will be tormented at all times forever.

"And the devil that deceived them was cast into the lake of fire and brimstone, where the beast and the false prophet *are*, and shall be tormented day and night for ever and ever" (Revelation 20:10, KJV).

The end quest Satan brings all who follow him to eternity in the lake of fire. If the devil is cast into the lake of fire at this time, then what is the use in following this rebellion that ends up burning its adherents? This is a torment that is day and night, and it is forever.

Satan has tried all these centuries to force God's hand into a position where he must change his mind. God is always right and never had to correct himself. Repent because hell lasts just as long as heaven. God made you for heaven, will you choose heaven? All who go to hell decide to go there.

Therefore, consider Satan's end and how his followers fair. Make your choice for eternity and strive to walk in that choice.

The Dead Outside of Jesus Christ

What happens to those outside of Jesus Christ? Do they have a bright future? Will they hold to positions after Jesus Christ reigns? Let's look at the future of all who are outside of Jesus Christ.

You can know what happens to those who die outside of Jesus Christ by reading Revelation 20:11–15. Let's examine what happens to those who die without putting their faith in Jesus Christ.

God almighty judges those who die outside of Jesus Christ.

"And I saw a great white throne, and him that sat on it, from whose face the earth and the heaven fled away; and there was found no place for them" (Revelation 20:11, KJV).

Here is the Revelation picture of the great white throne judgment. We see that the glory and terror of God almighty cause the heavens and earth to disappear forever. This is the one who sent Jesus Christ to redeem humanity. God judges the many who rejected Jesus Christ and his sacrifice for their sin and said no to God. Now all those who rejected God's offer of mercy must stand before him and receive their sentence of eternal damnation. Here is the great white throne. Could it be that the pure brilliance now illuminates all things and reproves the dark hearts of those who will be judged? All of the earth gives up its dead to be judged, and then the earth disappears. If a soul has not received Jesus Christ as their Lord and Savior, they shall be judged at this judgment.

We must pass this probationary period by receiving and believing on the Lord Jesus Christ and what he did on our behalf. Failure to do so means we failed the purpose of our probationary period (to learn to exercise faith in God). Every day is a choice to make Jesus your Lord if you have not done so yet, and it's a chance to be a servant who is faithful to God.

All judgment will be based on those two criteria. Have you thought about how your life has been lived out? Has your life reflected God the way Jesus expressed it through his life? It's not too late to turn to God and believe in Jesus Christ and make some changes.

Every dead person will give an account of their rejection of Jesus Christ and all the wicked deeds they had done.

> And I saw the dead, small and great, stand before God; and the books were opened: and another book was opened, which is *the book* of life: and the dead were judged out of those things which were written in the books, according to their works. And the sea gave up the dead who were in it, and death and hell delivered up the dead who were in them: and they were judged every man according to their works. (Revelation 20:12–13, KJV)

Here the dead are those outside of Jesus Christ. They died in their sinful and unforgiven state because they rejected the good news. The books were opened, which recorded their deeds, and they were judged for the degree of eternal punishment. The book of life was opened to show that none of these placed their faith in Jesus Christ. All the dead who die outside of faith in Jesus Christ stand before God to give account to God for their behavior at this great white throne judgment. They are judged according to their works. This cannot mean that if they do well enough, then they will enter heaven. Instead, the actions they did prepares the degrees of punishment received because they rejected heaven by rejecting Jesus Christ.

God is not unjust in this because they had all their life to choose Jesus. How shall we escape if we neglect so great a salvation? How can we avoid the condemnation of hell for rejecting Jesus Christ?

You must choose Jesus or Satan. Will you choose today?

All who reject Jesus Christ will be cast into the eternal lake of fire because they were not found in the Lamb's book of life.

"And death and hell were cast into the lake of fire. This is the second death. And whosoever was not found written in the book of life was cast into the lake of fire" (Revelation 20:14–15, KJV).

We must enter into a personal relationship with Jesus Christ, and then our life will be recorded in the Lamb's book of Life. To put this off is to continue to say no.

Those who said no were cast into the lake of fire. They were thrown into the lake of fire violently. Whoever was not written in the Lamb's book of life suffers this fate, both small and significant.

There is no more place for them in God's program because they said no to God and his will for their lives.

Think about this before you despise God's grace again. Turn to God and live. Do not choose eternal punishment as your option instead of God's plans for you.

Therefore, by knowing what happens to those who die outside of Jesus Christ, we should receive Jesus Christ as our Lord and Savior and commit our lives to him in love and service.

DIVISION 3

The Future State

CHAPTER 21

G od's vision for the believer.
What hope has God laid out for his followers? Is it just a place with no torment? Is it just a gathering place? God has a great future for his followers.

As we read Revelation 21:1–4, we come to know what God's vision is for man. Let's look at what God's vision is for humanity.

God's vision is for man to live in a sinless state and on a new unpolluted earth.

"And I saw a new heaven and a new earth: for the first heaven and the first earth were passed away; and there was no more sea" (Revelation 21:1, KJV).

God presents heaven and his creation with a marvelous new earth. The old earth and heavens have passed away. This earth has no sin or corruption or anything to remind the people of God about the sorrows of past rebellion; everything is in a perfected state. The Bible says it's "new heaven." The astronomer would love to see what God is going to make. The olden days have gone including the old heaven and earth. There remains nothing to remind us of the previous days, except the nail-scarred hands of Jesus Christ.

That sinless state will be our new nature because God lives with his creation. Where God dwells, sin cannot. All creation will be new.

This is a place where all people's dreams come true. Will you be there?

God will bring heaven to be a part of this new earth permanently.

"And I John saw the holy city, New Jerusalem, coming down from God out of heaven, prepared as a bride adorned for her husband" (Revelation 21:2, KJV).

After the earth is replaced or renovated, God will bring the holy city upon the planet and will dwell with humankind forever. It is impossible to imagine the scope of all that will take place during that long eternal journey. Make sure you're a part of it. When the holy city comes to earth, God is going to make his abode with us literally. God also patiently waits, and as he consummates all things, so his city will be among men.

There are two eternal journeys to choose from heaven or hell; they both go on forever. One is good, and the other is bad. What choice do you make? Eternal joy (faith in Jesus Christ) or eternal punishment (rejection of Jesus Christ), these are our choices. Which is for you?

Let's come to God by faith in Jesus Christ so we can participate in this tremendous eternal joy. This is what God made us for.

God will take up residency with humanity on this new earth.

"And I heard a great voice out of heaven saying, Behold, the tabernacle of God is with men, and he will dwell with them, and they shall be his people, and God himself shall be with them, *and be* their God" (Revelation 21:3, KJV).

God comes with all of heaven to dwell with man. Do you see why having God in your life means everything to you? He is our hope of this grand eternal vision. The verse declares that the tabernacle of God is with men. God will be with us and be our God.

This is God's vision, and he is in the process of bringing it to pass. Paul said this world is passing away.

Are we growing in the things of God then? Put the struggle and effort to grow in Jesus Christ.

God will wipe all tears away because the former things are no more.

"And God shall wipe away all tears from their eyes; and there shall be no more death, neither sorrow, nor crying, neither shall there be any more pain: for the former things are passed away" (Revelation 21:4, KJV).

At this time, God will wipe away every remembrance of the pain and struggle that sin and Satan attacked us with. There will be no more death; people will go on and live forever. There will be no more pain. Nothing will ever grieve us because the former things have passed away.

This will be the eternal state of those who place their hope of eternal life in Jesus Christ. God will wipe away all tears. Humanity cannot make up such a grand vision. This revelation is God interposing on man's behalf.

Do you choose God's vision? Make a choice today. Both life and death are before you. Make sure you know what you prefer.

So now that we acquired what God's vision is for man, a precious eternity with love, life, power, and all good things. Why would we tell God no and choose Satan over this opportunity?

Participation in God's New Order

Will you be a part of God's new order that is coming? Can you imagine yourself in God's new heaven and new earth? Can you see yourself within a heaven and earth that has everything new in it? Let's look at how you can be a part of the new order.

In Revelation 21:5–8, we learn how we can participate in the coming new created order of God. Let's see how we can join the new created order.

God says that a newly created order will emerge.

"And he that sat upon the throne said, Behold, I make all things new. And he said unto me, write for these words are true and faithful" (Revelation 21:5, KJV).

We have heard men say things like "it is a new world order," etc. Such things mean nothing until God steps in with his plans. Men have tried to change the world but miserably failed 100 percent of the time. God failed zero times. It is the true and faithful one who backs up the Word with power. God says to behold because he makes all things new. I don't know about you, but I can't wait to see God's new created order. Everything today will be gone. God will keep his promise, and he will not suffer us to be in the pain of remodeling the old.

After God's creation of humankind has emerged from the order that's awaiting the manifestation of the sons of God, God will unfold eternity's plans for us.

I don't know about you, but I want to participate in this plan. Will you ask God to save you and be a participator?

Participants must partake of God's offer through the person of Jesus Christ.

"And he said unto me, it is done. I am Alpha and Omega, the beginning and the end. I will give unto him that is athirst of the fountain of the water of life freely" (Revelation 21:6, KJV).

God's design and plan as the originator and completer is "it is done!" It is going to come to pass; you can be sure God will keep his Word. God will give of this plan and program to whoever asks God through Jesus Christ. Jesus is the beginning and the end, the originator of all things and concluder of things also. That's why we must ask Jesus to make a place for us in his program.

The invitation is good if you respond and do it promptly; putting it off is saying no to the opportunity before you.

Again, I say ask Jesus into your life and let him bear your sin burden. He will make you ready for heaven.

The responsibility of the participant is to overcome to receive the heavenly privilege.

"He that overcomes shall inherit all things; and I will be his God, and he shall be my son" (Revelation 21:7, KJV).

God says you can be his child and inherit all he has planned for you if you will overcome. To overcome means to press on in faith in the reliance of Jesus Christ and his sacrifice on your behalf. The condition is that you be sure you remain in Jesus Christ and be active in him. Keep believing that he is God the Son, and he will keep his promise of saving those who believe. God is offering to you himself and all he has.

Do you long for God and his provision? To have God is to obtain infinite eternal value. Satan overthrew himself by rejecting the true God and life; he, thus, lost all of God's will.

Don't throw away this opportunity before you. Be responsible for overcoming in Jesus Christ, and you will obtain.

Those who refuse to repent and believe in Jesus Christ will not enter the new order but be consigned to eternal hell.

"But the fearful, and unbelieving, and the abominable, and murderers, and whoremongers, and sorcerers, and idolaters, and all liars, shall have their part in the lake which burns with fire and brimstone: which is the second death" (Revelation 21:8, KJV).

The second death is defined; it is eternal separation from God, his will, his people, his plan for your life, and to be tormented by fire for eternity! All who have rejected repentance and faith in Jesus Christ will suffer this fate. Therefore, any fear, liars, and whoremongers, etc. will miss God's good will. Anyone who sins and won't repent and turn to Jesus Christ will go to the second death. Those who refuse God will be set apart for destruction.

Because they said no, they choose to live in eternity without God. Their choice, nor do they want to change it. Eternity will not change their wills.

You can reach your community for Jesus if you so choose. Show them how to receive Jesus Christ and go to heaven.

Participate in the coming new created order by God. If you RSVP, you can avoid the evil snares.

Visualize Heaven

Can we imagine what heaven is like? What if we could picture heaven in our minds? Would you contemplate being part of it? Let's attempt to grasp an understanding of heaven.

We should want to visualize the characteristics of the eternal city. As we read Revelation 21:9–14, let's see what overarching features this City has.

Only those that are holy will even have a chance to look upon this city.

"And there came unto me one of the seven angels which had the seven vials full of the seven last plagues, and talked with me, saying, come hither, I will show thee the bride, the Lamb's wife. And he carried me away in the spirit to a great and high mountain, and showed me that great city, the holy Jerusalem, descending out of heaven from God" (Revelation 21:9–10, KJV).

John was privileged to view the holy city. But it was an angel who poured out plagues that showed John the city. Hence, all those who were overthrown by the diseases will never see the city. The angel told John to come, and he would show him the city. It will be a privilege for all those who view this city, for only God's saved and faithful people will see it. John was allowed to view the eternal city. This is the secret hope God places in men's hearts too long for this as their home. Not all will make it there.

No unclean thing can look at or enter the holy city. The next couple of passages demonstrate its brilliance.

It is worth your effort to make peace with God through Jesus Christ, so you can see the city.

To look upon the city is to view most precious things.

"Having the glory of God: and her light *was* like unto a stone most precious, even like a jasper stone, clear as crystal" (Revelation 21:11, KJV).

The greatness and brilliance of the heavenly city will be breathtaking. God's glory will radiate through and from it. It will appear to be a wonder of the most precious jewel. The city shines with the glory of God. God's brilliance is what lights the whole city like a precious jewel. To behold it will be grand. It will be translucent and pure. Can you imagine being a citizen of such a place? This is God's best for those daring and willing to follow Jesus. Have you yet decided to follow Jesus?

Would you love to see this breathtaking holy heavenly city? Commit yourself to the King of the city and follow him and his ways. He said no man could come to the Father but through him.

The city's walls and gates (named after the tribes of Israel) are incredibly high.

"And had a wall great and high, *and* had twelve gates, and at the gates twelve angels, and names written thereon, which are *the names* of the twelve tribes of the children of Israel: On the east three gates;

on the north three gates; on the south three gates; and on the west three gates" (Revelation 21:12–13, KJV).

The walls and gates make the city impenetrable (because of God, of course), but it means that never, never, ever will any unholy or unclean thing enter her. The twelve gates are ascribed with the twelve tribes of Israel. The high walls show it to be a mighty fortress. It has twelve foundations because such a city would need a strong foundation, which consists of twelve layers ascribed to the twelve apostles.

Can you imagine these walls 1,580 miles high? What can penetrate that mainly when God protects the city?

You have a choice to be inside or outside the city. It all depends on your response to the good news.

The city's foundations are twelve foundations (named after the twelve apostles).

"And the wall of the city had twelve foundations and in them the names of the twelve apostles of the Lamb" (Revelation 21:14, KJV).

The twelve foundations are earmarked with the names of the twelve apostles in remembrance of their sacrifice to Jesus. Can you believe they would have their names there? Serving God is a memorial of what God has done through you.

Let's consider giving our lives in service to God. God will remember you for it.

So conceptualize what it will be like in this great city and allow yourself to be stirred to get real with God.

The Eternal City

What is the eternal city like? Is it like an earthly city? Are there things unique to it? The eternal city is unique.

Revelation 21:15–21 helps us know what characteristics are specific to the eternal city. Let's see what aspects are particular to the eternal city.

The city is extremely large.

"And he that talked with me had a golden reed to measure the city, and the gates thereof, and the wall thereof. And the city lieth foursquare and the length is as large as the breadth: and he measured the city with the reed, twelve thousand furlongs. The length and the breadth and the height of it are equal" (Revelation 21:15–16, KJV).

This city seems to be a huge cube. Perhaps that on every level there are floors? The walls are approximately 1,400 miles in width, length, and height. This is a vast city which could be compared to the size of the USA. The walls and gates (with angels guarding them) stress that no unclean thing shall enter. We are made able to come through Jesus Christ's shed blood on our behalf.

This city has all the traffic of God's holy angels and humans doing God's business throughout the heavens. Perhaps they report back to God on the work.

We will be a part of this in Jesus Christ. Let's do business for him now.

The walls and design of the city are unique.

"And he measured the wall thereof, a hundred *and* forty *and* four cubits, *according* to the measure of a man, that is, of the angel. And the building of the wall of it was *of* jasper: and the city *was* pure gold, like unto clear glass" (Revelation 21:17–18, KJV).

Everything about this city, its walls, streets of gold, size, shape, the people, it's brilliance, all demonstrates that it is the abode of God and his people. It has walls of jasper, and it's a city of pure gold. This all speaks of the royalty and glory of the Creator and his holiness and majesty! The Lord God Almighty reigns! It's incredibly unique because God lives there, holy people live there, brilliance is there, and it's the most crucial place in the universe. The walls are 144 cubits or two-hundred-foot-thick beautiful Jasper stone for decoration. The city is made of pure gold, demonstrating royalty.

The people there are God, angels, the redeemed of the earth, as well as other created beings. God made all this for his eternal pleasure and purpose.

Please be a member and participator in this city! You must respond to the invitation of receiving Jesus Christ as your Lord and Savior to enter.

The foundations are designed with unique types of stones.

> And the foundations of the wall of the city *were* garnished with all manner of precious stones. The first foundation *was* jasper; the second, sapphire; the third, a chalcedony; the fourth, an emerald; The fifth, sardonyx; the sixth, sardius; the seventh, chrysolite; the eighth, beryl; the ninth, a topaz; the tenth, chrysoprase; the eleventh, a jacinth; the twelfth, an amethyst. (Revelation 21:19–20, KJV)

These stones may be hard to find throughout the universe, but for the heavenly city, it's no problem for God. God provides according to his will. The city is filled with every kind of precious stone. Precious means of a high value costly. Every foundation had a covering with its precious stone.

The uniqueness of the followers of Jesus is that their names are bountifully remembered on these foundations. God built the city, and he calls or called his people, twelve disciples, and all others, and he knows how to honor their labor and decision for him.

Followers of God are precious, and they are covered with the righteousness of Jesus Christ. God has an eternal plan for them.

The gates are designed out of pearl.

"And the twelve gates *were* twelve pearls; every several gates was of one pearl: and the street of the city *was* pure gold, as it were transparent glass" (Revelation 21:21, KJV).

These substances are things we have not acquainted with super large pearls and transparent gold. So heaven will be a place with substances that are not yet known to man. Yet all the highest value! Each of the twelve gates is made of a single pearl! Now where did that come from? God must have made it. They are pure goldlike transparent glass! The gold is so pure that you can see through it!

Heaven is a place only holy beings' dwell. This is God's best for those who follow Jesus Christ. To follow Jesus Christ is a response and decision you must make to the good news.

Time is running out. Will you decide to receive Jesus Christ as your Lord, Savior, and follow him?

So contemplate the characteristics of the heavenly city, so you stay motivated to press on in your discipleship to Jesus Christ.

God Is the Life of the Future

What role does God play in the new earth and the eternal city? God is the life of the city and the new earth. He is the light of the city and the new earth. God will be the all preserving element for eternal things (things that last forever).

In Revelation 21:22–27, we learn that God is the life-giving essence of the eternal city. Let's look at how God is the essence of the eternal city.

The temple of the eternal city is God himself.

"And I saw no temple therein: for the Lord God Almighty, and the Lamb are the temple of it" (Revelation 21:22, KJV).

The center of Jewish life was centered around the temple of God. Now being in heaven is centered around God himself as the temple of worship is himself within the eternal city. John said he did not see a temple. No sacrifices are going on there. For all that enter, there have been cleansed by Jesus Christ's blood. The Lord God Almighty and the Lamb are the temple! The Lord God Almighty and the Lamb will be the center of activity and worship and reverence! People will come in their processions to worship God.

This is because, at the heart of the earthly temple, services were the worship and reverence of God. The whole design and purpose of the temple was God's plan, to set people right with himself and to be worshipped by the people.

How can anyone like heaven or enter there who does not love God! It will be well if we make our peace with God now!

The light of the eternal city is God himself.

"And the city did not need of the sun, neither of the moon, to shine in it: for the glory of God did lighten it, and the Lamb is the light thereof" (Revelation 21:23, KJV).

Every square inch of the eternal city will radiate the glory of God, and that glory will light up every room and space. No need for a sun or moon because God determines all set times, seasons, and events. God's glory causes all manner of osmosis needed to produce any life required. Life comes from him. The brilliance of God and the Lamb lights up the city.

This is the natural light of God. At that time, that should be in our hearts today. The light that lights our path.

Let God illuminate your life. Study the Word daily and turn on the light in your soul. You'll find God's light will radiate through you.

The eternal city will be the guiding light and principle for all nations.

"And the nations of them which are saved shall walk in the light of it: and the kings of the earth do bring their glory and honor into it" (Revelation 21:24, KJV).

This city will be the center metropolitan of the new earth, and all inhabitants will pour all their best gifts into it. The nations will walk by the light of God radiating from the eternal city. God will radiate all over the earth from the city to give the inhabitants light. The nations will bring in their best offerings. The people will offer their very best unto the Lord and his holy city.

The principle is that of offering our very best to God and what can we do for the joy of the King of kings and Lord of lords? This type of thinking will be the joy of the earth's inhabitants.

This needs to be our mind-set today! How can I offer my best in service for the glory of God?

The city gates will always be open for the nations to bring in their glory and honor into it.

"And the gates of it shall not be shut at all by day: for there shall be no night there. And they shall bring the glory and honor of the nations into it" (Revelation 21:25–26, KJV).

All nations will work to produce their best services in hopes of presenting them to the king. The best of the countries will come and be given to God. Everyone's very best is brought, and know that this will bring God's very best for them! The heavenly city will always be open for this transaction!

No sleep may be needed anymore. The rest will be as natural as breathing.

What are we offering to God that he will pour his favor into our lives? He who is faithful with small things unto God will be blessed with the larger. No wonder they work their tails off to present their best to God; God is the source of life and all good things. Is serving God the center of our motives? To serve him not for the blessings, although God blesses us abundantly, we serve God because it's part of our love and worship to him.

The city will not permit any person who is vile or unsaved to enter it.

"And there shall in no wise enter into it anything that defiles, neither *whatsoever* worketh abomination, or *market* a lie: but they which are written in the Lamb's book of life" (Revelation 21:27, KJV).

If there is any evil on earth, it will not enter the eternal city! Nothing impure shall come. This city is like living with pure oxygen in all aspects. As John again mentions the Lamb's book of life, I believe John is telling us the importance of getting our names written in the book during our earthly probationary period. Our eternity is at stake; if we want to be a part of God's plan, repent toward God and believe in Jesus Christ.

Let us realize that after our probationary period (this life), our eternity is set! We can't change it afterward. Therefore, we know enough to get right with God by repenting and exercising faith in Jesus Christ. The book of Revelation is about getting right with Jesus now and enduring in faith in him to the end!

Please take the opportunity to receive Jesus as your Lord and Savior. As you invite Jesus into your heart, a spiritual transaction takes place, and your name is written in the Lamb's book of life. You will have a place reserved for you in the eternal city.

So know that God is the life-giving essence of the new earth and it's godly new Jerusalem. Let this cause you to pursue God.

CHAPTER 22

G od's sustainment method.
How will God sustain his new earth? Will he make it like earth as we know it? Will it support all life? Earth's the prototype of what heaven is. God is sustaining all things.

We learn in Revelation 22:1–5 how God will sustain the nations of the new earth. Let's see how God will sustain the countries of the new earth.

The river of life will proceed from God's throne.

"And he shewed me a pure river of water of life, clear as crystal, proceeding out of the throne of God and of the Lamb" (Revelation 22:1, KJV).

Here again we see the ruler of the universe, the Lord God Almighty sustaining all things, and now we know the origination of the water of life. It comes from the throne of God. The water is pure and clear as crystal. The pureness of God purifies the water I presume. Somehow this river that flows from the throne is life-giving and sustains the nations. God is the water's source, and the water comes from his throne.

It seems fitting that such water originates from God. People have always sought life-giving water.

Will you be partaking of the water of eternal life? If you turn to Jesus Christ, then he will be this source in you.

Many trees of life produce fruit and leaves for healing the nations.

"In the midst of the street of it, and on either side of the river, *was there* the tree of life, which bare twelve *manner of* fruits, *and*

12

yielded her fruit every month: and the leaves of the tree *were* for the healing of the nations" (Revelation 22:2, KJV).

God has a unique sustainment system that the earth modeled in a fallen way. Life-giving trees to nourish the nations are on each side of the river. Down the middle of the street is this great river of life. It flows somehow in the street, possibly a gutter in the center. The trees of life are sustaining tree that gives fruit and leaves for healing the nations. These leaves and fruit will be the medicine for the countries.

No doubt that there will be representatives picking up their rations of fruit and leaves so that they can be sustained.

Would you like to taste of this tree? Let's strive to enter in. Push in through faith in Jesus Christ. That is, let us continue in faith in Jesus Christ.

No more curse will be on the people.

"And there shall be no more curse: but the throne of God and the Lamb shall be in it, and his servants shall serve him" (Revelation 22:3, KJV).

There will be no curse in the city because all people will be doing God's perfect will. All people will joyfully be serving the Lord. Sin and disobedience will not be present because the throne of God and the Lamb shall be in the city, and God's presence will assure holiness. God will have a lot going on and his servants will do his bidding.

This service will be the highest goal of our existence. Today, to serve God and others is our most top objective.

Do you share this attitude? Perhaps it's time to make an attitude adjustment. Yes, God helps us in all of life, so let's be glad to serve God and love others.

Each person shall have God's name written on their forehead.

"And they shall see his face; and his name *shall be* in their foreheads" (Revelation 22:4, KJV).

Each person will be given a name only they know, and God's name identifies them as belonging to God. Each one of these persons will personally see, know, and worship God. God's name will personally be written upon them.

This means they are identified as God's very own children. Between parent and child is attachment and a certain sharing of life, etc. We will have such attachment with God, as well as him living within us.

It is expedient to identify with Jesus Christ and to stand for God here and now; then on that day, God will stand for you.

God will be the light for all people.

"And there shall be no night there, and they need no candle, neither light of the sun; for the Lord God giveth them light: and they shall reign forever and ever" (Revelation 22:5, KJV).

The climax of why Revelation was taught to the early suffering Christians is the truth and vision of the fact that along with Jesus Christ, they also will reign forever and forever in God's brightness. The verse tells us that God will be our light. We function at our best when under God's presence. The vision is that the saints reign forever with Christ. This is the vision for those who endure for Jesus to the end.

Since this is an age of persecution, our future will be that of the ruling. This is the reversal of roles at the end of the age.

Keep pressing on in Jesus Christ, even if it costs you your life. Then you will reign with Jesus Christ.

So take note of the eternities sustainment method set up by God. This is better than the suffering of those who reject the plan of God. Choose wisely who you will serve.

You're choosing your eternal disposition now.

How do you want to be known in eternity? A bum on the street begging? Would you like to be an authoritative ruler? You are choosing your role by your response in this life.

In Revelation 22:6–11, we see that we are determining our eternal disposition right now. Let's see why choosing God's path is essential to a beautiful destiny.

Very shortly, destinies will be sealed.

"And he said unto me, these sayings *are* faithful and true: and the Lord God of the holy prophets sent his angel to shew unto his servants the things which must shortly be done" (Revelation 22:6, KJV).

God is sending this message within the book of Revelation to warn us to both get saved and get prepared. God is the God of the prophets. God inspires true prophecy. God shows the future to various individuals. Those who follow God will undergo suffering, but God has a glorious ending prepared for them and retribution upon their enemies. Soon all these things in the book of Revelation will come to pass. We must not delay putting our spiritual house in order.

This prophecy seals eternal destinies! To those who heed and respond, there will be a glorious future. But to those who dismiss this as fanaticism, there will be a tragic ending.

What eternal ending are you writing for yourself by your response? Make sure you know what you're choosing.

You do well to allow God's Word to pursued you to live godly.

"Behold, I come quickly: blessed *is* he that keepeth the sayings of the prophecy of this book" (Revelation 22:7, KJV).

By keeping the words of the prophecy of this book, you prepare and keep your spiritual house in order. Read this book to prepare for the end and to live with zeal for Jesus Christ and to warn others. Jesus says that he is coming soon. Jesus was speaking and expressing that he will soon appear and take his people out, then the end will run its course, meaning the tribulation will happen, and everything in the book of Revelation will happen. You will be blessed if you keep the words of the book of Revelation. Act on what you hear!

Let this book sink deep into your heart and inspire you to follow more earnestly the master, Jesus Christ. Our call is to be saved, follow Jesus, make disciples, and warn others.

How will you respond to the book of Revelation? What changes, steps, and goals must you implement to grow into the type of person Jesus Christ is calling you to be?

Each of us is called to worship and serve God as our reason for being.

"And I John saw these things and heard *them*. And when I had heard and seen, I fell down to worship before the feet of the angel which shewed me these things. Then saith he unto me, see *thou do it* not: for I am thy fellow servant, and of thy brethren the prophets, and of them which keep the sayings of this book: worship God" (Revelation 22:8–9, KJV).

We should be inspired through this book to live lives that honor and worship God. Just as John fell to pray a created person and was rebuked, make sure you do not do that. If your godly, you'll refuse to worship others or be worshiped from anyone else and direct them to worship the one true God.

We are created to worship Jehovah God only. I fear many, even myself, has not been prompt enough to worship God.

Set specific times aside daily to worship God. This will fulfill your reason for being.

We are warned of the nearness of when the things in the book of Revelation will come to pass.

"And he saith unto me, Seal not the sayings of the prophecy of this book: for the time is at hand" (Revelation 22:10, KJV).

Revelation is a stern warning to keep our hearts right with God. I beg you to examine your heart and life and adjust according to God's Word. This book was not sealed up so that we could read and take heed. The book of Revelation is understandable. We are warned that the events are imminently near.

This warning is to prepare us to walk in fear of God. The fear of God must cause us to adjust and develop.

Will you get to and stay in a state of readiness? This is the response that God is seeking.

Each person will go living either by good persuasion or bad until the end, and in such, a state will their eternal state be sealed forever.

"He that is unjust, let him be unjust still: and he which is filthy, let him be filthy still: and he that is righteous, let him be righteous always: and he that is holy, let him be holy always" (Revelation 22:11, KJV).

What is the persuasion you allow yourself to live under? That will be the nature and character of your eternal settings. Those who do wrong and those who do right are encouraged to continue to do so that they may receive their reward. God will come back and catch everyone within the context of what they allow their hearts to follow. You are choosing who your master will be.

These works adorn your eternal disposition forever. If you're going to heaven and you slacked off toward God's cause on earth, you'll be known by that in heaven.

Put forth your very best as unto the Lord.

Therefore, realize that you, while in your earthly sojourn, are determining your eternal disposition! Make the very best of it.

Turning to Christ

Is it too late to turn to Jesus? You can still respond to God's invitation. Refuse to exclude yourself from heaven. By turning to Jesus, you'll preserve your soul.

We see in Revelation 22:12–17 that it is essential we turn to Jesus Christ and continue with him. Let's see why we must turn to Jesus Christ and remain with him.

We must turn to Jesus Christ because soon, Jesus will appear in glory and will reward every man according to how he lived.

"And, behold, I come quickly; and my reward *is* with me, to give every man according as his work shall be. I am Alpha and Omega, the beginning and the end, the first and the last" (Revelation 22:12–13, KJV).

According to your faithfulness, beliefs, and conviction, self-application, you shall be rewarded. God is the author of all things; therefore, we should live to obtain his favor on the day we give our account. Jesus says he is coming soon. We only have so much time to work. Jesus tells us he will reward us according to what we have done. Whatever we used in building God's program will be generously rewarded. Because Jesus is the beginning and end and the Maker of heaven and earth, he has full rights to judge what he made.

We don't know exactly when Jesus is coming again, but it will be so soon that we must prepare and stay in a state of readiness. How then have we been living? Are we living like Jesus or like Satan?

What kind of reward will you get? It will be a reward in keeping with how you lived.

All who obey the Word of God are commanded and given the right to enter the holy city and partake of the tree of life.

"Blessed *are* they that do his commandments, that they may have right to the tree of life, and may enter in through the gates into the city" (Revelation 22:14, KJV).

If you repent and follow God's Word placing your trust in Jesus Christ, then you will be accepted into heaven. You'll get to partake of the tree of life, and you'll be perpetually allowed to enter and exit the eternal city. We must have our robes washed. We must make repentance and exercise faith in Jesus Christ if we have the right to the tree of life. If we do trust in Jesus, then we will go in and out of this great city.

We must obey the Word for the attitude we need to have toward God. Psalms 119 describes how the Word is the delight of those who follow God.

Would you love to live forever in the blessedness of God's holy city and people? Seek to know and do or obey God's Holy Word.

All who reject the gospel and live for themselves will find themselves excluded from the holy city.

"For without *are* dogs, and sorcerers, and whoremongers, and murderers, and idolaters, and whosoever loveth and maketh a lie" (Revelation 22:15, KJV).

Those who reject the gospel and refuse to turn to God to be healed of their sin will be shut out of the new earth and heaven and holy city. The verse tells us that outside are the dogs; this is those who exclude themselves from God and are called dogs. Also, all peoples who are involved in the vices mentioned in the verse will be those who are excluded from the holy city.

If people put someone or something else before God, then they will lose out. The rich fool would not give up money for Jesus.

We must accept and live out the gospel message. To forfeit the saving message is to reject God's will.

Jesus Christ, the Bride, and the Holy Spirit extend you an invitation one more time to come and partake through a born-again experience (repentance toward God and faith in Jesus Christ) with Jesus Christ because shortly the opportunity will close.

"I Jesus have sent mine angel to testify unto you these things in the churches. I am the root and the offspring of David *and* the bright and morning star. And the Spirit and the bride say, Come. And let him that heareth say, Come. And let him that is athirst come. And whosoever will let him take the water of life freely" (Revelation 22:16–17, KJV).

God sends this testimony to warn and prepare Christians and to lead the unsaved to experience Jesus through the born-again experience. We must partake and stay in Jesus Christ for the hope of eternal benefit. God sends his messenger to reveal his testimony to us. The bride and Spirit both testify of Jesus Christ. The bride works under and with the Spirit in this work. The testimony is to compel you not to wait any longer but act and respond by faith in Jesus Christ. If you want to partake, then do so.

You cannot be sure of the last time you'll receive the invitation, so you must respond before the unannounced day of Christ return or before you die. Call out to God to forgive you and give you life eternal.

Quit putting off the chance to be saved. Eternity is too long to be lost.

So turn to Jesus Christ and continue with him; God is going to come back and would rather you choose Jesus Christ as your hope of life.

Final Warning

Are there some final warnings in Revelation? If we are born again, does God have some warnings for us? Can we treat God's Word anyway we want? Let's see the last final warning within the Bible.

Revelation 22:18–20 reveals how we should heed God's final warnings in the last three verses. Let's examine what the final warnings are and how to take heed accordingly.

God warns us not to add to the things written in his book.

"For I testify unto every man that heareth the words of the prophecy of this book, if any man shall add unto these things,

God shall add unto him the plagues that are written in this book" (Revelation 22:18, KJV).

We are warned not to add to the writing of the book of Revelation. We must rightly divide the word of truth without adding or taking away from what it's saying. There is a great danger in misusing or abusing God's Holy Word. Do not add to the Bible. Let it speak its message. Be an interpreter who interprets correctly. Do not rewrite the Bible and change anything, or you're in trouble with God.

You do not want to miss heaven on account of this. This is a warning not to change the truth by adding or taking away from the Holy Word.

If you're responsible for handling the Word of life, don't add too it your words because you'll be changing the meaning of what it is saying, especially if you are a Bible translator.

God warns us not to take away the things written within it.

"And if any man shall take away from the words of the book of this prophecy, God shall take away his part out of the book of life, and out of the holy city, and *from* the things which are written in this book" (Revelation 22:19, KJV).

We are warned not to chop off and remove God's words and meaning. His intent must stand. Preach the whole counsel, do not say something that should be taught, and do away with it if it's in the Bible and given to you by God to preach. This is a stern warning to those trifling with God's Word, who write translations. God says if you change the Word, he will take away your chance to the tree of life. God will see to it that the one cutting off God's counsel loses out on eternal hope.

There are many today rewriting the Bible wrongly. There are Bible writers who take Jesus the Son of God out of the Bible, etc. This is wrong.

Do not cut out any part of God's counsel. Then you'll preserve your place in heaven.

God warns again that he comes quickly; therefore, do what you will for God now.

"He which testifies these things saith, Surely, I come quickly. Amen. Even so, come, Lord Jesus. The grace of our Lord Jesus Christ *be* with you all. Amen" (Revelation 22:20–21, KJV).

Jesus again makes clear that the time is near, and we are to prepare and get ready now. We don't have any more time to waist. Let's repent and believe the good news. We should be praying for Jesus to come.

By the end of our lives or the rapture of the Church, many will find they waisted their life away. My friends, it is too late to do something after your time is gone.

Learn to use each day to gain the time by glorifying God in it. This will be how to acquire or invest in God for eternity.

So heed the final warnings. Don't presume and abuse the Word. Don't waste your opportunity to live for God. Know that Jesus Christ is coming soon, so prepare and stay ready.

In conclusion, it is my sincere hope that you are inspired to press on to live for and serve your Lord and Savior Jesus Christ. Indeed, he will come as the King of kings and Lord of lords, so let's be ready to meet him.

ABOUT THE AUTHOR

Gerald Melton has studied in four Bible training institutes. He has a diploma of religion, ministerial studies diploma, advanced counseling certificate, and a pastoral and congregational leadership certificate.

Gerald Melton's journey began with Jesus Christ at age nine when his mother led him to receive Jesus as his Lord and Savior. He left Michigan to join the army and fought in the first Persian Gulf war. It was during this time he had to learn to put God first. Meeting with church groups during his time in the military helped him to discover a real walk with God and develop a passion for Jesus.

Since the '90s, God has been revealing his will to Gerald through Bible college training and life experiences. It has been his pleasure to discover God through the challenges of life. Many times, God has assisted Gerald through rough waters.

Gerald has discovered that having Jesus as one's friend is the utter joy of life. God is willing to direct and instruct each follower of Christ to their destination in his will.

As you read Gerald's study of the book of Revelation, please let Jesus talk to you about how the text applies to you so you can get the most God has for you in it.

My theme:

1) Be saved & pray that all your loved ones + friends will be saved before Tribulation
   2nd half: worse by far

7 Revelation focals to Jesus

3) Jesus wins in end.?
   we win

Chapt #1 – Tabernacle 4)
   Fall Feast Days

for class
Feat Day –
marriage (Jewish

CPSIA information can be obtained
at www.ICGtesting.com
Printed in the USA
FSHW011042300420
69760FS